Stephen Richard Glynne

Notes on the churches of Kent

Stephen Richard Glynne

Notes on the churches of Kent

ISBN/EAN: 9783337262037

Printed in Europe, USA, Canada, Australia, Japan

Cover: Foto ©Lupo / pixelio.de

More available books at **www.hansebooks.com**

NOTES

ON THE

CHURCHES OF KENT.

BY THE LATE

SIR STEPHEN R. GLYNNE, Bart.

WITH ILLUSTRATIONS.

LONDON:

JOHN MURRAY, ALBEMARLE STREET.

1877.

PREFACE.

THE Notes on 312 Churches in Kent which are contained in this volume, form part of a series embracing the whole of England and Wales. This series, it must be premised, deals only with the old parish churches of the country dating anterior to the Restoration; though the author's acquaintance with churches in general extended with almost equal minuteness to a vast number both at home and abroad beyond this limit.

The survey which it embodies, comprises upwards of 5,530 churches, and was spread over the whole of Sir Stephen Glynne's life. The precise date of its commencement does not appear; but in his early youth the forms of churches specially attracted his attention, and Ecclesiology soon became his chief pursuit. The Kentish Notes were commenced in 1829, and a considerable portion of the work was done prior to 1840, including all those descriptions to which no date is prefixed: the remainder was carried on year by year without intermission, a certain number of weeks or months being regularly devoted to it, until 1874, when death overtook the author at the age of 66, while actually engaged in his long-matured undertaking.

Neither is it known whether Sir Stephen Glynne intended to publish his Notes; but, inasmuch as they were left in so finished a state as to make publication possible, his relations have not hesitated to embark, at any rate by way of experiment, upon that enterprise. Such a publication, containing so vast an amount of first-hand information, would seem to be not only a worthy monument of his life and labours, but a work of deep historical interest,—an interest much enhanced by the fact that the constant process of rebuilding and restoration of churches must often vary, if it does not sometimes efface, the old and original features, which it was Sir Stephen Glynne's chief aim to trace out and record.

The labour of accumulating such a mass of details as are here given may be readily conceived; but it was, in the truest sense, a labour of love, and the very act of exploring the country to its furthest recesses, and acquiring all sorts of local information by the way, was a process thoroughly congenial to the author. It mattered little to what extent successive modifications had interfered with the original design of the church under examination; Sir Stephen Glynne would at once, as if by instinct, read its architectural history, and a very short time usually sufficed for the jotting down of brief memoranda respecting the fabric and its appurtenances, to be afterwards drawn up into the full but compendious form in which they are here presented. And herein he would rely almost wholly on his own knowledge and observation, the aid of the Incumbent being rarely invoked or required.

This is hardly the place to speak of Sir Stephen Glynne's personal qualities,—of that rare simplicity and fidelity of character which endeared him to a wide circle of friends. But it may be observed that the calm temper and judgment which distinguished him in all matters of daily life, was of no little value in dealing with vexed questions of archaeology, and must needs give weight to his conclusions thereon. He was, moreover, one of the most accurate of observers. His details have never been questioned, and have always been highly valued by the most competent judges. His memory, too, was marvellous. The details of the 5,530 churches he has described were not merely committed to paper, but were continually carried in his head, so that he could at any moment give off-hand a clear and accurate account of any one of them; and amid a miscellaneous company he would often be able to tell them more about their own churches than they knew themselves. Yet his knowledge extended far beyond the limits of his favourite subject; and on all matters of topography, county and personal history, and such like, he was a well-nigh infallible guide. These pursuits, it should be added, attractive as they were, were never permitted to interfere with the sedulous discharge of duties belonging to him at home as magistrate and Lord-Lieutenant, and left ample room for frequent exchanges of hospitality, and for other occupations agreeable to his refined taste, and to the tenour of a well-ordered and exemplary life.

It now only remains to tender very grateful thanks to the Ven. Archdeacon Harrison for the interest and trouble which he, in conjunction with the Rev. Canon Scott Robertson, Honorary Secretary to the Kent Archæological Society, has taken in preparing this volume for the press. Certain supplementary notes have been appended by them, chiefly descriptive of recent alterations. The illustrations have also been inserted by their care.

W. H. G.

Oct., 1877.

INDEX OF CONTENTS.

ACRISE—St. Martin.
ADISHAM—Holy Innocents.
ALDINGTON—St. Martin
ALKHAM—St. Anthony
ALLINGTON—St. Lawrence
APPLEDORE—St. Peter and St. Paul.
ASH (BY SANDWICH)—St. Nicholas
ASH (JUXTA WROTHAM)—St. Peter and St. Paul
ASHFORD—St. Mary
ASHURST—St. ——
AYLESFORD—St. Peter.
BADLESMERE—St. Leonard.
BAPCHILD—St. Lawrence
BARFRESTON—St. Mary
BARHAM—St. John.
BARMING—St. Margaret
BEAKESBOURNE—St. Peter
BEARSTED—Holy Cross
BECKENHAM—St. George
BETHERSDEN—St. Margaret
BETTESHANGER—St. Mary
BEXLEY—St. Mary.
BIDBOROUGH—St. Lawrence.
BIDDENDEN—All Saints
BILSINGTON—St. Peter and St. Paul
BIRCHINGTON—All Saints.
BISHOPSBOURNE—St. Mary
BOBBING—St. Bartholomew
BONNINGTON—St. Runwald.
BORDEN—St. Peter and St. Paul.
BOUGHTON ALUPH—All Saints
BOUGHTON MALHERBE—St. Nicholas

Index of Contents.

	PAGE
BOUGHTON MONCHELSEA—St. Peter	248
BOUGHTON-UNDER-BLEAN—St. Peter and St. Paul	235
BOXLEY—All Saints	251
BRABOURNE—St. Mary	53
BRASTED—St. Martin	234
BREDGAR—St. John	161
BRENCHLEY—All Saints	324
BRENZETT—St. Eanswith	252
BRIDGE—St. Peter	131
BROMLEY—St. Peter and St. Paul	271
BROOKLAND—St. Augustine	263
BUCKLAND (BY DOVER)—St. Andrew	97
BYRLING—All Saints	294
CANTERBURY—Holy Cross Church (Westgate)	18
St. Peter's Church	18
St. Margaret's Church	19
St. Mildred's Church	19
St. George's Church	20
St. Mary Magdalen's Church (Burgate)	21
St. Dunstan's Church (without the Westgate)	21
The Cathedral Church	23
St. Mary Bredin Church	181
St. Mary's Church, Northgate	182
St. Alphage's Church	182
St. Martin's Church	183
St. Paul's Church	134
CAPEL LE FERNE—St. Mary	50
CAPEL—St. Thomas à Becket	186
CHALK—St. Mary	313
CHALLOCK—St. Cosmus and St. Damian	232
CHARING—St. Peter and St. Paul	157
CHART PARVA—St. Mary	156
CHARTHAM—St. Mary	225
CHATHAM—St. Mary	345
CHELSFIELD—St. Mary	150
CHERITON (NEAR FOLKESTONE)—St. Martin	119
CHEVENING—St. Botolph	302
CHIDDINGSTONE—St. Mary	325
CHILHAM—St. Mary	132
CHILLENDEN—All Saints	187
CHISELHURST—St. Nicholas	322
CHISLET—St. Mary	144

Index of Contents.

	PAGE
CLIFFE AT HOO—St. Helen	347
COBHAM—St. Mary Magdalen	336
COLDRED	138
COWDEN—St. Mary	179
CRANBROOK—St. Dunstan	77
CRAYFORD—St. Paulinus	323
CRAY (NORTH)—St. James	343
CUXTON—St. Michael	339
DARENTH—St. Margaret	306
DARTFORD—Holy Trinity	274
DAVINGTON—St. Mary Magdalen	193
DEAL—St. Leonard	101
DENTON—St. Mary	255
DETLING—St Martin	3
DITTON—St. Peter	291
DODINGTON—St. John	199
DOVER CASTLE CHURCH—St. Mary	241
DOVER—St. Mary's Church	48
St. James's Church	49
DOWN—St. ——	273
DYMCHURCH—St. Peter and St. Paul	265
EAST FARLEIGH—St. ——	278
EAST LANGDON—St. Augustine	98
EAST MALLING—St. James	153
EAST PECKHAM—St. Michael	299
EASTRY—St. Mary	104
EASTWELL—St. Mary	233
EDENBRIDGE—St. Peter and St. Paul	324
EGERTON—St. James	155
ELHAM—St. Mary	95
ELMSTEAD—St. James	260
ELMSTONE—St. ——	242
ELTHAM—St. John the Baptist	273
ERITH—St. John	341
EWELL—St. Mary and St. Peter	139
EYNESFORD—St. Martin	301
EYTHORNE—St. Peter and St. Paul	246
FARLEIGH, see EAST and WEST.	
FARNBOROUGH—St. Giles	303
FARNINGHAM—St. Peter and St. Paul	306
FAVERSHAM—St. Mary of Charity	13
FOLKESTONE.—St. Mary and St. Eanswith	51

Index of Contents.

	PAGE
Foot's Cray—All Saints	320
Fordwich—St. Mary	27
Frindsbury—All Saints	335
Frinstead—St. Dunstan	162
Gillingham—St. Mary	120
Godmersham—St. Lawrence	122
Goudhurst—St. Mary	286
Great Chart	69
Groombridge—St. John	181
Guston—St. Martin	45
Hadlow—St. Mary	145
Halling—St. John	338
Ham—St. George	147
Harbledown—St. Michael	169
Hardres, see Upper.	
Harrietsham—St. John the Baptist	89
Hartley—All Saints	250
Hartlip—St. Michael	173
Hawkhurst—St. Lawrence	79
Hawkinge—St. Michael	111
Headcorn—St. Peter and St. Paul	113
Herne—St. Martin	28
Hernhill—St. Michael	238
Hever—St. Peter	326
Higham—St. Mary	342
High Halden—St. Mary	223
Hinxhill—St. Mary	159
Hoath—St. Mary	30
Hollingbourne—All Saints	83
Hoo—St. Werburgh	259
Horsmonden—St. Margaret	284
Horton Chapel, in Chartham	227
Horton Kirby—St. Mary	275
Hougham—St. Lawrence	142
Hucking—St. Margaret	167
Hythe—St. Leonard	60
Ifield—St. Margaret	341
Ightham—St. Peter	296
Isle of Grain—St. James	202
Ivychurch—St. George	262
Iwade—All Saints	192
Kennardington—St. Mary	211

	PAGE
KENNINGTON—St. Mary	73
KESTON—St. ——	273
KINGSNORTH—St. Michael	217
KINGSTONE—St. Giles	130
KNOWLTON—St. Clement	186
LAMBERHURST—St. Mary	283
LANGLEY—S., Mary	112
LEEDS—St. Nicholas	81
LEIGH—St. Mary	151
LENHAM—St. Mary	76
LEVELAND—St. Laurence	230
LEYBOURNE—St. Peter and St. Paul	154
LINTON—St. Nicholas	76
LITTLEBOURNE—St. Vincent	167
LONGFIELD—St. Mary	310
LOOSE—All Saints	160
LUDDENHAM—St. Mary	195
LUDDESDOWN—St. Peter and St. Paul	341
LULLINGSTONE—St. Botolph	146
LYDD—All Saints	64
LYDDEN	138
LYMINGE—St. Mary and St. Eadburga	93
LYMPNE—St. Stephen	239
LYNSTEAD—St. Peter and St. Paul	198
MAIDSTONE—All Saints'	1
MALLING, see EAST and WEST	
MARDEN—St. Michael	85
MARGATE, alias ST. JOHN'S IN THANET	35
MEOPHAM—St. John the Baptist	276
MERSHAM—St. John Baptist	57
MILSTEAD—St. Mary and Holy Cross	163
MILTON, JUXTA CANTERBURY—St. Nicholas	181
MILTON (NLNT GRAVESEND)—St. Peter and St. Paul	227
MILTON (NLNT SITTINGBOURNE)—Holy Trinity	7
MINSTER IN SHEPPEY—St. Mary and St. Sexburga	136
MINSTER IN THANET—St Mary	32
MOLASH—St. Peter	231
MONGEHAM—St. Martin	102
MONKTON—St. Mary	31
MURSTON—All Saints	10
NACKINGTON—St. Mary	181
NETTLESTEAD—St. Mary	289

	PAGE
NEWCHURCH—St. Peter and St. Paul	206
NEWENDEN—St. Peter	219
NEWINGTON (BY HYTHE)—St. Nicholas	92
NEWINGTON (BY SITTINGBOURNE)—St. Mary	6
NEWNHAM—St. Peter and St. Paul	197
NEW ROMNEY—St. Nicholas	63
NONINGTON—St. Mary	187
NORTHBOURNE—St. Augustine	103
NORTHFLEET—St. Botolph	311
NORTON—St. Mary	195
NURSTEAD—St. Mildred	342
OARE—St. Peter	194
OFFHAM—St. Michael	293
OLD ROMNEY—St. Clement	268
ORLESTON—St. Mary	216
ORPINGTON—All Saints	151
OSPRINGE—St. Peter and St. Paul	13
OTFORD—St. Bartholomew	303
OTHAM—St. Nicholas	85
PADLESWORTH—St. Oswald	257
PATRICKSBOURNE—St. Mary	26
PECKHAM, *see* EAST and WEST.	
PEMBURY—St. Peter	185
PENSHURST—St. John	281
PLUCKLEY	115
PRESTON (BY WINGHAM)—St. Mildred	243
PRESTON (BY FAVERSHAM)—St. Catherine	16
POSTLING—St. Mary and St. Radegund	52
QUEENBOROUGH—Holy Trinity	179
RAINHAM—St. Margaret	172
RIDLEY—St. Peter	249
RINGWOULD—St. Nicholas	99
RIPPLE—St. Mary	118
ROCHESTER—The Cathedral Church	315
St. Nicholas Church	318
St. Margaret's Church	319
RODMERSHAM—St. Nicholas	12
ROLVENDEN—St. Mary	217
ROMNEY, *see* NEW and OLD	
RUCKINGE—St. Mary	207
ST. LAWRENCE (IN THANET)	37
ST. MARGARET AT CLIFFE	46

Index of Contents.

	PAGE
St. Mary Cray	321
St. Nicholas at Wade (in Thanet)	30
St. Paul's Cray—St. Paulinus	321
St. Peter's (in Thanet)	36
St. Stephen's (near Canterbury)	110
Saltwood—St. Peter and St. Paul	59
Sandhurst—St. Nicolas	219
Sandwich—St. Peter's Church	38
St. Mary's Church	39
St. Clement's Church	39
St. Bartholomew's Hospital	41
Seale—St. Peter	301
Selling—St. Mary	237
Sellinge—St. Mary	210
Sevenoaks—St. Nicholas	300
Sevington—St. Mary	91
Shadoxhurst—St. Peter and St. Paul	211
Sheldwich—St. James	229
Shorne—St. Peter and St. Paul	313
Sibertswold	138
Sittingbourne—St. Michael	9
Smeeth—St. Mary	57
Snargate—St. Dunstan	253
Snodland—All Saints	294
Southfleet—St. Nicholas	308
Speldhurst—St. Mary	204
Staple—St. James	107
Staplehurst—All Saints	87
Stelling—St. Mary	259
Stockbury—St. Mary	1
Stone by Dartford—St. Mary	328
Stourmouth—All Saints	228
Stouting—St. Mary	261
Sturry—St. Nicholas	28
Sundridge—St. ——	346
Sutton-at-Hone—St. John	147
Sutton, next Ripple—St. Peter and St. Paul	189
Swalecliffe—St. John	134
Swanscombe—St. Peter and St. Paul	309
Swingfield—St. Peter	256
Tenterden—St. Michael	68
Teynham—St. Mary	177

Index of Contents.

	PAGE
THANINGTON—St. Nicholas	168
TILMANSTONE—St. Andrew	241
TONBRIDGE—St. Peter and St. Paul	279
TONG—St. Giles	196
TROTTESCLIFFE—St. Peter and St. Paul	277
TUNSTALL—St. John	165
ULCOMB—All Saints	170
UPCHURCH—St. Mary	175
UPPER HARDRES—St. Peter and St. Paul	228
WALDERSHARE—All Saints	45
WALMER	117
WALTHAM—St. Bartholomew	258
WAREHORNE—St. Matthew	215
WATERINGBURY—St. John	290
WESTERHAM—St. Mary	280
WESTWELL—St. Mary	74
WEST CLIFFE	47
WEST FARLEIGH—All Saints	278
WEST MALLING—St. Mary	292
WEST PECKHAM—St. Dunstan	208
WEST WICKHAM—St. John	272
WHITSTABLE—All Saints	135
WILLESBOROUGH—St. Mary	72
WINGHAM—St. Mary	108
WOMENSWOLD—St. Margaret	188
WOODCHURCH—All Saints	212
WOODNESBOROUGH—St Mary	42
WOOTTON—St. Martin	209
WORTH (BY SANDWICH)—St. Peter and St. Paul	126
WOULDHAM—All Saints	340
WROTHAM—St. George	295
WYE—St. Martin and St. Gregory	123
YALDING—St. Peter and St. Paul	288

LIST OF ILLUSTRATIONS.

	PAGE
EXTERIOR OF BRABOURNE CHURCH	54
HEART SHRINE IN BRABOURNE CHURCH	55
BRASS OF THOMAS GODFREY, LYDD CHURCH	66
BRASS OF PETER GODFREY AND WIFE, LYDD CHURCH	67
GREAT EAST WINDOW OF HAWKHURST CHURCH	80
HAWKHURST CHURCH FROM THE SOUTH-EAST	80
HAWKHURST CHURCH; EAST END OF SOUTH CHANCEL	81
NORTH CHANCEL OF HAWKHURST CHURCH	81
SOUTH DOOR OF STAPLEHURST CHURCH	88
ST. MARY'S CHURCH, ELHAM	96
MINSTER CHURCH AND ABBEY GATE-HOUSE, IN SHEPPEY	137
LOW SIDE WINDOW IN DODINGTON CHURCH	200
AUMBRY AND PISCINA, WAREHORNE CHURCH	215
LEADEN FONT, BROOKLAND CHURCH	264
SIR THOS. CAWNE'S WINDOW, IGHTHAM CHURCH	297
EAST WINDOW OF SOUTH AISLE, STONE CHURCH	329
ONE PANEL OF MOULDED STRING-COURSE ON THE NAVE WALLS OF STONE CHURCH	329
CAPITAL OF WINDOW MONIAL, IN THE CHANCEL OF STONE CHURCH	330
BOSSES ON CUSPS OF THE CHANCEL ARCADING, IN STONE CHURCH	331
MOULDING OF CHANCEL ARCH, STONE CHURCH	333
NORTH-WEST BAY OF CHANCEL, STONE CHURCH	334

Kentish Archaeological Society –
Sittingbourne Literary & Scientific
Association –

NOTES ON THE
CHURCHES OF KENT.

MAIDSTONE.

Aug. 1882. B.A.

ALL SAINTS'. 1829.

THE church is a very large and beautiful specimen of the best Rectilinear work, without any of earlier date.* The exterior is plain but good, and being constructed of good stone has suffered no mutilation, nor is there any bad modern insertion. The nave and chancel have side aisles, those of the chancel being narrower,† the tower stands on the south side of the nave, and in its lower stage forms a porch; it has an embattled parapet, and a turret at one of the angles. The side aisles are also embattled, but not the clerestory. The west-end has three large windows, the centre one of six lights, the others of five; those of the side aisles are of four lights in the nave; in the chancel of five, and very wide.‡ The clerestory is continued along the nave and chancel, and has a range of two-light windows.§ There is an octagonal staircase turret on the

---

* The chancel, erected by Archbishop Courtenay, about 1395; the nave, probably later.

† The aisles are of remarkable width, but those of the chancel less wide than in the nave. The length is stated to be 227 feet, of which the chancel is 63; the width of the nave and aisles 94.

‡ The east window of the chancel was carried up to a considerably greater height, in 1871, under the authority of a faculty from the Archbishop's Court, and filled with stained glass, as a memorial.—H.

§ The clerestory windows of the chancel differ from those of the nave, the latter having flat arches, the former more approaching to Curvilinear tracery. The tracery of the aisle windows in the chancel also appears of earlier date than those of the nave.

north side, and in the north-east angle of the chancel is a fine niche. South of the chancel is an elegant vestry of two stories, having a doorway with label and quatrefoils in the spandrels.* The other doors are mostly plain. The interior is very light and beautiful, and the proportions very fine; the aisles are very broad, and the nave has on each side six very elegant arches, the piers of which are light, with mouldings carried down the front, and shafts attached, with octagonal capitals, whence spring the arches. The arch to the chancel is very wide; the chancel is divided from each aisle by three pointed arches similar to those of the nave.† In the chancel are several ancient stalls with turn-up seats. On the south of the altar is a beautiful monumental chapel, with rich tabernacle work, and niches which have groining beneath the canopies; parts of it retain traces of rich painting and gilding, and within it is an altar tomb with panelled sides.‡ The effect of this fine monument is injured by a modern monument being erected against it. On the north of the altar is some wood screen work now tastelessly covered with whitewash.§ There is also in the chancel the vestige of a fine large brass.||

The font is octagonal, panelled with shields. The gallery in which stands the organ is placed one arch distant from the west end.¶

On the south side of the churchyard are the remains of the

* The vestry has been carried up externally to the same height as the side aisles, in order to form an organ chamber within.—H.

† Since 1844, All Saints', Maidstone, has been greatly improved by the entire removal of the galleries and the substitution of oak benches for the former absurd and inconvenient pews.

‡ The original painting is represented, together with engravings of the windows and other architectural details of the church, in the "History and Antiquities of All Saints' Church, Maidstone," by J. Whichcord, 1845.—H.

§ The whitewash was, of course, removed when the church was restored in 1844.—H.

|| There are several mural brasses of the 17th century. A stone bench runs along the aisles under the windows.

¶ This gallery having been taken away, the large space, which before was shut out, now forms part of the body of the church.—H.

College, of which considerable portions remain of good Rectilinear character. There is a good gateway tower embattled, having as is generally found, two arches of entrance, one large, the other smaller, and the ceiling within groined in stone. The windows are all square-headed, of two lights with labels, and the roof of most part is high and sloping; at the northwest angle is a square tower of three stages.

A large new church (Holy Trinity) has been erected in the upper part of the town, of fine stone, in the plain Grecian style with a lofty spire. It is very capacious; contains an organ, galleries, &c.* The ancient archiepiscopal palace remains standing, on the north side of the churchyard, a handsome old stone house of Elizabethan period,† with large square mullioned windows, and projecting windows in the roof surmounted by gables. Opposite to this is a fine ancient barn with plain square windows.

DETLING.
ST. MARTIN.

This church, though small and destitute of architectural beauty, is most beautifully situated on the declivity of the range of chalk hill which runs across Kent; and the view which it commands over a great extent of rich and lovely country is most delightful. The whole is built of rough flints, and has a nave with a low north aisle, a chancel with north chapel, and at the west end a low square tower, the upper part of which is of wood, &c., with a Rectilinear west window of three lights. There is a plain Early English door on the south side, above which is a trefoil niche of later date. The tower contains two bells. The

---

* Since these notes were written, several churches have been built in the parish of Maidstone: St. Peter's Church, originally the Pilgrims' Chapel, recovered from desecration, restored and enlarged; St. Stephen's, Tovil; St. Philip's, St. Paul's, St. Faith's, St. John's, and St. Michael's, new churches. H.
† The residence [1829] of Lady Frances Riddell.

windows throughout the church are Rectilinear and square-headed. The nave has on the north side two plain Early English arches without mouldings, the pier square, and quite plain, and having attached to its west side the font, which is octagonal, upon a central circular shaft, and four other smaller ones detached around it. The aisle is low, the tiled roof being carried down almost to a level with the ground. The chancel has a plain large pointed arch to its north chapel, and contains a modern Gothic monument to Mr. and Mrs. Foote, 1788. The north chapel is Rectilinear, and has a trefoil niche with label and piscina. Against the east wall is inserted a slab with a cross, probably moved from elsewhere. Within this chapel is a very beautiful carved desk, an exquisite specimen, such as is seldom found, these desks being very rare. It appears to be of early Rectilinear period; it is of square form, supported upon a light octagonal shaft, the whole of wood. Each of the sloped sides of the desk is enriched with pierced tracery of varied character, there being on one side a beautiful circle. This elegant specimen is unfortunately not duly appreciated, and is in want of much repair.

STOCKBURY.

ST. MARY.

This is a spacious church, in the form of a cross, with a nave having side aisles, transepts, and chancel, and a tower at the west end. There are several portions deserving of great attention, and a great deal of singularly elegant Early English work. The exterior is plain and without battlement, the south transept mantled in ivy; and on the north, near the transept, is an octagonal turret. The tower is Rectilinear, with square belfry windows, and a circular turret at the south-east corner. There is no clerestory, but the interior is spacious and handsome. The tower arch is open and lofty. The nave is divided from each aisle by four Early English arches. On the south the pillars

are circular and very slender, with octagonal capitals; on the
north, the capitals are circular, and the last shaft against the
west wall has an impost with rude foliage. The south transept
is much larger than the north; both transepts have lancet Early
English windows, some of which have shafts and others not;
there is also a Rectilinear window on the north side. Each of
the transepts opens by two most beautiful Early English arches,
with singularly light and elegant piers; each being formed of
two entire shafts of Purbeck marble set lengthways, upon a
square base; the capital has rich foliage surmounted by a square
abacus. A continuation of these transept arches is carried on
each side along the walls of the chancel the windows being set
within them, there being no aisles. The pier between the
transept arches and those of the chancel has been strengthened
by the addition of a square shaft in front; an aperture behind
this pier communicating between the chancel and transept.
The shafts next to the nave, from whence springs the transept
arch, are double; and the capitals have the richest foliage, of
the finest and most delicate execution; the two arches on each
side of the chancel are rather more acute, and spring from very
slender single shafts upon square bases and good capitals; the
arches are well moulded, and within them in the wall are set
plain lancet windows. The arrangement of these arches is very
uncommon, and singularly beautiful; the piers being so slender
and the capitals so finely executed. The whitewash has been
taken off from some of the marble shafts.* The east window of
the chancel is Rectilinear of four lights. There is a good deal of
wood screen work in the chancel and transepts, and on the south
side of the altar is a trefoil niche and drain. The font is of
square form, upon a square pedestal raised on steps, but covered
with whitewash. There are five bells in the tower. The situation of the church is highly picturesque, it being placed at a

* This church was restored with great care and knowledge by the late vicar
(1831—1875), the Rev. David Twopeny; whitewash, of course, removed, &c.—H.

distance from any houses upon a ridge of hill looking over a beautiful woody valley; the north side of the churchyard commands a fine view over the river Thames, and there is a fine yew tree in the churchyard.

NEWINGTON.

ST. MARY.

This church is principally Curvilinear of very good character, with a Rectilinear tower of lofty proportions, embattled, and with an octagonal turret on the south. The west doorway has plain mouldings and shafts, and over it is a two-light window; there are several tiers of small square windows on the south side, and the belfry has windows of two lights. The walls of the church are principally of flint; the south side of the nave is embattled, but not the other parts. The windows of the south aisle of the nave are fine Curvilinear of two and three lights, with ogee heads having finials. The other windows of the nave and chancel are also Curvilinear and very good, except one in the north chancel, which is an Early English lancet. The nave has an aisle on each side, and the chancel one on the south; the nave is wide, but without a clerestory, and divided from each aisle by four pointed arches with octagonal piers, the whole of which, together with the walls, are completely covered with glaring whitewash.* The chancel is divided from its south aisle by two plain pointed arches of Early English character—the pier square, having at each angle shafts set in a hollow with foliated capitals, the foliage being continued along the whole pier. Eastward of these is a third smaller arch in the wall opening to the south aisle. On the north side is a small doorway opening to a vestry which has Early English lancet windows. Within the arches of the chancel is some very fine wood screen-work, apparently of

---

* Beneath the whitewash some effective wall-painting has been discovered around the north doorway.—R.

Curvilinear period, and there is a rich Rectilinear wood screen between the south chancel and the south aisle of the nave. In the south chancel are the door and steps to the rood-loft. Beneath the east window of the south chancel are the remains of an ancient altar, near which is a good niche with crocketed ogee canopy trefoiled, and a piscina with a shelf. The beams of the roof in the south chancel are richly carved with very bold foliage. There is also a pew with some handsome wood carving, *temp.* James I., and an altar tomb, the sides of which are enriched with trefoil arches. The font is a plain octagon, but has a large wood cover * of the age of Elizabeth, in which the Gothic and Italian forms are mixed; but the effect is handsome. The eastern pier on the north side of the nave has a singular octagonal projection, upon which is a Rectilinear niche.† There are six bells.

The churchyard is surrounded by orchards, with a fine bank of wood on the north side, forming a very pleasing picturesque scene.

MILTON (next Sittingbourne).
HOLY TRINITY.

This church stands at some distance from the town and overlooks the channel of the Thames. The north side of the churchyard is planted with extremely fine trees, having a very fine effect. The church itself is principally Curvilinear, with portions of later date—the greater part is of plain flint work with rough stone intermixed; the church consists of a wide and lofty nave and chancel, each with a south aisle. The south chancel belonged to the Northwoods and is of greater pretension than the principal one, having two sedilia. At the west end is a plain square tower of unusually large dimensions, with a turret

---

* This is a "buffet" cover similar to that in Ticehurst Church; it cannot be raised, but three of its sides form a door which opens outwards upon hinges. R.

† This church contains four monumental brasses, and possesses a remarkable chest thickly banded with iron. R.

at the north-east angle, a Curvilinear window on the west side, and small single windows in tiers above it; on the west side is also a doorway of good Curvilinear character, having deep mouldings and shafts, and surmounted by a triangular canopy, the intermediate space being filled with pierced tracery. There is a plain south porch. The nave is particularly wide and lofty, and the interior of grand proportions, though without a clerestory. The south aisle has Curvilinear windows of two lights, and at the west end one of three. On the north of the nave they are square-headed, Rectilinear, and of two lights with transoms. The nave is divided from the aisle by three large pointed arches with octagonal piers. There is no chancel arch from the nave; and the chancel is divided from its south aisle by two pointed arches with pillars more slender than those of the nave. The south chancel is loftier than the aisle of the nave, and has externally some neat flint work. The east window of the chancel is a fine large one of five lights, apparently of early Curvilinear work, and south of the altar is a feathered niche with ogee head and drain; there is also in the chancel the brass of a knight; on the north side is a vestry with small Rectilinear windows. The south chancel has an east window with ogee head having a finial—the tracery has been modernised; in this aisle are two stalls ascending eastward, the heads ogee and feathered, and springing from shafts of Purbeck marble with bell capitals. Eastward of these is a small niche and drain of similar character. There is likewise a slab with a cross flory, and a turret with staircase and door opening formerly into the rood-loft. In the wall is a brass plate to the memory of "Thomas Alefe and Margaret his wyfe," 1529. The font is a plain octagon. The whole interior is kept very neat, and the whitewash has been taken off some of the ornamental portions.* There are no galleries; the pulpit is made to look very gaudy with gilding. The tower contains five bells.

* The chancel has been restored, and also the south chancel, with the tracery of its east window restored. H.

SITTINGBOURNE.

ST. MICHAEL.

This church is built of flint and stone, and consists of a nave with side aisles, north and south transepts, and a chancel with a south chapel. The tower at the west end is embattled, with a corner turret, and has a lancet window on the west side, and a belfry window of two lights, of later date. The nave has no clerestory, and its side aisles are embattled, but not the chancel. The south porch is of two stages, and has a stone groined ceiling. Many of the windows have been deprived of their tracery,* but the south transept has one very large Rectilinear one of five lights, with a transom, and in the south chancel is a fine one of three lights of early Curvilinear character, with shafts having foliated capitals; in the same part is also a buttress charged with a fine niche having a crocketed triangular canopy. The two east windows have lost their tracery. The interior is very neat and well kept. The nave is divided from each aisle by three pointed arches, the piers alternately circular and octagonal. The north transept or chapel opens to the chancel by two Early English arches, the pillar circular, with the capital richly moulded; upon this pillar is a trefoil niche. Eastward of this north chapel is the vestry, having square Rectilinear windows, and divided from the chancel by two very elegant pointed arches † with deep architrave mouldings, within which is a plain stone screen ‡ containing a beautiful door of Curvilinear character, set in a square compartment, with fine mouldings and quatrefoils in the spandrels. The chancel is

---

* In the windows on the south side, and at the east end of the church, the original tracery has been restored, the western gallery removed, and the tower arch opened, the square pews taken away, the nave fitted up with open seats, and the chancel arranged chorally, the organ being placed on the north side of the chancel. H.

† They were simply a mural arcade ; in the middle of each arch an original Early English lancet window has been discovered.—R.

‡ This was not a screen, but the outer wall of the Early English chancel, to which the vestry was a Rectilinear addition. R.

divided from its south aisle by two lofty Early English arches, with a central octagonal pier, having a detached shaft set on two opposite faces. Within these arches is a plain stone screen. A third arch of plainer character opens to the south transept, springing from moulded corbels of bell-form. In the north chancel beneath a window is a tomb under a flat arch, consisting of two compartments divided by a kind of shelf; in the lower is the effigy of a female, and the arch has in the mouldings a band of square flowers. The font is octagonal. On the alternate faces are shields and square bands of foliage, much varied; among them are oak leaves and acorns, and the shields are mostly charged with armorial bearings.* There is a gallery at the west end containing a good small organ played with keys.

MURSTON.
ALL SAINTS.

This is a small church, consisting of a nave and chancel, with small side aisles, with a wooden turret over the west end of the nave.† There are lancet windows at the west end of each aisle, (one is trefoiled,) and a Rectilinear window west of the nave. There are no side windows to the aisles, but on the north side is a doorway with a "shouldered" arch. The interior is gloomy, and the nave divided from each aisle by two pointed arches, those on the south Early English, with a circular pier having a square Norman capital. On the north are two pointed arches with an octagonal pier. The chancel has on each side two Early English arches, with pillars like that south of the nave. There are two windows at the east end of four lights with Rectilinear tracery. The chancel aisles are higher and wider than those of

---

* Those of Archbishop Arundel occupy one shield; others bear instruments of our Lord's Passion.—R.

† Murston Church has been rebuilt on a more central site. The arches of the old church have been worked into the new.—H.

the nave. There is a pointed doorway on the south side, and a little wood screen work in the north chancel.* The font is attached to the wall west of the arches on the south of the nave, and is a plain square mass. The church commands a view over the channel of the Thames and the marsh between.

BAPCHILD.
ST. LAWRENCE.

This church is built of flints, and consists of a nave and chancel each with a north aisle; with a tower standing on the south side of the nave,† surmounted by a shingled spire. The tower is plain, and has small Early English lancets. The nave is divided from the aisle by four low semicircular arches, with no architrave mouldings; the pillars massive and octagonal, with square Norman capitals. The aisle of the nave is very low. That of the chancel is much loftier and wider, and is divided from the chancel by two Early English arches with a circular pillar. In the nave the windows are mostly square-headed, and of Rectilinear character; but one on the south side is a lancet with an obtuse head. The chancel has three lancet windows on the south side; and the chancel and its aisle have each at the east end a Rectilinear window, of three and four lights. In the east wall of the chancel, on each side of the Rectilinear window, are two Norman windows stopped up. In the north chancel are two Early English niches with a circular shaft.‡ The north chancel is said to have belonged to the Sinclairs, and the windows contain a few fragments of stained glass.

* Within which was a monumental brass to John Eveas, who died in 1488, and to Mildred his wife. This brass still remains in that fragment of the ancient church, which is used as a mortuary chapel since the re-building of the church on a new site.—R.
† At the east end thereof.—R.
‡ Forming the graceful canopy of an Early English piscina, wrought in the engraved pier at the east end of the chancel arcade. Upon the north wall of

RODMERSHAM.
ST. NICHOLAS.

This church is principally Rectilinear, with several windows of Curvilinear work, the nave has side aisles, and the chancel a south chapel with a high tiled roof; part of the nave has an embattled parapet; and at the east end of the north aisle is an octagonal turret.

The tower is of flint and stone, embattled, with an octagonal corner turret; the belfry windows are square-headed, and on the west side is a Curvilinear window of two lights. The south porch is plain, but contains a stoup.

The west window of the north aisle is Curvilinear, of two lights. Some other windows are Curvilinear, but most are Rectilinear. The east window appears to be of the former character. The nave has three pointed arches on each side with octagonal pillars.

The chancel contains the ancient wood desks and seats, and also a fine wood screen dividing it from the south chapel. In continuation of which, south of the altar, are three seats in wood, with elegant canopies and a cornice of Tudor flower. It is very rare that instances of wooden stalls south of the altar are to be found. The south chancel is enclosed by a wood screen, and has two plain niches of Early English character, with a central circular shaft having a foliated capital and abacus.

On each side of the east window is the pedestal of a niche. The font is octagonal upon a square base. Many of the windows contain portions of rich stained glass. The tower has four bells.* The churchyard is beautifully surrounded by orchards.

the chancel aisle is a pretty arcade of mural arches Early English, and a string course ornamented with the five-leafed flower. A carved wall-plate of very early character remains in the north-west corner of the chancel roof.—R.

* The church is about to undergo a careful restoration and rearrangement of the interior, with open seats, 1876.—H.

OSPRINGE.
ST. PETER AND ST. PAUL.

The external appearance of this church is much injured from the tower having been destroyed.* It is, however, a tolerably good structure of flints, and has much Early English work; consisting of a nave with aisles, a south transept, and a chancel. There are lancet windows at the west end of the north aisle, and in the chancel, which last are stopped. On the north side of the nave they are mostly Rectilinear, in the south transept they are Curvilinear, one of which of two lights has an ogee head with a finial. There is also a square one of three lights. The east window is early Curvilinear of three trefoiled lights; there is also a trefoil head window in the gable of the south transept. The north porch of the nave has an Early English door, with lozenge moulding on the imposts. There is a Norman doorway † on the north of the chancel with the chevron and roller moulding; and the string above it has billet ornament. The south aisle is embattled; and there is an octagonal turret on the south side near the rood-loft. The nave is divided from each aisle by four plain Early English arches with square piers. The transept opens to the chancel by two pointed arches with a plain pier. There is an organ at the west end.

FAVERSHAM.
ST. MARY OF CHARITY.

This is a very spacious church, but has been much altered and modernised.‡ The plan comprises a nave with aisles, large

---
* A new tower has since been erected. R.
† There is a larger Norman doorway in the north aisle of the nave.—R.
‡ A detailed account of this church, in regard, particularly, to the work which has been done in "re-seating, re-arranging, partially restoring, and generally improving the interior, the exterior having been recased with flint a few years before," is given in the "Canterbury Diocesan Church Calendar," 1876. R.

transepts, also with side aisles, a chancel with a chapel on each side. At the west end of the nave is a modern tower of light-coloured brick with stone corners, surmounted by a light and airy stone spire supported on flying buttresses, in imitation of that of St. Dunstan in the East, London. The effect is light and good, but neither the design nor the execution will bear criticism. The clerestory of the nave has been rebuilt in brick, and the parapets are plain. At the west end within the tower is a good Curvilinear doorway with mouldings and clustered shafts. On the north and south of the tower terminating each aisle is an apartment; that on the south side is now used as a school, and beneath it is a crypt of very early English work with pointed arches and circular pillars. On the north side is a square apartment with lancet windows, supposed by some to have been a gaol, but more probably the depository of the altar vessels, vestments, &c.; above it is an apartment said to have been formerly occupied by the sexton.

The original walls of the church are of flint and stone; the windows in the north aisle Curvilinear of two lights, in the south Rectilinear. In the transepts are some of both characters. At the end of the south transept is a very fine Curvilinear one of five lights, and those on its west side have ogee heads externally, but all the transept windows in each style are of good character. The chancel is tiled; several of its windows were Curvilinear of two lights, but now mutilated. The east window of five lights has also been much spoiled.*

There is a porch south of the nave, having a stone groined ceiling, and near it a circular turret.

The interior is spacious, light, and handsome, though the original arches and pillars of the nave have been destroyed and

* The tracery of these windows has been, of course, restored; the exterior of the windows in the clerestory of the nave has been conformed to the architecture of the church, the pews replaced by open seats, and the western gallery taken down. "In an ecclesiastical sense, the works in the nave and transepts were of an interesting character, from the various discoveries that were made." For particulars, see "Dioc. Calendar," *sup. cit.*—H.

replaced by Tuscan columns, and the clerestory is entirely modern.* The pews are very handsome and uniform, and at the west end is a neat gallery containing a good organ. The transepts have each of them side aisles, and a double row of three arches with pillars alternately circular and octagonal. The middle aisle of the nave is paved with marble. The chancel opens to each chapel by a wide pointed arch, with mouldings carried down to the ground. Several of the ancient wood stalls remain, and have fine carving about them. On the north side is a vestry of Rectilinear character, having small square-headed windows, and a wood roof. Within the vestry is a very fine and curious ancient wood chest, with singular carving apparently of Curvilinear work. The altar screen † is of woodwork, and is a pretty good imitation of Gothic work; the altar itself is a marble slab supported on iron work. On the north side of the chancel is a fine Rectilinear altar tomb, panelled, with shields charged with armorial bearings, among which is seen the chevron between three trefoils; the canopy is very rich, with three ogee arches, having crockets and finials; the spandrels have beautiful pierced panelling, and there is a cornice of Tudor flower, the buttresses terminated by crocketed pinnacles.

In the south chancel in the wall is a rich feathered arch, which had a crocketed triangular canopy, now destroyed, and supported on slender shafts, with foliated capitals. Within is a slab in shape of a coffin, and the arch is flanked by crocketed pinnacles. In the centre of the chancel is a fine large brass of William Thornbury, vicar of Faversham, who died soon after 1480.

* In 1851, on the removal of "many repeated coats of whitewash," some mural paintings were discovered in St. Thomas's Chapel, in the north aisle, which are described and figured in a paper by Mr. Williment, in "Archaeologia Cantiana", vol. i., pp. 150-3. More recently, "a painting, representing the murder of Becket, has been discovered upon the north wall of that chapel. In the north transept an octagonal pillar, in the eastern arcade, is completely covered with paintings descriptive of incidents in the life of the Virgin Mary." "Archaeologia Cantiana," vol. ix. p. lxi.—H.

† This was replaced by a stone reredos, when the church was restored. R.

There is also a smaller one to another vicar, John Redborne, 1531. In the south transept is a large and fine brass to Henry Hatche, merchant and jurat of Faversham, whose figure, with that of his wife, is represented beneath a rich screen, with the following inscription, partly concealed by a pew: "Under this stone lyeth buryed the body of henry hatche merchant of the ffyve ports whyche was durying his lyffe a greate benefactor to this Churche   yere of our lorde god M.CCCCXXXIII and also lyeth the body of Johan the wyfe of the sayde H. H., whych Johan departyd the   day   of   in the yere of our lord god MCCCCC   on whose soules Jesu have mey. Amen."

There is also a monument of John Castlock, late jurat and mayor, who died 1613, and Alice his wife, with some lines inscribed, and several other brasses and monuments, chiefly to merchants and members of the corporation.*

The ancient tower stood at the intersection of the nave and transepts. The alterations in the nave were made in 1755, at the expense of £2500; the tower and spire are more recent. The length of the church is 160 feet by 65. The transept 124 feet.

PRESTON.
ST. CATHERINE.

This village adjoins the town of Faversham so closely as to form a part of it. The church is a low building, but very interesting, and principally of good Early English work. The walls are wholly of flints, and the roof tiled. The plan consists of a nave, with south aisle,† a chancel, and a very

---

* At the time the church was under restoration, "a number of brasses were found in different parts of the church, though, unfortunately, none of them are quite perfect. Some of the inscriptions they bear are not to be found in any history of the town, nor in Weever. . . . They have all been preserved, and refixed in the church." "Dioc. Calendar."—H.

† The church has since been restored, and a north aisle has been added to the nave.—R.

low tower on the south side of the east end of the nave. The
tower scarcely rises above the roof of the nave, has a plain unfinished top, belfry windows single lancets, and another lancet
in the lower part on the west side, with a rectangular label
over it. The nave has on the south side three Curvilinear
windows of two lights, and on the north some lancets and one
square Rectilinear one. The west window is likewise Rectilinear. The nave opens to its side aisle by two large dissimilar
pointed arches, with no mouldings, one lofty, and the other
wide and low; the pier between the two arches is very massive
and square, and there is a thick wall between the western arch
and the west wall.

The chancel arch springs from corbel heads. The chancel
has on the north side five lancets, some walled up, the arch
mouldings deep and fine, and supported upon shafts: on the
same side is inserted one Curvilinear window. On the south
are three lancets, and one two-light Curvilinear window, a string
runs beneath the windows, and on the north side is an ogee
arch in the wall deeply moulded, with a finial. On the south
of the altar are three stone stalls of extreme richness, but much
mutilated,* the back part being entirely diapered with flowers
carved in diamond compartments, the canopies and feathering are
sadly mutilated, but at each extremity is a shaft with very rich
capital of foliage, of Curvilinear character. Above runs a hollow
band, filled with heads and pieces of foliage. There are traces
of painting and gilding; and eastward of the stalls is an elegant
ogee niche, feathered and crocketed, with a piscina, and small
shafts with foliated capitals, set against buttresses which are
enriched with bands of square flower, and crowned by pinnacles.
In the chancel is a slab with a brass to the memory of Valentine
Baret, and Cicely his wife. He died in 1410, she in 1442,
both figures in very perfect condition; also one to William
Mareys, the figure in armour and in fine preservation, with

* Since restored by the Dean and Chapter of Canterbury, the impropriators.
—H.

a sword and spurs, but no helmet: from his mouth proceeds a scroll inscribed in black letter "Misericordias dñi in eternum cantabo," and beneath his feet, "Hic jacet Willm̄s Mareys quōdā honorād Armiger regis henrici V^ti ac deinde Armiger revēndi in xpo patris ac dñi dñi henrici* Cardinalis Anglie q̄ quidem Willm̄s obiit ultimo die mēs^s Augusti A° Dñi M°CCCC° lix° cui^s aīc" &c. &c. There is on the north side a sumptuous altar tomb of marble to Roger Boyle and his wife Joan, erected by their son Richard Boyle, first earl of Cork; with figures of others of the family. There is a good deal of wood screen work, and some fine carved desks. The font is square, upon a cylindrical base surrounded by four round shafts.

CANTERBURY.

HOLY CROSS CHURCH (*Westgate*).

This church† is built of flints, and is a plain structure of the two later styles, consisting of a nave and aisles, a chancel and a square embattled tower at the west end of the south aisle, containing five bells: the windows are mostly Curvilinear, some with flat arches. The chancel has square-headed Rectilinear windows. The nave has on each side four pointed arches with octagonal pillars. The font is a plain octagon, upon a shaft of the same form: the cover is of rich wood tabernacle work. At the west end is a good organ.‡

ST. PETER'S CHURCH.

This church consists of three equal aisles; the centre one being divided from each of the others by a row of four plain pointed arches with no mouldings, and square piers entirely

---

* Henry Beaufort.—H.   † Built by Archbishop Sudbury, *circa* 1380.—R.
‡ This church has been thoroughly repaired, restored, and rearranged; the tower, more recently, has been rebuilt. A new organ has been placed in the south aisle.—H.

plain. At the west end of the south aisle is the tower opening by a low pointed arch. Most of the windows have been modernised, but the western one is Rectilinear, and one on the north is Curvilinear, with square head, and filled with good stained glass. On the north side of the altar is a feathered ogee niche; there is also on the south side an opening into the aisle. The font is square and plain.

ST. MARGARET'S CHURCH.

This church is deformed in its plan and utterly devoid of any architectural beauty.* It consists of three aisles with no chancel, and a plain embattled tower at the west end of the south aisle. The east wall is not in a straight line, but expands upon the south side.† The windows are partly Rectilinear, but many barbarously altered and modernised. The interior is sadly wanting in symmetry; the tower occupies the west end of the south aisle, and beyond it are two ill-formed wide pointed arches with octagonal pillars. On the north are four arches of different proportions with octagonal pillars. A neat organ has been erected on the south side. The font is octagonal, cased in wood: the shaft has at each angle small Early English columns.

ST. MILDRED'S CHURCH.

This is perhaps the best parish church in Canterbury: it consists of a nave and chancel, each with north aisle, and a tower standing between the two north aisles.‡ The chancel has also a chapel on the south side. Most parts are built of flints, the tower plain and rude. On the south side of the nave are some good and light Curvilinear windows, with flat heads and

---

* Much alteration has subsequently taken place in St. Margaret.
† The deformity created by one corner of the south chancel aisle having been levelled off to widen the street, has been skilfully dealt with by Sir G. Gilbert Scott setting back the east wall of that aisle and giving an apse to the main chancel. H.
‡ The tower was taken down many years ago. H.

labels: on the north side are two plain lancets. The west window is Rectilinear, of three lights; as are the three eastern windows, the central one being of five lights with good tracery. The south chancel has some rude chequered flint work, with a cross worked in the west gable. The nave is divided from the aisle by two pointed arches, with an octagonal pillar. The tower opens to the chancel by a similar arch; as also does the north chancel. The chancel opens to its south chancel (which belonged to the Atwoods, formerly resident in Stour Street, and eminent in the corporation) by a large Tudor arch now walled up. The chapel now is used as a lumber room.* Between the nave and chancel is seen an aperture for the rood-loft. Over the east end of the nave is a wooden ceiling, coved and painted blue. North of the chancel is a Rectilinear vestry. Upon one pier of the nave is a niche and bracket. The font is an octagonal one, panelled with quatrefoils upon a pedestal. There are several handsome modern monuments, and a good organ has been erected in the west gallery. The churchyard commands a very pleasing view, and is surrounded by the ancient walls of the city.†

ST. GEORGE'S CHURCH.

This church consists of a nave and a north aisle, and at the west end a square embattled tower surmounted by a very small leaden spire.‡ Some of the windows are Curvilinear, with square heads; others are Rectilinear, of which the south ones are good. The tower-arch springs from circular shafts, and the nave is divided from the aisle by five pointed arches, with some early piers—one square and one circular, with a Norman capital: the eastern pier is lighter and octagonal. The font is a very good

---

* The church has been well restored and re-seated within, and a new organ placed on the north side of the choir.—H.

† Early Tudor carving adorns the north door of the nave.—R.

‡ A new chancel has been built, and a north aisle added to the church: the arches having been taken from the church, recently taken down, of St. Mary Magdalene, Burgate (the parish united to St. George's).—H.

Early English one of octagonal form; the pedestal also octagonal, and surrounded by shafts having bell capitals. One of the east windows contains some good stained glass. In the vestry is a curious painting of Guy Fawkes, date 1632 inscribed "In perpetuam Papistarum infamiam."

ST. MARY MAGDALEN'S CHURCH (Burgate).

This small church contains little worthy of remark, and consists of two equal aisles divided by a row of four pointed arches with slender octagonal pillars, having square capitals, apparently Norman. Some windows are square-headed, of Rectilinear character; others are Curvilinear. There is a low tower with pointed roof engaged with the west end of the northern aisle, and ranging with the street. The font is good Early English, almost exactly resembling that of St. George. There is a sumptuous monument to John Whitfield who died 1691.*

ST. DUNSTAN'S CHURCH (without the Westgate).

This church stands in the suburbs, and is a pretty structure, with very fair portions of the two later styles. It consists of a nave and chancel, each with a south aisle, and a plain tower, standing at the west end of the south aisle. The west window is a good Rectilinear one of three lights; on the south side are some early Curvilinear ones of two lights, and on the north one lancet. The nave is very wide, and is divided from its aisle by four good pointed arches, with mouldings carried down the face of the piers, to which are attached circular shafts. The chancel has one trefoiled lancet on the north, and is divided from the south chapel by two pointed arches with an octagonal pillar. The south chapel has a flat wood ceiling, and has late windows with

---

* This church, with the exception of the tower, has been taken down, and the area enclosed. The materials, including the arcade and columns of Kentish rag, have been used in the enlargement of the sister church of St. George the Martyr. The monument of John Whitfield is preserved under the tower.—H.

flat arches. It is the burial place of the Ropers: in it is buried the head of Sir Thomas More, whose daughter [Margaret] married one of that family, and is interred in this chapel. It contains two Rectilinear altar-tombs: one with the sides richly panelled; the other plainer, beneath a flat-arch canopy. The font is octagonal, on a shaft; and has a wooden cover of very rich tabernacle work.

Of the other Canterbury churches, few are worthy of the least remark. *St. Martin's* is an Early English structure, with some earlier portions, built on a more ancient foundation—consisting only of a nave and chancel, with a tower. The font a superb Norman one.[*] *St. Paul's* has some Curvilinear windows. *St. Alphage* has been much mutilated and modernised, but neat within, and contains an organ.[*] *All Saints'* and *St. Mary Northgate* are modern Gothic structures, with towers, but deserve no attention. *St. Mary Bredin*[†] is very small and mean. *St. Mary Bredman* is modern and quite plain. *St. Andrew's* is a plain structure of brick with a tower. Both the last mentioned contain organs.

Of the Abbey of St. Augustine[‡]—the gateway is a most magnificent specimen of the Curvilinear style, and undoubtedly the finest work of the sort that is to be found. The front is flanked by two lofty octagonal turrets rising above the roof, finished by a battlement, and enriched with panelling, some of which is pierced for windows. The centre contains a wide arch for the gate springing from shafts, and the mouldings filled with square flowers. The woodwork of the door itself is finely sculptured. The spandrels each contain a quatrefoiled circle. Above the gateway arch is a series of rich niches with crocketed pyramidal canopies, and feathering continued over each of the side turrets; there are also two rich windows of two lights

---

[*] For St. Martin's and St. Alphage, *vide infra.*—H.
[†] The church of St. Mary Bredin has been entirely rebuilt on an enlarged scale and a new design.—H.
[‡] Built 1297 to 1309.

introduced in the range. Above, there is a fine band of panelling and a rich battlement. Of the other portions of the Abbey some fragments remain, especially some fine Norman parts of what is called Ethelbert's tower.

THE CATHEDRAL CHURCH.

This magnificent and highly interesting building would take a volume to describe adequately; and it has already been so much noticed and illustrated by engravings, that it will suffice to make very few remarks. The plan, though intricate, is very regular; comprising a nave and choir with side aisles, a western and an eastern transept, a spacious chapel behind the choir called Trinity Chapel with a semicircular end, beyond which again is a circular space called Becket's crown. There are several other chapels, both north and south; but they almost invariably are placed quite regularly, answering to each other. A magnificent Rectilinear tower arises from the intersection at the western transept, and the west front is flanked by two towers. The northern was formerly a Norman one, but, being ruinous, was taken down, and is now* being replaced by one to correspond with the south tower, which is a very good Rectilinear one, with panelled battlements and eight pinnacles. The whole of the western portion, as far as the choir, is Rectilinear of good character; the exterior plain, without battlement, but the buttresses crowned with pinnacles, and there are flying buttresses to the clerestory. The west front is plain, but has a large window and good door. Attached to the south side of the south-west tower is a rich and beautiful porch with panelling and niches. The interior of the nave is very fine: the arches very grand, the piers rich, the groining of this part is also of the richest description. The central tower is open to a considerable height, and has a light and beautiful effect. There is a very considerable flight of steps up to the choir, beneath which is a very large and beautiful crypt, or undercroft, the largest in England. The eastern portion,

* 1830.—H.

including the choir with the chapels, has highly curious Early English work, parts just emerging from Norman with many singularities; yet the arches of the choir, and all the lower portions, may be considered Norman, but late in the style. The screen of stone between the nave and choir is a most splendid Rectilinear one. The arches of the choir are semicircular, but lofty and with very rich mouldings; the piers mostly massive, in some cases, clustered; the capitals have very rich foliage. The clerestory of the choir has long lancets in each division, with fine mouldings, and shafts with foliated capitals. The groining of the roof is plain, but good. The aisles have some lancet windows, and some with semicircular heads, all having shafts; these aisles have also an upper tier of curious windows with trefoil heads. There is much ancient stained glass, of splendid colouring. The Norman and Early English forms are much intermixed, and the ribs of the groining have chevron ornament. The eastern transepts have three heights of windows, and beneath the lowest externally a range of intersecting arches continued all along the choir aisles. In the upper tier of the south-east transept, is a plain circular window; and attached to the same transept is a square Norman tower with several tiers of arches. St. Anselm's Chapel, (south of Trinity Chapel) is also Norman, but has, inserted, a fine Curvilinear window. The chapel of Henry IV. (north of Trinity Chapel) has an exquisite fan-groined roof.

The monuments are very numerous; that of Archbishop Theobald is very Early English, the sides enriched with trefoil arches and shafts. Those of Archbishops Meopham and Peckham are fine Curvilinear specimens; that of Warham is late and good Rectilinear; that of Chicheley is earlier. The undercroft exhibits great variety, and is of immense extent; the greater part is Norman, but there is much later work in the groining and other decorations; it contains also a chapel dedicated to St. Mary, and the tomb of Archbishop Morton.

On the north side of the cathedral there are very extensive

portions of the monastic buildings, in very perfect condition; including the cloisters, which are quite perfect, and of Rectilinear character, with groined ceiling and fine canopies to the windows. The chapter house is a large fine space and has a very large rich window of seven lights of Rectilinear tracery.

The treasury, situated on the north side of Trinity Chapel, is a very fine Norman specimen, with ranges of intersecting and other arches. The registry * is approached by a most beautiful and rich Norman staircase, the arches and capitals exquisitely sculptured. There are many other fine portions of Norman and other styles among the prebendal houses and other buildings surrounding the cathedral,† and many fine gateways, &c.

BEAKESBOURNE.
ST. PETER.

The church is small, consisting of a nave, a small south transept, and chancel; and a small modern tower at the west end. The north doorway is Norman with chevron ornament and shafts; there is a plain semicircular arch in the north wall which seems to have opened to a transept now destroyed. There is a similar arch opening to the south transept. In the nave some windows are Norman, but most of them are Rectilinear. The chancel has, on the north, three lancet windows of plain work; on the south one obtuse lancet, and some of late date; at the east end two lancets, on the piers of which, in the inside, are very elegant moulded Early English brackets: a string runs beneath the northern windows. The font is a plain octagon.

* The Registry was removed to another building many years ago; the room occupied by it now forms the Library of the King's School.— H.
† The remains of the ancient buildings of the priory, on the north side of the cathedral, particularly the infirmary, and its chapel, the dormitory, &c., have been brought into view, within the last few years, by the removal of prebendal and other houses, which, after the dissolution of the priory, had been built into them. H.

This small and insignificant village, though at such a distance, is a member of the port of Hastings, and within its jurisdiction, being exempt from the county magistrates.

PATRICKSBOURNE.
ST. MARY.

July 1881. F.A.S.

This church is remarkable for its singularly beautiful specimens of Norman work. It consists of a nave and chancel; the nave having a south aisle, the central portion of which is occupied by the tower, which forms a south porch, and has one of the richest doorways that is to be found, and in excellent preservation. The door itself is flat at the top, and the head of the arch filled with sculpture, representing in one compartment the figure of St. Peter, together with grotesque figures of birds and beasts: the shafts have rich capitals of the finest workmanship. The arch has three tiers of moulding; one of which has scrolls mixed with heads and animals, one has pieces of foliage set alternately with gryphons and other animals, the third moulding is of much plainer character: the whole is crowned with a high pediment, within which is a small semicircular opening.

The tower itself is plain in the upper story, and surmounted by a shingled spire. There is another good Norman doorway on the north with shafts, but much smaller than that on the south side.* At the west end of the south aisle is a Norman window: the other windows of the nave are mostly Rectilinear, or Curvilinear with square head. Parts of the exterior have been lately restored, the interior is newly and handsomely pewed.† The part of the aisle westward of the tower is occupied as a receptacle for rubbish and opens by plain semicircular arch to the nave. The tower and the part eastward

---

* The two fine Norman doorways, as well as the exterior of the church generally, are engraved in the "Antiquarian Itinerary," vol. vi.

† The church has been more completely restored and put in order since these notes were written.—H.

of it open each to the nave by pointed arches, that of the tower having the billet ornament. The chancel opens to the nave by a semicircular arch with shafts. The east end of the chancel has in the upper part a curious circular wheel window, apparently of Norman work, the mouldings having the chevron ornament: below this are three narrow windows with semicircular heads, the central being the highest, but these are now stopped up.* There are some other Norman windows in the chancel, and one inserted of Rectilinear character. The south door of the chancel, now stopped, is small, but handsome, having several ranges of moulding with the chevron and other ornaments, and the shafts have rich worked capitals. Above it is a small statue, rather mutilated. On the south side of the altar is a Curvilinear niche, with crocketed triangular canopy and tracery.

The churchyard is sequestered, and beautifully shaded with trees.

FORDWICH.

ST. MARY.

This church consists of a nave with a north aisle, and a chancel; at the west end is a plain tower without buttresses, surmounted by a shingled spire; the tower appears Early, and has a lancet window. There is one plain, obtusely-pointed window north of the nave; the other windows of the nave are Curvilinear, with square heads and labels, the tracery good. The nave is divided from its aisle by three rude, pointed arches without mouldings, and the piers square.

The chancel has one Norman window, and some square-headed Rectilinear; at the east end a Curvilinear one of two lights. The font is Norman, of square form, moulded with plain, small, semicircular arches; it stands upon a circular pillar with square base.

* These windows are now opened.—H.

STURRY.

ST. NICHOLAS.

This church is of Early English origin, but has lost much of its original character by insertions of later date. It consists of a nave with aisles, a chancel, and a plain embattled tower at the west end of the nave.

There is a wooden south porch, with open panelling, and good feathering in the gable. The south windows of the nave are square headed, of Curvilinear or Rectilinear character. On the north are some windows of two lights, the tracery of which seems to be Curvilinear. The nave is divided from each aisle by four very plain, pointed arches without mouldings, of Early character, and resembling those at Fordwich: the piers square, with imposts. The chancel has one obtuse lancet on the south; and, on the north one, with a trefoiled head and dripstone. The east window consists of two trefoiled lancets with a central shaft. On the north of the chancel is a vestry. The whole church is neatly kept and very well ventilated, and there is an organ at the west end of the nave.*

HERNE.

ST. MARTIN.

This is a large and handsome church, comprising a nave and chancel, each with side aisles, the tower standing at the west end of the north aisle, and engaged in the west front.† The walls are chiefly built of flints. The tower is principally Early English, having a plain parapet; and the two upper stages have each two trefoiled lancet windows on each side. On the west side a Curvilinear window of three lights has been inserted. There is an Early English north porch, having two plain trefoil

---

* This church has been thoroughly restored; the organ removed from the west end, &c.—H.

† Of Herne Church is a good engraving, with description, in Brandon's "Churches."

lancet windows on each side. The north aisle is embattled in its whole length. The northern windows of the nave, and all the south windows of the whole church are Curvilinear of two lights; those of the chancel having very flat contracted arches. At the west end of the nave is a fine large Rectilinear window of five lights, with a transom; and at the west of the south aisle is a small one with square head of three lights. The tower has to the lower story a stone groined ceiling, with plain intersecting ribs, and opens to the nave and to the aisle by very elegant Early English arches having fine mouldings and clustered shafts. The nave is very wide, and has on each side four pointed arches, including that of the tower on the north; the piers are light and of octagonal form. There is no clerestory. The chancel has a fine Curvilinear east window of five lights, and is divided from each aisle by two pointed arches with piers, as in the nave. The chancel extends a little beyond the aisles; and there is a window on each side of the altar, the northern square-headed Rectilinear, the southern is Curvilinear. There is a great deal of good wood screen-work in the chancel, and some carved stalls. On the south of the altar are some remains of stone stalls, with an embattled cornice running over them, but much concealed by walling and monuments placed in front. The south chancel is divided from the south aisle of the nave by a good Early English arch, and has a Rectilinear window of four lights at the east end. The north chancel is large and handsome, and has two east windows of Rectilinear character. It communicates with the chancel by an opening in an oblique direction.

There are in Herne Church several brasses, one of a female has this inscription: "Orate specialit^o p Aiā Dñe Xp̄ine dudū vxoris Mathei Phelip Ciuis et Aurifabri ac quondā Maioris Cinitatis Londoñ que Migrauit ab hac valle Miserie xxv^o. die Maii A^o dñi Millñio CCCC^{o}lxx^o Cuius Aīe ppiciet^o Dē Amē."

The font is an octagon, with panelling and shields, the pedestal enriched with very beautiful panelled tracery. A large barrel organ is erected in a gallery in the south aisle of the nave.

The situation of the village is very pleasing, in a wooded valley, at the distance of near two miles from the sea.

HOATH.
ST. MARY.

This church is but a small, mean fabric, consisting merely of a nave and chancel, and a wooden turret over the west end. There are some lancet windows; at the east end is a double lancet with a circle between the heads. The west window was Curvilinear of three lights, but the tracery has been sadly mutilated.* There are a few others of Curvilinear character, and some of Rectilinear date. On the south of the altar is a plain niche with piscina and shelf. In the nave is a small brass with the figures of a man and a woman, of the 16th century;† there is another in the chancel‡ inscribed "Hic jacet Isabella Chakbon cuius anime ppicietur deus Amen." The arch to the chancel is pointed.

ST. NICHOLAS AT WADE (in Thanet).

This church is a very good building, consisting of a nave with aisles and clerestory, a chancel with side aisles, and a lofty tower at the west end of the south aisle. There is a variety of good work of every style. The whole of the nave, south porch, and tower are embattled; the latter has an octagonal corner turret, a very common feature in Kent, and on the south side an elegant Curvilinear window of two lights, having shafts in the mullions. The south porch is of two stages, and contains a niche and stoup. The windows of the nave are mostly Curvi-

---
* This church has been restored and re-seated.—H.
† Antony Maycot, 1535, and wife Agnes, with two sons and five daughters.—H. ‡ 1430.—H.

linear upon the south side; and the west window is a very good one of three lights, but the upper part walled up.* At the west of the north aisle is a lancet window; the others in the north aisle, as well as those of the clerestory, are Rectilinear. The north chapel of the chancel is embattled, and loftier than the aisle of the nave; the south aisle has a tiled roof. The windows of the chancel are mostly Curvilinear; that at the east end a rich one of five lights, but there is one plain lancet in the south aisle.

The interior of the nave has a grand appearance, and there is much variety in the arches on each side. Upon each side they are five in number, including that which opens to the tower on the south side. The northern arches are all pointed with octagonal piers. On the south, the three eastern arches are Norman, varying in character; one of them much enriched, having a kind of wavy ornament running round one of the mouldings, as well as the toothed ornament; the piers are square, with shafts attached, from whence spring the arches; these have fine and varied capitals with square abaci; in some there is foliage, in others the scroll or heads; the fourth arch is pointed and very acute, that to the tower also pointed, with rich architrave mouldings, rising from octagonal shafts. A similar arch on the east side of the tower opens into the south aisle. Some of the windows have portions of rich stained glass. The chancel is divided from its north aisle by two plain Early English arches, with a circular pillar having the abacus and an Early capital; to the south aisle there is only one wide pointed arch. On the south side is some fine wood screen work, part of which appears to be of Curvilinear period. The space inclosed within the altar rails is unusually large, and the altar table and screen very neat. There is a small doorway, set very high up, south of the chancel arch, as if to communicate with the rood-loft. The font is of lead, and of octagonal form upon a circular base.

* This church has lately undergone a complete restoration. H.

MINSTER IN THANET.
ST. MARY.

This is unquestionably one of the very finest churches in the county, and is a very large cruciform structure; the nave being a fine and perfect specimen of pure Norman work, the chancel of beautiful Early English, and the transepts also of the latter style, but plainer. At the west end of the nave is the tower, of Norman work, without buttresses, and having a large square turret attached to the south side. There are three stages of windows with semicircular heads, of rather plain character, the parapet is embattled, and crowned by a well proportioned shingled spire. The nave has a leaded roof, the aisles are embattled, most of the windows are modernised,* but one of the original Norman windows remains on the north side. The nave is wide and lofty, and is divided from each aisle by five handsome semicircular arches, the three eastern of which have the chevron and billet ornaments in the mouldings, the others are much plainer; the pillars are circular; some of the capitals on the north side enriched with foliage, the bases of the pillars are square; the tower opens to the nave by a semicircular arch, springing from shafts, above which in the tower is a window of the same form opening to the nave. The transepts are Early English, and the exterior plain: some of the buttresses have triangular heads. The north transept has two lancets at the north end, two on the east and one on the west side, and opens by a good arch with shafts to the north aisle. The south transept has also some lancets; but a rectilinear window is inserted at the end. The springs of groining in the chancel are begun, rising from shafts which stand upon the string beneath the windows. In the north transept is an arch in the wall for a tomb. The space at the intersection of the body and the transepts, seems originally destined for the erection of a tower, and

* The church has been completely restored, with the tracery of the windows, &c.—H.

has stone groining of plain character. The chancel has a very fine effect within, and its ceiling is entirely groined in stone: the ribs merely cross each other without bosses, and spring from shafts with moulded bell capitals. Upon each side of the chancel are four lancet windows without shafts; but at the east end is a fine triple lancet window having very deep mouldings, and clustered shafts with bell capitals. Some of the shafts are gone which sustained the ribs of the groining, but the capitals remain, and along the line of the capitals is carried an elegant band of Early English ornament, consisting of quatrefoils and circles. All the ancient stalls remain in fine condition, with handsome wood carving. The altar table is not enclosed by rails. The whole church is in good order, well cleaned and preserved, and the fine arches and pillars of the nave divested of their coats of whitewash. The font is an octagon, but cased in wood. The churchyard is surrounded by fine elms, and commands an extensive view on the north over the marsh, with Ash Church.

BIRCHINGTON.

ALL SAINTS.

This is a good church, consisting of a nave with aisles, a chancel with side chapels, and a tower crowned with a shingled spire, upon the south side of the chancel. The nave is wide, but the side aisles narrow; the greater part of the church is Rectilinear, with good windows of two and three lights. The tower is, however, Early English, and opens upon three sides by plain pointed arches rising upon imposts, some of its windows are of lancet form. The nave is divided from each aisle by five pointed arches springing from octagonal pillars; there seems to have been a stone arch thrown across the south aisle from one of the piers, which is consequently strengthened. There remain some portions of the rood-loft screen. The chapel south of the chancel, and adjoining the tower on the east, is now the vestry, and contains a curious old wood chest, and the brass of an ecclesiastic.* The chapel on the north opens to the chancel by pointed arches, and is called the Quex Chapel, from an ancient family now extinct, formerly possessors of the estate of the same name in this parish. In this are several brasses and handsome monuments. One brass represents two figures, one considerably smaller than the other, thus inscribed—"Hic jacet Johēs Queke." 1449. Another represents a female figure, with a smaller one kneeling at her feet. There is also one of small size to Margaret Cryspe, wyfe of John Cryspe 1533, beneath which is represented an infant in swaddling clothes. Another represents eight sons and seven daughters. There is a panelled altar-tomb to one of the Crispe family,† the panelling containing shields charged with various armorial bearings; upon it are the effigies of a man and woman. The other tombs to the Crispes are of later date, mostly of the gorgeous but heavy style of James I. One of them to Henry Crispe and Marie his wife (1618) is sculptured with figures of their children, some of whom carry sculls, seeming to mark that they died before their parents. Another monument to the same family has six compartments, each containing a bust in bas-relief. The font is an octagon, supported upon a central cylindrical shaft, and having four smaller ones at the alternate sides.‡

MONKTON.

ST. MARY.

This is a small church, comprising only a nave and chancel, with a tower at the west end; but there was formerly a north aisle opening to the nave by five pointed arches, which may be

* John Heynys, vicar of Monkton, obiit 1523.—R.
† Sir Henry Crispe (obt. 1575) and his first wife Catherine Scott.—R.
‡ The church has been well restored.—H.

seen in the wall of the nave; and there is likewise a fragment of the west wall of the same aisle. There are a few Norman windows walled up on the south, the others are all Rectilinear insertions. The tower and the chancel arch are Early English. The former is plain, and without buttresses: in the lower part are plain lancets; in the belfry story two trefoiled lancets on each side; the parapet without battlement; the arch from the tower to the church is pointed, upon imposts. That to the chancel springs from shafts with early capitals, upon which are small plain brackets of stone. The font is octagonal, and cased in wood. The pulpit large with wood carving, temp. James I. At the west end is a gallery with an organ.*

MARGATE, alias ST. JOHN'S.

This is a large low building of not much beauty, the exterior being almost wholly modernised, and the interior disfigured by shabby irregular pews and unsightly galleries.† The length is considerable, and both nave and chancel have side aisles. The tower, which stands at the west end of the north aisle, is modern. A vestry, with embattled parapet forms the eastern termination of the north aisle. The windows are mostly moderuised, but some few have the original Rectilinear tracery, and some south of the chancel are trefoiled lancets, having to the interior very good mouldings and shafts. The nave is seven bays in length, the space of one bay on the north being occupied by the tower. The arches are of various character: on the south they are all pointed, some of very plain Early English character without mouldings; the piers are mostly octagonal; the eastern arch springs from a shaft with rich foliated capital. On the north the two eastern arches are semicircular, the rest pointed; the

---

* This church has been entirely re-seated and put in order.—H.
† This church has just undergone a complete repair and restoration; galleries removed, and church re-seated, 1876.—H.

piers all circular with square abacus and early capitals. The chancel has two arches on each side; on the north, of Early character without mouldings, and a massive circular pier; on the south the arches are of more advanced period, with an octagonal pier. The font is octagonal, panelled, with shields and roses. There is, in the western gallery, a good organ presented to the church in 1797.

ST. PETER'S (in Thanet).

This is a large long church, in many respects resembling Margate, consisting of a nave and chancel, each with side aisles and tiled roofs; and at the west end of the north aisle a lofty tower much out of proportion with the lowness of the body. The walls are mostly of flints; there are considerable portions of Norman and Early English work, and some of later date. The tower has an octagonal turret attached to the north side; on the west side is a Curvilinear window of three lights; the belfry window is of two lights, and the whole is surmounted by a battlement. The windows are, some Curvilinear, some Rectilinear, many of which have lost their tracery.* There is one trefoiled lancet on the south side. There is a small north door with some Early English nail-head ornament. The south porch is embattled. The tower opens to the north aisle by a fine pointed arch with good mouldings. The arrangement of the arches in the nave and chancel is dissimilar on the two sides, and irregular; in the western part of the nave the divisions are formed by blank walls, which seem original; beyond which, on the north, are four very plain semicircular arches, with circular columns having square capitals and bases, and ornaments in the angles of the bases. On the south side are three arches:

* This church has been thoroughly restored, with the tracery of the windows, throughout; the pews replaced by open seats, and the western gallery removed, &c.--H.

one, nearest the west, pointed and very plain, with a square Early pier having shafts set at the angles; the other two arches are pointed, with circular pillars as on the north, and the eastern arch rises from a semi-column attached to the pier. The fourth arch on the south opens to the chancel, and is a good Early English one, with toothed ornament in the mouldings. The south aisle is only continued a little way along the chancel; but the north aisle extends to the east end, and opens to the chancel by three rude Early pointed arches with square piers. The chancel has the roof coved, and divided into panelled compartments by wooden ribs with bosses of good carving: beneath runs a cornice of wood carving, with pieces of foliage, &c. The pews are neat and uniform, and the altar handsome. There are some monumental brasses of the fifteenth century; and, in the west gallery, a good organ.

ST. LAWRENCE (in Thanet).

This church consists of a nave with side aisles, small transepts not extending beyond the body, a chancel with side chapels and a tower rising from the centre. The exterior is plain and not remarkable. The tower partakes both of Norman and Early English work; the arches upon which it is supported, opening to the body, transepts, and chancel, are pointed; the eastern and western having fine architrave mouldings and clustered shafts with capitals of Early English foliage. The other two arches are plainer with square pilasters. In the eastern arch there is some of the chevron ornament. On the south, outside the tower is a range of four semicircular arches of Norman character, with shafts. The belfry windows consist of two single lights on each side; the parapet is embattled. The nave is divided from each aisle by three plain, pointed arches, the columns massive and circular, with square capitals of early date. The chancel has on each side two plain, Early, pointed arches, with square piers having shafts at the angles; on the south is also a third arch, smaller and lower. The roof of the chancel is coved and panelled; with ribs, bosses, and flowered cornice running beneath, as at St. Peter's. In the north chancel is a wooden screen, and some ancient books, including Foxe's Book of Martyrs, and others. There are some brasses—one to Nicholas Manston, armiger,* 1444. In the south chancel is an ogee niche trefoiled, with a stoup. The whole church is fitted up with pews and galleries painted with most glaring white. The windows are all Rectilinear, but many mutilated.†

SANDWICH.
ST. PETER'S CHURCH.

This church has undergone considerable mutilation, and has at present a very unsightly, patched appearance. It consists now of a nave and chancel with a north aisle, and a tower placed between the nave and chancel. The south aisle is destroyed, but part of its outer wall is standing, and the arches are visible, built into the south wall of the nave. The walls are mostly of flints; the tower is large, but the upper part is modern and built of brick. There is a Rectilinear north porch embattled; all the windows of the nave have been sadly mutilated. The interior is spacious and lofty; and the nave is divided from its aisle by three pointed arches with octagonal pillars. The chancel is divided from its aisle by two similar arches, and those which support the tower are of like character. There is no vestige of very early work about the church. The chancel has a fine Curvilinear window on the north side, of three lights, but unfortunately walled-up. In the north aisle is an ogee arch for a tomb, flanked by buttresses with pinnacles; there are also the effigies of a man and woman, and a slab with a cross flory and inscription in Lombard letters. A small altar-tomb is

* With collar of SS.—H. † This church has been much improved.—H.

panelled with trefoils containing heads, and bears the mutilated effigy of a knight. There is one good carved pew-end. In the west gallery is an organ.

ST. MARY'S CHURCH.

This church is an unsightly and deformed building, having been greatly modernised and altered from its original plan. The exterior is much patched and repaired with brick. The nave and south aisle are thrown into one, under the same roof, and the arches removed; the north aisle is now divided from the nave by a row of six modern wooden arches; but there remains, against the wall, an ancient Norman pillar of clustered shafts with fine capitals. The chancel is thrown into one space with its aisle, exactly as the nave; and at the east and west ends of the church are two windows of plain tracery without feathering, possibly modern. The west window of the north aisle is a good Curvilinear one of three lights; and there are two others on the north side with an ogee canopy and finial, and Curvilinear tracery of two lights: the others are mostly modern, except one lancet on the south side. At the west end, above the two windows, is the trace of a small Norman window, walled-up. Beneath some of the windows externally runs a string-course. On the south side is a small low tower crowned with a wooden turret, and forming a porch. On the north side of the chancel is an ogee feathered arch in the wall: there are some vestiges of brasses, and a slab with inscription in Lombard letters too much worn to be decyphered. There is also a Norman pillar in the chancel wall. The font is an octagon, with quatrefoil panelling. There is a neat Grecian altar-screen, and the interior is very tolerably neat generally, but the exterior is mean and hardly resembles a church.

ST. CLEMENT'S CHURCH.

This is a large and handsome church, consisting of a nave and a chancel, each with side aisles, and a very fine Norman tower rising between the nave and chancel. All the other parts are of later date, but the tower is an uncommonly beautiful specimen of enriched Norman: it is supported upon four lofty semi-circular arches, with good mouldings, opening to the interior, with clustered shafts having sculptured capitals; within the original arches, north and south of the tower, are inserted pointed Early English ones, rising from shafts with bell capitals and bases, probably for the purpose of strengthening the original arches. Above the arches, and open to the interior, runs a tier of semicircular arches, the piers formed alternately by single and clustered shafts. The tower has, above the roof, three tiers of semicircular arches all round, and set very close, with good mouldings, and shafts having enriched capitals; the top of the tower is unfinished, but the Norman enrichment is singularly beautiful. The nave is light and lofty with a clerestory and side aisles, and of Rectilinear character. The windows have been sadly mutilated, in many instances; that at the west end is large, but the tracery is gone.* Above it is a square tablet, containing a pierced quatrefoil; and below it a doorway with mouldings and label. There is a large north porch, the outer doorway of which has octagonal shafts. The nave is divided from each aisle by three elegant arches, finely moulded, and the mouldings are continued down the piers, which have shafts attached to the extremities. The clerestory windows are of two lights with contracted arches. The ceiling is of wood with plain panelling. At the north-west angle of the tower is a staircase turret of square form, entered from within by a small Norman doorway, having the head of the arch filled with scroll work and other ornaments. The chancel is separated from each aisle by two pointed arches. Those on the north are Early English, without moulding, and the pier is circular, with square base. On the south they are much wider, with mouldings, and a light octagonal pillar having the base square. In the chancel

* The church has been carefully restored, with the tracery of the windows, &c.—R.

aisles are some Curvilinear windows, and some of later date; some have been well restored, and others mutilated. The chancel extends a little eastward of the aisles; the stalls in the chancel are perfect; and on the north side is a small door, with label, opening obliquely to the aisle. At the east end of the south aisle is a small low vestry. On the south pier, between the tower and chancel, is a large niche of Rectilinear character, once very rich, but mutilated, having fine feathering and a band of foliage, with vestiges of red paint and gilding. The font is Rectilinear, of octagonal form; the sides ornamented alternately with roses, and shields with arms; the pedestal has a niche on each side. In the nave is a large brass, mutilated. The church is very well attended to, within and without, being well drained, the earth removed from the walls, and the whitewash scraped from off many of the ornamental parts.

ST. BARTHOLOMEW'S HOSPITAL, SANDWICH.

The chapel of this hospital is an Early English structure, consisting of two aisles; of which, the northern does not extend to the west end of the other aisle, but has on the west side two lancet windows, with a quatrefoil circle between their heads. There is, at the west end, a doorway having toothed ornament in the mouldings. There is also a south door of similar character with shafts. The windows on the south side consist, each of double lancets; those in the chancel have very fine mouldings with shafts, and the whole north side of the chancel has a series of arches with shafts. The east window consists of three lancets. The arches which form the divisions between the aisles are plain and pointed; in the nave the pier is square, in the chancel octagonal.*

* The repair and restoration of this chapel is now about to be undertaken. 1876. H.

WOODNESBOROUGH.
ST. MARY.

This church consists of a nave with side aisles, and a chancel, with a square tower at the west end of the nave. The tower is very plain, and of Early English character, without buttresses, the divisions of the stages marked by string-courses; the west door has the shafts rather mutilated. The divisions between the nave and aisles are formed by a double row of arches, four on each side. Those on the south are pointed, but very plain, and the piers square; on the north they are semicircular, with piers alternately circular and octagonal. The windows of the nave seem to have been chiefly of Curvilinear character, of two lights; but many have lost their tracery.

The chancel has, on the north, one lancet window, and others consisting each of two trefoiled lights, one being of Rectilinear character; and at the east end is a Curvilinear window of three lights, of early character, with good mouldings. On the south side of the chancel are three beautiful stone stalls, of Rectilinear character, each having a crocketed ogee head, and in each of the spandrels a circle containing a quatrefoil with foliage. Each arch has feathering, and beneath the canopy is some elegant groining; the divisions are formed by clustered shafts. Above the whole runs a parapet of small battlements. There is also a small feathered niche in a square compartment having a piscina. The situation of the church is picturesque, surrounded by trees, and the churchyard enclosed by an old wall mantled with ivy.

BARFRESTON.
ST. MARY.

This small church is quite a gem as a specimen of highly enriched Norman work.* It is exceedingly small, consisting

* This church has been expensively restored since 1830.

only of a nave and chancel. There are engravings of it, showing several of the details, in Britton's Architectural Antiquities, Vol. 4, which represent them more clearly than any description can do. A bold block cornice runs all round beneath the eaves of the roof, *externally*. The nave has on each side two windows, the heads of which are semicircular; in the interior there runs a string-course, filled with toothed ornament, carried over the windows. On the exterior of each side there is a range of arched recesses, in line with the windows, but varying in character, those on the south being pointed, and those on the north semicircular. Beneath the whole runs a hollow string-course filled with the chevron ornament. Upon each side of the nave there is a doorway with semicircular arch; that on the north is small, but has some chevron and other ornaments; that on the south is very rich and beautiful, the mouldings filled with very elaborate sculpture. The outer one contains fourteen figures within compartments formed by circular borders of foliage, the figures representing human beings in different attitudes and employments, some very grotesque. The second band of moulding contains a range of twelve smaller figures, some representing animals, also within foliated compartments. Within these again are two bands of chevron and scroll work. The door itself is square-headed, a transom worked with rope ornament extending across the arch, the head of which is filled with elaborate sculpture. In the centre is represented Our Saviour enthroned on a cloud, around which is a good deal of foliated and scroll work, with medallions, in which are heads of saints and bishops. The capitals of the shafts are also finely sculptured. In the interior, on the north side, a sculptured string-course is carried beneath the windows and over the door. At the west end is a Rectilinear window. Between the nave and chancel is an elegant semicircular arch in the centre, with fine chevron work in the mouldings, and springing from shafts which are also ornamented with the chevron, their capitals resemble Corinthian foliage, in line with which runs a cornice on both sides. Upon each side of this arch is a smaller one of similar form, also springing from shafts, and having chevron ornament in the moulding. These arches are now stopped up. The chancel is of still richer character than the nave. On the north side it has two windows, with semicircular heads, and an arcade of four semicircular arches ranging with them, exactly like those on the same side of the nave; but on the south the arrangement is nearly the converse of what is found on the same side of the nave, the two windows having pointed ogee heads trefoiled, and four arched recesses with semicircular heads. One of these differs from the rest, having shafts and a band of chevron ornament, and containing within it some rude sculpture that seems to have represented a building. A string-course with zigzag work runs externally below the windows all round the chancel, which is of lower elevation than the nave. On the south is a doorway much smaller than that of the nave, but having the chevron and scroll ornaments and shafts. In the interior of the chancel an embattled ornament runs beneath all the windows, the battlement being T-shaped. The east end externally exhibits in the lower part two arched recesses of semicircular form, with flat buttresses between them, above which runs an arcade of semicircular arches, alternately larger and smaller, the three smaller ones being pierced for windows, resembling the north side of the nave and chancel. Above is a rich band or cornice of scroll-work, over which the end terminates in a pointed gable containing in the centre a circular wheel window, the outside border enriched with foliage. From the centre of the window, which is a circle, issue eight radii; the intervals between them are formed into trefoiled compartments. Upon each side of this window is a circular compartment containing sculpture, one of a horseman, the other of a gryphon. In the interior there is a fascia, with lozenges and heads, running above the windows. There is a small square recess or cupboard on each side of the chancel. The furniture of the interior is very rustic and plain.

WALDERSHARE.
ALL SAINTS.

This is a mean church, and consists of a nave, a chancel with north and south chapels of late date, and at the west end a low massive tower not rising above the roof of the nave, but surmounted by a wooden spire. In the tower is a lancet window; in the nave is one of Norman character, and some of later date inserted. The side chapels of the chancel are of brick, of late Rectilinear work with square-headed windows. That on the south side belongs to the family of North, and contains a gorgeous tomb of the seventeenth century. In the north chapel is a still more stately monument of like period. The font is a plain octagon. The churchyard is very beautiful and sequestered, surrounded by trees and brushwood, and contains some fine yews.

GUSTON.
ST. MARTIN.

This church is very small and of mean appearance, comprising only a nave and chancel with a small wood turret over the west end. Several portions are Norman, among which are some windows and the north doorway, in which the door itself has a flat arch on impost mouldings, and the arch above it is moulded and springs from shafts. The arch to the chancel is removed, but there is a wooden screen of late date. The south door was Norman, but it is now stopped up. The east end of the chancel has three plain Norman windows, one set high up in the gable, the others lower down, similar to the arrangement at Barming. The two lower windows have, externally, masonry of a sort of long and short work carried round them, terminating in a point above the head which is itself semicircular. Most of the windows have semicircular heads; but those on the south of the chancel

are pointed lancets. Others are modern. The roof has th
common plain tie-beams. Against the east wall is a bracket.
The font has a small octagon moulded bowl, on a pedestal of
like form.

ST. MARGARET AT CLIFFE.

This is a very fine Norman church of the best character, and
with very rich portions. It consists of a lofty and spacious
nave, with side aisles, and a chancel. At the west end is a
tower, some part of which is modern, it having some time since
become very ruinous.* The nave has a high roof, and a plain
parapet, beneath which runs a cornice of square Norman ornaments. The clerestory externally presents a range of Norman
arches having piers with shafts attached, and every third arch
pierced for a window. This range of arches was continued
uninterruptedly round three sides of the tower, but on the west
side it is stopped by the modern work. The west doorway of the
tower is one the finest Norman specimens in the country : the
arch is surmounted by a triangular pediment, resting on imposts,
having a kind of finial at its apex, and richly wrought with
the billet ornament; the space between the pediment and the
head of the arch is sculptured with a kind of scroll work ; the
arch itself has several tiers of rich mouldings, one with scroll
work, another containing medallions, each filled with a head, a
third has the embattled ornament, and a fourth some foliage; there
is also in the centre of one band of moulding a piece of sculpture
representing three figures beneath semicircular arches. The
tower is very massive and opens to the nave by a pointed arch
with shafts of Norman character. The north doorway is surmounted by a semicircular arch, and has several bands of
moulding enriched with the lozenge, embattled and rope orna-

* The church has been very carefully restored ; whitewash taken off, the
modern altar-piece removed, &c.—H.

ments: the capitals of the shafts are clogged with whitewash; the head of the door itself, within the arch, is nearly flat. The side aisles are narrow, but the centre aisle is spacious and lofty, and has on each side four very fine lofty arches of semicircular form, all having mouldings enriched with the chevron, and a kind of embattled ornament; two of the piers on each side are cylindrical, having the abacus with nail-head ornament; the other two piers consist each of clustered shafts of different dimensions, there being on the east and west sides two large semi-columns, and on the other sides two small shafts with a kind of flat pilaster between them. The clerestory presents to the interior a range of plain Norman windows. Of like character are some of the windows in the aisles, but others have shafts. The chancel is plainer than the nave, but opens to it by a fine Norman arch, springing from shafts having fine sculptured capitals, and nail-heads in the abacus. On each side of the chancel are four plain Norman windows, and at the east end three smaller ones, all without mouldings. The interior is wainscoted, and has a gaudy modern altar-piece. The pews are neat; the font a plain octagon.

WEST CLIFFE.

This very small and neglected church is only used for service very rarely.* It consists of a nave and chancel with a small low tower on the south, the lower part of which forms a porch. The west end has had three lancet windows arranged as at Guston east end, but now walled up and a Rectilinear window inserted. Most of the windows of the nave and chancel are plain lancets, but a few on the north side have semicircular heads. In the tower is one trefoiled. The nave is divided from the chancel by an acute pointed arch, springing from shafts with Norman capitals. The south doorway has a semicircular arch, and near it is a stoup for holy water.

* West Cliffe Church has been repaired, and is now used regularly for service. E.

DOVER.

April 1864

1829.

ST. MARY'S CHURCH.

This is a spacious church of Norman origin, and exhibiting in the tower and several of the interior portions excellent specimens of that style; but the exterior has been sadly modernised and many frightful windows inserted.* A most unsightly effect is also produced by the addition of a new slate roof along the whole length of the north aisle. The walls are of flints, and the whole is plain excepting the tower. The church consists of three very long parallel aisles of equal length, the eastern division forming the chancel; at the west end is a massive tower surmounted by a small leaden spire: the tower is rich in ornament, but the flint work is somewhat decayed; at each corner it has a flat buttress, and on each side are four tiers of semicircular arches, varying in character and dimensions: those in the upper tier are at intervals pierced for windows to the belfry; in the next tier the arches are narrow, and the spaces about their heads are filled with scale work; the lower tier has large arches, each subdivided into smaller ones, all rise from shafts; the parapet is plain, but beneath it is a course of the common square ornaments; the strings between the stages are enriched, and in the upper part of the tower on the north side are two circular apertures as at Old Shoreham. The tower opens to the nave by a semicircular arch springing from clustered shafts with square capitals. The north aisle is wider than the south aisle, and the absence of clerestory windows materially injures the appearance both of exterior and interior, the roof being too low. The three western arches within the nave are semicircular, springing from circular piers with square capitals; the next pier on each side is large and square, and the fourth arch is semicircular with a band of embattled ornament running round the outer moulding; the next pier is circular, and from

* St. Mary, Dover, has been much repaired and otherwise improved since 1840.

it springs a very wide arch which appears to be made up of two thrown into one.* The chancel has, on the north, two Early English arches, with a circular pillar having an octagonal capital; on the south side is one pointed arch, and one very low pointed opening. There are a few lancet windows still remaining, and one in the chancel has mouldings and shafts. The interior is roomy and spacious, but not elegant, and much crowded by pews and galleries.† At the west end is a large organ. The Corporation seat is situated behind the altar. The font is octagonal, of Norman character, with semicircular arches on each side; the pedestal is square.

ST. JAMES'S CHURCH.

This church has no very imposing appearance, being much patched and modernised in the shabbiest manner.‡ It consists of a nave with added south aisle, a chancel, and a low tower placed between the nave and chancel. This is an Early arrangement and the only Norman remnants that yet exist are seen in the tower and the west doorway. The latter is large but plain and rude, having a semicircular arch, with three broad courses of moulding with a kind of horizontal band at the spring of the arch. The door-case has a square head. The south aisle is probably a late addition, but extends past the tower along part of the chancel: the west gable includes both nave and aisle. All the southern windows, the eastern, and several on the north are of the vilest modern kind. There is a Norman doorway, now closed, on the north, the arch on shafts having spiral mouldings and lozenge ornament above the capitals. The tower is low and without buttresses, but on the north side is a large projecting stair turret; there is a lancet belfry window and a plain battlement;

---

* The original pier was restored, in the general restoration of the church, with extension of the chancel, &c. - H.
† These have all been removed, and open seats substituted; the organ and the corporation seat moved, &c.—H.
‡ The church has been recently restored, and a new church built. H.

the walls of the whole church of rough flints, the tower with stone corners. On the north side of it there is a rude northern window, now closed. Internally the tower has a stone groined roof of plain character, with strong ribs simply crossing. The east and west arches under the tower are however pointed, with zigzag mouldings and shafts which are clearly of Norman character. The interior is ugly enough, with flat ceilings, and encumbered with very high lumbering pews and a large west gallery in which is an organ. The homeliness of the modern south wall and windows defies description. A large obtuse arch is opened between the aisle and chancel. The chancel is neat but modernised, and raised up several steps from the sloping nature of the ground. Immediately behind rises the Castle cliff. The chancel has a tiled roof, and on its south side a trace of Norman window. The nave roof is of modern slates.

CAPEL LE FERNE.
ST. MARY.

This small and solitary church stands among the fields, away from the village, and is with difficulty found. It consists only of a nave and chancel; with a low tower at the west end, of Early English character, having a plain top without finishing; it is divided by string-courses, and has a west door set within an Early English arch having mouldings and shafts somewhat rude. The ground has risen considerably against the walls of the church. The windows north of the nave are Curvilinear, of two lights; those on the south are Rectilinear with square heads and labels. In the chancel all are Rectilinear, of three lights, with square heads. The most remarkable feature is the curious triple arch that forms the division between the nave and chancel, an arrangement of very uncommon occurrence. A kind of screen is formed in stone, having three well-formed open pointed arches, rather small but with good mouldings, and springing from light octagonal shafts; the centre arch is the highest of the three. In the upper part of the screen, above these, is a single pointed arch. On the south side of the chancel are two small niches with trefoil heads, with a cylindrical shaft between them; one of the niches is set in a slanting direction. The font is a plain octagon, on a pedestal of like form. The arches of the doors and windows are, as is often the case, absurdly painted black and yellow.*

FOLKESTONE.

April 1884.

ST. MARY AND ST. EANSWITH.

This was originally a cruciform church, but the transepts have been cut short. The tower rises from the centre of the cross, and is of Rectilinear character, with an embattled parapet, and an octagonal turret on the south side; the rest of the church is chiefly Early English, with some later insertions. There is, on the north side, a plain Norman doorway without shafts. The exterior has suffered much mutilation, and has a ragged appearance; the walls are chiefly of flint. Most of the windows of the nave are modern, of the vilest description. The west end of the church is wretched patchwork, the nave having been cut short on that side, probably by the damage done by a storm, and the west wall rebuilt in most niggardly incongruous style. In 1705, the west end of the nave was blown down, to the length of two arches, and only *one* was rebuilt.† The nave has side aisles, from each of which it is divided by a row of three pointed Early English arches, of plain character and without mouldings, rising from circular columns. In the centre of the church, under

---

* The church has been much improved.—H.
† The church has been well restored, 1870, the nave extended two bays to the west, and all the wretched modern work replaced by some of appropriate character; the whole of the nave fitted with open seats, the chancel stalled for a surpliced choir, and a very fine organ placed on the south of the tower.

the tower, are four pointed arches, the piers of which have shafts with octagonal capitals, and the arch mouldings carried down between them, apparently of Rectilinear work. Beneath the tower is a stone groined ceiling. The chancel is large, and much the handsomest portion of the church, having some rich Early English work. It has an aisle on each side not extending to the east end, from each of which it is separated by two pointed arches, with circular pillars having capitals of rude foliage almost of Norman character. The east end of the chancel has three large equal lancet windows, which have rich and deep mouldings in the architraves, and shafts with bands round them, and fine foliated capitals. On the north and south sides of the altar are smaller lancet windows with similar mouldings and shafts; these windows are enriched only in the interior, to the outside they present a perfectly plain appearance. In the north wall is a very beautiful tomb of early Curvilinear period; the canopy is singularly elegant, and consists of a large ogee arch, richly crocketed, and formerly terminated by a finial now broken; the canopy has also a band of pierced trefoils carried round it beneath the crockets, and the interior surface has fine double feathering. The tomb itself is enriched with a range of niches with ogee canopies, each containing a small image. Upon it is the effigy of a knight.

The font is a plain octagon, raised upon steps. The chancel has on the outside an embattled parapet. The interior is plainly fitted up. (An organ has been added lately, 1843.)

POSTLING.

ST. MARY AND ST. RADEGUND.

This small, obscure village is in a remote situation, amongst very bad roads. The appearance of the place is wretched and poverty-stricken. The church is small, consisting only of a nave and chancel, with a low tower at the west end. It is almost wholly of Early English work, with a few inserted windows. The tower is very plain, with a pointed doorway, and some simple lancet openings; the upper part is of wood. There is one square-headed Rectilinear window on the south side of the nave; the other windows are all lancets, but they differ in size; and some have trefoiled heads. The east window of the chancel has three trefoiled lancet lights within a pointed arch.

The arch between the nave and chancel is plain and pointed; in the wall near it are stone brackets which probably once supported the rood-loft. There are a few remnants of old seats; the font is of square form, upon a pedestal of similar form.

The only interesting object about the church is an inscribed stone tablet, let into the north wall of the chancel.*

This is evidently original, and very curious, but unluckily the date of the year does not appear.

BRABOURNE.

ST. MARY.

This is a very curious church, abounding in good Norman work, and some of singular character. It consists of a nave and chancel of considerable height, and a tower at the west

---

* The inscription is given here from the careful copy made in Bryan Faussett's "Collecta." "A small square stone in the north wall of this chancel, with the following inscription . . . which I thus interpret:—

" XIX KL SEPTBR	19 Kalendarum Septembris
S EVSEBII CFSR	Sancti Eusebii confessoris
&C. HEC ECCLA	&c. hæc ecclesia
FVIT DEDICATA	fuit dedicata
IN HONORE SCE	in honore sanctæ
DI MATRS MARE	Domini Matris Mariæ.

I take the word Die to be understood in the second line; and the &c. in the third, to mean et Martyris.—The sense then is plain and easy. Dr. White Kennet takes notice of this inscription in his 'Par. Antiq.,' p. 609. His father (Basil Kennett)," as Bryan Faussett adds in a note, "was Vicar of Postling, as appears from a memorandum in the Register-book of that parish."—H.

An engraved facsimile of this tablet will be found in the *Journal of the British Archæological Association*, vol. x. p. 183. R.

end, massive but very low, and scarce rising above the body. This was the original form, but an aisle of Early English character is added on the south side of the nave, and a chapel on the south side of the chancel, of Rectilinear character. The general effect of the exterior is not elegant, on account of the disproportionate size of the tower to the body. The tower has a west doorway with a Norman arch over it with shafts; but the inner arch is pointed. The tower is otherwise very plain,

EXTERIOR OF BRABOURNE CHURCH.

and is strengthened by huge buttresses. The windows of the nave and chancel on the north side have round heads, and are set very high in the wall; beneath them runs a string-course, and between them are very flat buttresses. On the north side of the chancel is a small narrow doorway of Norman character, with billet ornament round the outer arch, which rests upon imposts, the head of the arch is filled with stone work arranged in rather a curious form. There are three pointed arches, with slender circular columns, between the nave and the aisle; and above is a clerestory with wide lancet windows. The arch to the tower is pointed, but very plain. The windows of the south aisle are Curvilinear of two lights, and beneath them runs a

HEART SHRINE IN BRABOURNE CHURCH.

string-course. The arch to the chancel is semicircular, and on the side facing the west is ornamented with an outer moulding of billets, and has shafts with rich capitals; towards the east the arch is plain, but rests upon imposts curiously wrought with scroll work. The chancel has two original windows on the north side, one containing ancient stained glass; there runs along a great part of the interior of the chancel a rich string-course, in character resembling that at Barfreston; and upon it stand shafts with rich capitals, probably designed for supporting the groining of the roof, which was never completed. There is a semicircular arch in the north wall, stopped up. The east window is Rectilinear of four lights, and immediately under it is a tomb of marble with a handsome canopy of the seventeenth century, to some of the family of Scott. On the north side is another tomb of elegant Rectilinear workmanship, the tomb itself panelled with compartments containing shields with various charges, among them the arms of Scott; the canopy consists of a flat arch with quatrefoil panelling in the spandrels, surmounted by a cornice with small battlements and very fine panelling, the under part of the canopy is handsomely groined. On the south side of the altar is a Rectilinear niche in a square compartment with a piscina; also two arches in the wall, apparently for tombs, and between them a small niche with elegant triangular canopy with crockets and finial, and flanked by small pinnacles. The south chapel has good Rectilinear windows of two and three lights, and a niche with piscina; also a brass with a female figure well preserved and thus inscribed : " Of yr charite pray for the soule of dame Elizabeth poynynges late wyf to Edward Poynyngs the whych d. Eliz: decessed the xv dai of August y yere of our lord god MVXXVIII on whose soul Jhū have mercy. Amen." There are remains of other brasses, and a few old wooden seats of Rectilinear character. The font is a plain circular mass of stone.

SMEETH.

ST. MARY.

This church has a nave and chancel, each with a north aisle, and a plain modern tower at the west end. There are both Norman and Early English portions, with some of later date. The south doorway is Norman, with shafts and some curious ornament. The nave is separated from the aisle by three plain pointed arches with square piers, and the chancel opens to the nave by a semicircular arch, having the chevron ornament in the mouldings and shafts; on one side of this arch is a door which probably led up to the rood-loft. The chancel has a large plain pointed arch opening to the aisle. There are some Curvilinear, and some Rectilinear windows, some of the former without feathering. There is one lancet at the west end of the north aisle; and in the east wall of the chancel is a Norman window, now walled up. The east portion of the nave has a coved wood ceiling, enriched with panelling and bosses, and a cornice of Tudor flower running beneath it. In the north aisle of the chancel is an arch in the wall for a tomb, with ogee canopy and feathering. The font is a plain octagon.

MERSHAM.

ST. JOHN BAPTIST.

This is rather a handsome church, with some singularities, and portions of various styles. The nave is wide, and has an aisle on the south side; the chancel has also a south chapel, and the tower stands at the west end of the south aisle. A door on the south side is Norman, of rather plain character. The tower is Early English, very large and massive, and has plain lancet windows in every stage; it is surmounted by a heavy four-sided spire of shingles. The most curious feature about the church is the west window of the nave, which is of very large size, in all of thirteen lights, and the tracery is of a transition character from Curvilinear to Rectilinear ; a transom runs across the window, below which the lines are Rectilinear, but the upper part of the window has all the lines curved, and of very unusual design. The north windows of the nave are Rectilinear of two lights with contracted arches ; of those on the south, some are Curvilinear, some Rectilinear. The south aisle is divided from the nave by five Early English arches with circular pillars, having moulded capitals. The nave has a good wood roof, the beams of which are supported upon brackets, enriched with elegant pierced tracery. The chancel has some Curvilinear windows, and a little wood screen-work. Its south chapel is late Rectilinear, and opens to the chancel by a low arch. It belongs to the Knatchbull family, to whom it contains many modern monuments ; it has also a niche with a piscina. The chancel contains some more ancient monuments to the Knatchbulls, and some old helmets. There are three very sumptuous marble monuments of the sixteenth century or later ; one to Bridget, wife of Sir Norton Knatchbull, and daughter of John Astley, Esq., obt. 1625 : the figure is represented kneeling beneath a canopy, the curtains in front of which are being undrawn by angels.

The view from the chancel down the church, looking west, is very fine, the nave being of broad and lofty proportions, its wood roof very handsome, and the whole terminated by the magnificent west window, which, as well as some of the other windows, contains portions of ancient stained glass.

The font is of square form, each face sculptured with an ogee arch. In the west gallery is a barrel organ. A brick school room has been injudiciously built on the north side of the chancel.

SALTWOOD.

ST. PETER AND ST. PAUL.

The church is a plain structure, consisting of a wide nave with north aisle, a chancel, and at the west end a rude low tower, with the east and west walls finished by pointed gables, and a penthouse roof. The south doorway is Norman, of small size; the shafts are gone, but the capitals remain. The west wall of the north aisle is carried up much higher than the present roof of the aisle. The nave is divided from the aisle by two very plain pointed arches with a square pier between them, having an impost moulding. The arch to the chancel is Early English, and springs from circular shafts. The chancel has a good east window of Curvilinear character, with four lights, and on each side a smaller one of two lights. On each side of the east window, against the wall, is the bracket of a niche. On the south side is a fine niche with ogee canopy, crowned by a finial and resting on head corbels; the niche itself has trefoil feathering, and contains a piscina.

There are some portions of ancient wood carving among the pews. The font is an octagon, standing on a shaft of similar form; upon one of its sides is a shield inscribed . . . . . Marya in very early characters. In the north aisle is a brass to the memory of Thomas Brockhole and his lady, with this inscription:—" Hic jacet Thomas Brockhill Armiger, qui obiit III° die Januarii anno dñi millm̄o ccccxxxvii° et . . . . eius quoꝝ aiabs p̄picietur deus. A M. E N." The arms are a cross between twelve crosses fitchées, impaling a chevron between three spread eagles. In the chancel is the vestige of a large brass, at least six feet in length. There is also in the chancel a remarkably fine ancient chest, sculptured with beautiful tracery of either Curvilinear or Rectilinear character.

Of the castle there are considerable remains, and very picturesque. There were originally two circumferences of wall, of which portions remain; the inner one has a beautiful gateway flanked by two circular towers having small windows with feathered arches; and much covered with ivy. On the south side of the court are the remains of the chapel, having three large pointed windows, the tracery of which appears to have been Curvilinear and very elegant; there are also traces of a groined ceiling. Beneath the chapel is an apartment with small pointed windows. The whole is much overgrown with trees and ivy, and within the area is a garden and orchard; some parts are appropriated to the farm buildings.

HYTHE.*
ST. LEONARD.

This magnificent church, though of plain exterior, presents in the interior of the chancel one of the finest and best preserved specimens of enriched Early English work that can be found. The plan of the church is cruciform, with nave, transepts, and chancel; the nave and chancel have each side aisles and clerestory, and a singular effect is produced from the chancel being very much loftier than the nave. At the west end is a tower, the lower part of which is of Rectilinear character, the upper part modern with battlement and pinnacles. The walls of the church seem to be principally Early English; but there is a door of fine Norman character, on the west side of the north transept, having good plain mouldings and shafts. The north transept has a singular double roof; several windows both of Curvilinear and Rectilinear work are inserted in the nave and transepts, but the clerestory has trefoiled lancets. There is a Rectilinear porch on the south side, but within it is an Early English doorway with shafts. The south transept seems to be partly modern. The chancel is large and purely Early English, but the exterior is not enriched, its walls rising

* This church was well restored in 1875.- R.

considerably above the roof of the nave and have the appearance of a tower; at the north-west corner is a circular turret. The aisles of the chancel have lancet windows, some single, some double, having externally merely dripstones. The east window of the chancel has three lancets, the centre one being the highest. The clerestory windows are trefoiled lancets, but many are walled up. On the south side is a good doorway with deep mouldings. The nave is divided from each aisle by three arches, and a fourth on each side opens to the transepts. These arches differ in character: on the south three are alike, lofty and pointed with pillars alternately circular and octagonal; but the fourth arch (to the south transept) is plainer, and springs from clustered shafts. On the north side the two western arches are of plain character, the first pier a rude octagon, the next circular; the third arch is much loftier and more enriched with mouldings; and the fourth, opening to the transept, is of still richer work, with fine mouldings and springs from beautiful clustered shafts having bell capitals. Between the south aisle of the nave and the transept is a fine low semi-circular arch with billet ornament in the mouldings, and springing from pilasters having shafts in their angles. The nave is neatly pewed, and contains a good organ. The chancel is of more advanced Early English work, far richer than the nave, and forming a singular contrast in the richness of its interior, to the simplicity of the exterior. It is approached from the nave by an ascent of several steps, there being beneath it a spacious crypt; and the general effect of the interior is magnificent, the ornaments being well preserved and lately cleaned from paint. The arch opening to the nave is lofty, with elegant mouldings and clustered shafts having bell capitals. Upon each side, opening to the aisles are two fine arches, with toothed ornament in the architraves; the piers are of octagonal form and each surrounded by eight shafts of Purbeck marble quite disengaged, with a general moulded capital. Over the south arches is a triforium, which in each compartment consists of two moulded semicircular arches with mouldings and shafts, subdivided by a central shaft into two smaller pointed arches. On the north side the triforium has been walled up. The east window presents to the interior five lancets, diminishing on each side from the centre, within a large pointed arch in the head of which are two quatrefoils above the centre lancet; the three centre ones are pierced for windows, the mouldings of all are very delicate and rich and have the toothed ornament, the shafts are clustered but disengaged, and their capitals varied.

There are slender shafts in the angles of the east end, from which spring the beginnings of ribs for the groining which never was completed; the same appears in the side aisles, and in the north aisle the arch of the groining is formed. The windows of the north aisle are beautifully arranged in three compartments, each different from the other: the first towards the west is a single lancet; the next a double lancet with clustered shafts, and a quatrefoil between the heads; the third has two lancets within one arch with mouldings and shafts. The east window is a single lancet. The south aisle has one single lancet with mouldings and shafts, and also three very beautiful continuous lancets with fine mouldings, the inner arch trefoiled with rich toothed ornament and clustered shafts. On the north of the altar is a door opening to the north aisle. On the south are two ascending stalls with trefoil heads and label over them, the shafts single; eastward of these is a double niche of exactly similar form, with piscina. Beneath the east window runs a band of quatrefoil panelling, and in the south aisle is an ogee niche trefoiled, with an octagonal piscina. The shafts are nearly all of Purbeck marble, cleansed from paint, which adds much to the general effect. Under the chancel is a large crypt, entered on the south side by a deeply moulded doorway, from which the earth has been cleared away. The crypt is lighted by lancet windows on the east side; the groining is very good though plain, the ribs spring from shafts of Purbeck marble against the wall, and are supported on octagonal pillars. In this crypt is an immense quantity of human bones, about which are various traditions. The font which stands in the chancel is a fine Curvilinear one, of octagonal form, with trefoil panelling.

NEW ROMNEY.
ST. NICHOLAS.

This is a large and handsome church, consisting of three spacious aisles of equal length with separate roofs, and at the west end a massive tower of curious character with a mixture of Norman and Early English work. The aisles are carried up to the west wall of the tower, but the western portion including three arches is much narrower than the rest. The tower is very massive, and five stages in height: on the west side is a good doorway of Norman character with several mouldings, and shafts much enriched; in the next stage are three narrow windows with semicircular heads and toothed dripstones springing from pilasters with shafts attached. The upper parts are Early English: the third stage having on each side two pointed windows, the pier between having shafts attached; the next stage has one lancet window; the highest, two lancets, with shafts having foliated capitals. The buttresses are chiefly flat; but the upper part of that at the north-west angle is octagonal, and crowned by a large pinnacle of like form, having shafts at the angles. At each of the other angles of the tower are pinnacles, two of which are octagonal and one square; beneath the parapet of the tower runs a cornice of heads and a band of toothed ornament. On the top of the tower is the base of an octagonal spire that has been long destroyed. The tower has, on the north and south, semicircular arches opening to the aisles, and a pointed arch on the east side with billet ornament. Beyond the tower the nave is five bays in length, four of its arches are semicircular, all enriched with billet ornament, and the alternate ones also with the embattled ornament, the piers alternately octagonal and circular with square capitals and bases. Over three of the arches were plain smaller arches with semicircular heads now walled up, which seem once to have formed a clerestory. The fifth arch of the nave is pointed, and the chancel has three high pointed arches on each side, with light octangular pillars. All the windows are of early Curvilinear work, chiefly of two lights, but at the east end, which consists of three equal gables, the centre window is of five lights, the north and south windows each of three lights. In the low west portion are some bad modern insertions, but the general effect both within and without is very good; the exterior simple but handsome; the interior light and spacious though without a clerestory. Beneath the windows runs a string-course. Upon each side of the altar are stone screens, partly concealed by modern wainscoting. In the north aisle of the chancel are some brasses, and in the wall a feathered arch for a tomb; there is also one of plainer character in the south aisle. In a gallery at the west end is a barrel organ. The roof of the chancel within is boarded and painted. The windows of the side aisles are set closely and particularly numerous.

LYDD.

ALL SAINTS.

This is a very large church, consisting of a nave and chancel, each with side aisles, and extending 190 feet in length. At the west end is a very lofty and beautiful tower of Rectilinear character, which is seen far and wide over Romney Marsh. The tower is in height 132 feet. It is surmounted by a battlement, and has at the south-west angle an octagonal turret crowned by a large crocketed pinnacle; at the other three angles are smaller plain pinnacles. On the west side is a double doorway, and over it a large window of four lights included in the same arched compartment. Each of the compartments of the doorway has the spandrels panelled, and the effect is very elegant. The rest of the tower is of plain work, and built of flint and stone, the belfry windows of two lights with transoms, and above each of them a small feathered opening. The tower is open to the church by a fine lofty arch, and the lower storey has a rich groined ceiling of beautiful design. The external appearance of the church is injured by the body being much too low in proportion to the tower, and without a clerestory, though the length is quite sufficient.

The body is mostly of earlier period than the tower, and has both Early English and Curvilinear work. Each aisle has a separate roof, and has little ornament externally. The windows of the nave are mostly Curvilinear of two lights, excepting only some in the west portion of the north aisle, which are Rectilinear and square headed. In the chancel the windows are all Rectilinear, excepting some plain lancets, trefoiled, and one Curvilinear in the south aisle. The top of the east end of the chancel has been altered, and made flat. The nave has seven Early English arches on each side; the pillars circular and slender, with moulded capitals and large bases. The chancel opens to the nave by a plain pointed arch upon octagonal shafts, and by a similar arch to each of its aisles. The pews do not occupy the whole space in the nave, and there are no galleries. A few ancient carved ends of pews still remain. The chancel extends a little beyond the aisles, and has on each side three trefoiled lancets, with a string-course beneath them. In the nave are several brasses, one dated 1506, one to Thomas Godfrey and his wife, with three figures under a rich canopy, but the inscription mutilated. In the north aisle of the chancel is a pointed arch in the wall springing from circular brackets, within which is the effigy of a cross-legged knight, in chain armour, Sir Walter Menil, 1333. In the chancel is a brass of an ecclesiastic, with this inscription, "Hic jacet magist' Joh'es Mottesfont utriusque

F

BRASS OF THOMAS GODFREY, LYDD CHURCH.

juris Bacallauri' et nup Vicari' istius ecclie qui obiit vi⁰ die Novembris Anno dñi M⁰CCCC⁰XX⁰ cuius aīe ppicietur Deus,

BRASS OF PETER GODFREY AND WIFE, LYDD CHURCH.

Amen." From his mouth proceeds a scroll with "Miserere mei Deus sēdum magnā miām tuā." Around run the following verses:—

    Qui tumulos cernis, cur non mortalia spernis?
      Tali namq3 domo clauditur omnis homo.
    R gia Majestas, omnis terrena Potestas
      Tran et absq3 morā, mortis cum venerit hora.

Ecce corona datur nulli, nisi rite sequatur
Vitam justorum, fugiens exempla malorum.
Oh, quam ditantur qui cœlica regna lucrantur !
Vivent jocund' confessi crimina mundi." *

There are other monuments to jurats and officers of the corporation.

TENTERDEN.
ST. MICHAEL.

This is a large church, having nave and chancel with side aisles of considerable length, and at the west end a lofty and beautiful Rectilinear tower, so very similar to that of Lydd, that it seems to have been the work of the same architect. It has the double doorway and window arranged in the same manner, but here the window has a transom and a small niche on each side of it. The belfry windows are double, the pinnacles differ from those at Lydd, there being here at each angle of the tower an octagon turret surmounted by a large crocketed pinnacle. On the north side is a staircase turret. The tower opens to the church by a lofty arch. The body is much too low in proportion to the tower, and has a shabby external appearance, being rough, with the plaster peeling off, and almost all the windows barbarously deprived of their tracery.† There is no clerestory, but the south aisle of the nave is embattled. Some of the buttresses have triangular heads. In the north aisle, in a line with the chancel arch, is an octagonal turret. The south porch has a doorway with shafts. The nave is divided from each aisle by five pointed arches, with pillars alternately circular and octagonal. The roof of the nave is coved, boarded, and divided into panelled compartments, with very richly worked bosses. The

---

* From the accurate transcript of the Rev. Bryan Faussett's Coll. Paroch.—H.
† The tracery of the windows has been restored, galleries removed, and pews replaced by open seats.—H.

arch to the chancel is Early English, from shafts having foliated capitals. The chancel has two pointed arches on each side to the aisles, the pier on the south circular, on the north octagonal. The chancel extends beyond the aisles, and has a lancet window on the north. The aisles of the chancel have Curvilinear windows, some square-headed, but those at the extremities have good tracery, and one has shafts to its arch. The pews and galleries are crowded, the altar-piece Grecian and Modern. At the west end is a good organ, erected by subscription.

GREAT CHART.

This church has a nave and chancel, with equal aisles, and an embattled tower at the west end, with a good plain door and a two-light window over it. The walls are of stone, the windows are some Curvilinear and some Rectilinear. The nave and part of the chancel has a clerestory, with square-headed windows of two lights, and Rectilinear character. The nave is divided from each aisle by three pointed arches with octagonal pillars, and the chancel opens to the nave by a pointed arch thrown across from one pillar of the nave to the opposite; there are similar arches across the aisles. The chancel has on each side three pointed arches with octagon piers, lower and wider than those of the nave. Some of the windows contain pieces of stained glass. There is a little screenwork within the tower arch. The font is a plain octagon. A barrel organ is placed in the west gallery. In the north aisle is a stair turret and door, placed at a great height. In the north chancel is a curious covered pew, with wood carving, temp. James I., and in the same several brasses to the Toke family of Godington, one of which represents a man between two women, with this inscription,* " Orate pro animâ Johannis Toke, armigeri nuper de Goddyngton isti' p'roch' cui' corp' jacet

---

* "Over them is a label with this sentence, 'Sancta Trinitas, Unus Deus, mi- rere n bi.'" Collecta Parochialia, MS. of Rev. Bryan Faussett.

hic tumulatum; ac pro animabs Margarete et Anne uxor' suarum que q̃dm M̃gareta filia fuit natalis, dum vixit Johĩs Walworth nup in Comitatû Suff. et dicta Anna filia etiam naturalis Johannis Engham Armigeri, nuper de Syngleton, isti' Paroch'. Qui vero Johẽs Toke obiit vicesimo die Maii Anno Dñi millmo quingentesimo tercio decimo. Quorum aīmabus ppiciet' Rex altissimus." Another, date 1565, to John Toke. In the nave is a brass with the figures of one man * and five females. In the chancel is a marble altar-tomb of Rectilinear character to some of the Goldwell family, the sides panelled, and upon the slab are brass figures of a man and woman.† There is a small low building attached to the west end of the north aisle.

ASHFORD.
ST. MARY.

This is a plain spacious church in the form of a cross with a lofty tower rising from the centre. The whole is of Rectilinear work, having been entirely rebuilt by Sir John Fogge in the reign of Edward IV. The nave, transepts and chancel are all of equal height with tiled roofs. The nave and chancel have

---

* William Sharp, 1500, and five wives. See "Parsons' Monuments," p. 186.—H.

† "On the north side of the Communion rails is a very ancient altar-tomb, which has been magnificently inlaid with brass, of which nothing now remains but the figures of a man and a woman; out of the mouth of the man proceeds a label with this sentence: 'Pater de cœlis, Deus, miserere nobis!' Out of the mouth of the woman comes another, with these words: 'Fili Redemptor mundi, Deus, miserere nobis!' At their feet are two other labels, which proceeded from two groups of figures now lost, with these words: 'Spt̃s Ste, Deus, miserere nobis'—'Sancta Trinitas, Unus Deus, miserere nobis!'

"Mr. Weever says it had the following inscription on its brass verge, or border, and, betwixt every word, the figure of a well, alluding to the name: 'Animæ Willelmi de Goldwelle & Aviciæ Uxoris suæ, per misericordiam Dei, in pace requiescant: Qui quidem (sic) Willielmus septimo die mensis Maij. et dicta Avicia octavo die Aprilis, Litera Dominicalis B. ab hâc luce migrarunt. Ann. Domini M.CCCC.LXXXV. Quorum animaḃ Ppicietur Deus. Amen!'" Collecta' of Rev. Bryan Faussett.—H.

side aisles, but no clerestory. Those of the nave have lately been re-edified, and widened, but quite in character with the rest of the church.* The windows of the aisles are of three lights, some with transoms. The east and west windows are of five lights each, with fine tracery. The transepts have each at the end a large window of four lights. Under the east window is a niche with a mutilated image. Beneath the west window is a door with Tudor arch, and panelled spandrels, there is a similar door on the north side. The tower rises two entire stages above the roof, the lowest having a two-light window, the upper a three-light window on each side, and all with transoms; the whole is crowned with a battlement, and at each angle an octagonal turret and large pinnacle. There is an octagonal staircase turret leading to the tower in the angle between the north transept and aisle. The nave is divided from each aisle by three high pointed arches, with slender circular pillars; the roof is coved, and divided into square compartments by ribs with bosses at their intersections. There are galleries along both aisles, and one at the west end, in which is a good organ.† The side aisles open to the transepts by half arches, and the tower is supported on four high pointed arches springing from shafts with octagonal capitals. The chancel is divided from each aisle by three acute arches with slender circular piers with octagonal capitals. Some of the ancient wooden stalls with carved ends remain.‡ The south transept has a chapel on the east side, divided by three arches like those of the nave, the north transept has also a chapel. There are several handsome monuments, that of the Founder, Sir John Fogg (obt. 1490) is on the north side of the chancel; it is an altar-tomb, with the sides handsomely panelled; it has a brass plate with some

---

* The nave has more recently been lengthened, in exact accordance with the original architecture. H.

† A new organ has been placed in the North transept.—H.

‡ The stalls have been restored, the pews which formerly ran across them having been taken away.—H.

Latin verses much defaced. There is also a mutilated brass in the north transept to Thomas Fogg, Esquire, who died in the sixteenth century. In the south transept are three very large gorgeous marble monuments to the family of Smyth, in the style that prevailed in the reigns of Elizabeth and James I., of which they are fine specimens. One to Thomas Smyth, Esquire, of Westenhanger, and Alice his wife, 1591, engraved in "Neale's Churches," and all the inscriptions given there. One to Sir Richard Smyth his son, obt. 1628, the third to Sir John Smyth of Ostenhanger, Knt. (son of the latter), Obt. 1609.

In the chancel is a large brass, much mutilated, of Elizabeth, daughter to Henry Lord Ferrers of Groby, and wife to David le Strabolgie, Earl of Athol, obt. 1375. The figure is curious from the costume in the old French dress closely buttoned. She had a banner in each hand, now gone, said to have been charged with armorial bearings; and round the slab ran originally a fillet of brass with an inscription, of which only remains "Icy gist . . . . Countesse . . . . que mour '."*

The font is octagonal, panelled with quatrefoils.

WILLESBOROUGH.

ST. MARY.

This is a light and pretty church, consisting of a nave with a south aisle, a chancel, and a tower containing four bells, crowned by a shingled spire at the west end. There are portions of each of the three Pointed styles, and Curvilinear parts remarkably elegant. The tower is Early English, with trefoil lancet belfry windows, and a west doorway with mouldings and shafts having bell capitals. The windows of the nave are mostly Rectilinear

---

* The entire inscription was: ✠ " Icy gist Elisabeth jadye, countesse D'Athels, La Fille de Seignr de Ferrers, q̃ Deiu asoill q̃ mourust le 22 jour d'October, L'An de grē M.CCC.LXXV." Bryan Faussett's Collecta.—H.

of two and three lights; but there is one lancet on the north. The chancel is Curvilinear, and opens to the nave by a pointed arch springing from octagonal brackets with heads. The nave is divided from the aisle by five Pointed arches, with three octagonal and two circular pillars. The side windows of the chancel are of two lights, the eastern one of five lights, with rich tracery, and a good deal of fine stained glass. There is a good deal of ancient stained glass in the chancel. There is an arch to a south chapel with circular shafts, having octagonal capitals. On the south are three fine stone stalls varying in form and size; the two western having flat tops with cinquefoil feathering, and surmounted by a cornice of small battlements. The third is larger and higher with a similar cornice, but an ogee arch with feathering and pierced spandrels. The piers between them have small stone knobs for resting the arms; beyond them is a niche with ogee canopy and finial, with a piscina. The font is octagon, standing on a shaft formed of four clustered shafts, and there are detached shafts at each of the alternate angles. The pews are neat and new, and there is a large barrel organ.*

KENNINGTON.

aug. 1883

ST. MARY.

This church has a nave and chancel, each with south aisle, and an embattled stone tower at the west end; the latter is of Rectilinear work and has an octagonal corner turret. The windows of the nave are mostly Rectilinear, but there are one or two of Norman character. The aisle on the south of the nave is small, not extending to the west end, and opens to the nave by one pointed arch, and one half arch, with an octagonal pier. The chancel is very neat, opening to the nave by a pointed arch with circular shafts partly cut away. The chancel is divided

* This church has been restored and reseated.

from its south chapel by two pointed arches with an octagonal pier, and has on the north one lancet window and two square-headed Rectilinear ones, and an east window consisting of three lancets within a pointed arch springing from shafts with bell capitals; in these are portions of early and very rich stained glass, like that at Canterbury. The south aisle is wholly Rectilinear, and has also some stained glass, and a wood screen. There is a little more screenwork. The font is octagonal, on a shaft of like form, each side enriched with a different pattern, chiefly Curvilinear tracery, the quatrefoil, and fleur-de-lys.

WESTWELL.

Aug. 1883. F.A.

ST. MARY.

This is a large and very interesting church, comprising a nave and chancel with side aisles, and at the west end a plain Early English tower surmounted by a shingled spire. The tower has no buttresses; the belfry windows are trefoiled lancets, and on the west side is a lancet window and a doorway, each with fine mouldings, but without shafts. The whole church is Early English except some inserted windows, and contains many very singular as well as elaborate portions. The walls are of flint. The nave opens to the tower by a fine Early English arch with good mouldings, springing from small shafts resting on heads and having luxuriant foliated capitals. The nave is divided from each aisle by four well-formed pointed arches, with pillars alternately circular and octagonal. There is no clerestory; the windows of the side aisles are mostly Curvilinear, some having square heads, others are lancets, and many contain very fine stained glass. The chancel has two arches on each side similar to those of the nave, and forming a complete continuation of them; and the arches on both sides, especially on the south, have fallen out of the perpendicular. Between the nave and chancel is a curious stone screen, extending from one pillar to the opposite one, and apparently coeval with the rest of the arches. This screen consists of three arches, each of which is trefoiled, and springs from light cylindrical shafts; in the spandrels are circles, and the effect is very good. On the north side in a line with this screen is a turret with a staircase. The chancel is by far the richest and most elegant part of the church; its roof has good stone groining of simple design; the ribs merely crossing each other, and springing from brackets. The east window has three equal lancets, filled entirely with ancient stained glass of the richest colouring, exactly resembling that in the cathedral of Canterbury. Above this in the east gable, and opening into the space between the groining and the roof, are two lancets with a circle between their heads. On the south side of the altar are three stone stalls in a square compartment crowned by an embattled cornice; each has an ogee head, with panelled spandrels and circular shafts; one of them comes down much lower than the other two; beyond them is a cinquefoil niche, with a piscina; eastward of which is another kind of stone seat with a pointed arch, but intercepted by an inserted window. In the east wall are two arched recesses, one opening by a double arch. On the north side of the altar are three pointed arches in the wall, and above them a single lancet window. The corresponding window on the south is Curvilinear. The windows at the east end of each aisle are Rectilinear of three lights; on each of that in the south aisle is a rich niche of the same period, with beautiful groining and tabernacle work, but much mutilated. At the east end of the north aisle is a cinquefoiled niche. There are three slabs bearing ornamented crosses; one with Lombard letters much obliterated.

The font is enclosed in wood. The south porch is of wood of very late date and not enriched; the doorway opening to the interior has a label over it.

LENHAM.

ST. MARY.

This church consists of a nave and chancel, each with a north aisle, and at the west end a Rectilinear embattled tower with an octagonal corner turret. There are several Curvilinear windows in the nave, of which the interior arches have shafts, some other windows are Rectilinear. The tower opens to the nave by a pointed arch with shafts having octagonal capitals, and the nave has four pointed arches opening to the aisle, the piers of which are octagonal. The chancel has on the south side some lancet windows with the heads cut off, and under them runs a string-course. Between the chancel and its aisle are two Early English arches with a square pier having shafts set in the angles. On the south side of the chancel is a curious stone seat with resting places for the arms, and its arched head is cinquefoiled; there is also a square recess with a piscina. In the north wall of the chancel is a curious slab inserted, with the effigy of an ecclesiastic with the head upon a pillow, and divided into two compartments by a plain fillet. In the north aisle of the chancel is a panelled altar-tomb. There are several wood stalls in the chancel; the pulpit has rich wood carving of a mixed character with arabesque, and a cornice of grapes with vine-leaves; it is dated 1571. There is also a curious wooden desk or lectern of beautiful form, but simple character. The font is an octagon enclosed in wood; the pedestal has good Curvilinear panelling.

LINTON.

ST. NICHOLAS.

This is a small church, comprising a nave with a south aisle, a chancel with side chapels, and at the west end of the nave a plain embattled tower crowned by a shingled spire. The tower appears Early, but has a belfry-window of Curvilinear character. At the west end of the aisle is a plain lancet window; the northern windows of the nave are Rectilinear, those on the south are of richer tracery of the same period and have shafts to the inner mouldings. The nave is divided from the aisle by two pointed arches with an octagonal pillar. The chancel has pointed arches to each side aisle, that on the north is of Tudor form. The east window is Rectilinear of three lights, those in the south chapel are of like character, and in that chapel is a wood screen. The north chapel is of much later date and has large monuments to the family of Mann, some of the last century, others of the seventeenth century, in which the name is spelt Mayne. The font is a plain octagon. The south porch is plain. The church* stands very high and commands a magnificent view over the Weald.

CRANBROOK.

ST. DUNSTAN.

This is a large and beautiful church, 147 feet long by 72 feet broad, entirely of fine Rectilinear character, excepting a portion of the chancel. It consists of a nave (36 feet high) and chancel, each with side aisles, and a tower 94 feet high with a battlement and corner turret at the west end, resembling many of the neighbouring steeples. This tower has a very good western doorway with deep mouldings and shafts within a kind of shallow porch. Above it is a window of four lights; those of the belfry are square-headed. The whole of the exterior is regular and handsome; the nave has a clerestory, and the whole is embattled except the centre aisle of the chancel. The windows are chiefly of three lights in the aisles and clerestory of the nave, but those at the extremities of the aisles are of four and five lights, and some in the south chancel are of four lights. The dripstones of the windows rest upon corbels formed of

* The church has been carefully restored, and considerably enlarged.

figures of angels bearing shields. There is a porch on the south side of the nave, with a battlement, a door with good mouldings and circular shafts, a single window over it, and two other small trefoiled windows in the sides of the porch. In the south chancel aisle is a doorway rising above the sill of the window; the arch of Tudor form with a label, and trefoils in the spandrels. Above the label is a fine band of panelling, and in the arch moulding a half figure of an angel bearing a shield. In the north aisle of the nave is a small doorway set under a window, with panelled spandrels. In the north aisle between the nave and chancel is an embattled octagonal turret. The interior is very light and elegant; the nave is divided from each aisle by six arches of Tudor form, having good mouldings and lozenge piers with shafts at intervals and the mouldings carried down the intermediate spaces. Between each clerestory window is a shaft upon a corbel, whence it was intended that ribs of the groining should spring.

The chancel is plainer and lower, and opens to each aisle by two more simple arches and of earlier date, with piers of four clustered shafts. The chancel extends beyond the side aisles and has a fine Rectilinear east window of five lights, entirely filled with ancient stained glass of the richest colouring. On the north and south sides of the altar are windows of four lights, the tracery of which appears to be rather of Curvilinear character. The ceiling is coved and painted in bad taste; there is much modern wainscoting, a neat Grecian altar-piece, neat altar and marble pavement within the communion rails.* There are no galleries save one at the west end of the nave, in which is a fine organ. The tower contains a clock, a peal of eight bells and chimes.

In the chancel is a slab charged with a cross flory and an inscription in Lombard characters not easily deciphered.

* The modern wainscoting has been removed, with the Grecian altar-piece, and rearrangement of the interior undertaken, removing the pews and substituting open seats.—H.

There are in the chancel several helmets and banners of the family of Roberts of Glassenbury, to whom there are also some monuments. There is in the north aisle of the chancel an arched opening, in a pier, commanding the altar. The south chancel contains a slab with two figures in brass, one of which seems to be an ecclesiastic, the other a young child in swaddling clothes, between them a brass with a merchant's mark or monogram. There is in this aisle a third slab with an inscription in Lombard characters; also two altar-tombs of Rectilinear character with panelled sides, one of them is set in the south-east angle, and over it is a plain niche. There is also a large monument of later date containing a complete pedigree of the family of Roberts. At the east end of this aisle is a plain vestry of Rectilinear character. In one of the windows is the pedestal of an image.

On the south side of the nave is what is scarce to be found in any other church—a square baptistery of stone for the purpose of immersing such Baptists as desire to enter the communion of the church; it was erected in 1725 by the Rev. John Johnson, Vicar, and resembles a bath with a descent of several steps. It is said only to have been used twice.

HAWKHURST.

ST. LAWRENCE.

This is a large and handsome church,[*] consisting of a nave and chancel, each with side aisles of equal height and without a clerestory. The church is said to have been built by an Abbot of Battle, temp. Edward III. The chancel is clearly a part of the original fabric. There are large north and south porches and at the west end a square embattled tower, with an octagonal corner turret, of Rectilinear character and resembling many of the neighbouring steeples. The whole of the church,

[*] A careful and accurate account of the architecture of this church, by the vicar, the Rev. C nen Jeffreys, is to be found in the "Archæologia Cantiana," vol. IX. pp. 240-264, from which the engravings here inserted are taken. H.

GREAT EAST WINDOW OF HAWKHURST CHURCH.

HAWKHURST CHURCH FROM THE SOUTH-EAST.

HAWKHURST CHURCH; EAST END OF SOUTH CHANCEL.

NORTH CHANCEL OF HAWKHURST CHURCH.

including the porches, is embattled; both porches are of two storeys, the northern one is placed further to the east than is usual; the southern one has good plain groining and square-headed windows of Rectilinear character; the outer doorway has good mouldings and small shafts; it has also an octagonal turret. The windows of the nave are mostly Rectilinear of three lights; the nave is divided from each aisle by four pointed arches with octagonal pillars, and by one high pointed arch from the tower; the appearance of the interior of this part is much injured by the insertion of numerous unsightly galleries.* The chancel has two arches on each side, lower than those of the nave, being of a contracted form almost semicircular, and apparently of late date; the piers are octagonal. The east end of the chancel is one of the finest pieces of architecture in the county. The centre window is a large and beautiful one of five lights with Curvilinear tracery of a rich and singular character; above it in the apex of the gable is a circle not pierced, but with elegant feathering. Beneath the sill of the window is a small embattled building now unroofed,† which seems to have been a vestry and has had a door opening from behind the altar, now quite closed up; it is lighted by cinquefoil openings. The east window has fine mouldings and shafts in the interior arch; the side aisles have each an east window of four lights, and the north aisle has windows of three lights all with flat contracted arches, and tracery that has a late Curvilinear character, some of which contain portions of fine stained glass. In the south chancel the windows are mostly Rectilinear. There is an octagonal turret on the north side of the church in a line

* These galleries have been removed.—R.

† No roof had ever been placed upon this building until after Sir Stephen Glynne's visit. It was originally open to the sky, and there was no entrance to it from the church. The door-like traces in the east wall were examined carefully during the restoration of the church, and it was proved that the wall had never been pierced for a door. This little building was roofed in, and turned into a vestry in 1849; the construction of an entrance to it from the church was a work of great difficulty, well described by the vicar, Canon Jeffreys, in "Archæologia Cantiana," vol. ix. pp. 258 and 255. R.

with the chancel arch. The font is a fine Rectilinear one, of octagonal form, panelled alternately with shields and roses; the pedestal has buttresses at the angles.

HOLLINGBOURNE.
ALL SAINTS. 1831.

This is a tolerably good church, built principally of flints, and consisting of a nave with side aisles, and a chancel with north aisle, with a square tower at the west end of the nave, having a battlement, and square headed belfry windows, of Rectilinear character, but without buttresses. The church is chiefly Rectilinear, of which character are all its windows, except that at the east of the chancel, and that at the west end of the south aisle, which are Decorated, the first rather late and not good. Most of the other windows are of three lights, in the chancel of two, with varying but not remarkable tracery. The nave has on each side three pointed arches with octagonal pillars. There is no chancel arch; the north chapel appears to be nearly as late as the time of Elizabeth, and is chiefly remarkable for its embattled parapet, inlaid with courses of flint and stone, in a kind of checkered form, as is seen in Norfolk. This chapel is raised on steps, with a vault beneath, and contains a tomb of black and white marble, with rather a fine figure of a female, to Elizabeth wife of Thos. Culpeper, and d^r. of John Cheney Esqr., ob^t. 1638. This chapel is surrounded by black marble monumental tablets, some inscribed in memory of the Culpepers, and above them this inscription: "Deo Sancto et Misericordi sint gratiae et gloria in æternum. Amen." There is also a mural monument by Rysbrack to one of the Duppa family, good of its kind. The chancel also is full of marble monuments to Culpeper, and one, A.D. 1610, to Barnham. The font is octagonal, with a fine wood cover, and there is a handsome ancient pulpit of wood.*

* The embroidered velvet coverings, for the pulpit-desk and the communion-table, were wrought by the Ladies Culpeper during the Commonwealth, and presented at the Restoration. - R.

BEARSTED.
HOLY CROSS.

This church has a nave with north aisle, and a chancel, and at the west end a square embattled tower of Rectilinear work, having an octagonal stair turret on the south, and figures of lions instead of pinnacles. The whole building is of stone. The nave is separated from the aisle by four pointed arches, of which the two eastern are much wider, and of rather contracted form. One pier is circular, and two are octagonal. The aisle does not extend quite to the west end. Most of the windows are Decorated of two lights, that at the east end has three lights and is of very early tracery, and contains some ancient stained glass. On the north side of the chancel is one of singular form. There are a few lancets also, and one trefoiled. South of the entrance to the chancel is the turret for the stairs to the rood loft. The font is a plain octagon.

LEEDS.
ST. NICHOLAS. 1834.

Aug: 1882. K.A.

This church has a nave with aisles, a chancel with side chapels, and a remarkably massive low tower at the west end, crowned by a shingled spire. This tower is perhaps unrivalled in size, and is of very Early English character, with flat buttresses, two plain lancets on the west side, and a tolerable doorway with arch mouldings, and the capitals of shafts remaining. (The roofs of the church are tiled, and the walls chiefly of stone.) Near the west doorway is a stoup, and the tower opens to the nave by a semi-circular arch. Most of the windows in the nave are Decorated of two lights; in the chancel many are Rectilinear. The nave is divided from each aisle by three pointed arches on octagonal pillars. The chancel opens to its south chapel by a very obtuse arch, to the north chapel by a pointed arch. The roof of the chancel is of plain ribs. There is a wood screen across the body, and aisles at the entrance to the chancel, and one also in the north chapel. On the south side of the altar are three sedilia, divided by buttresses, and surmounted by a horizontal cornice. The east window has been modernized. In the north pier of the chancel is a small aperture filled with pierced panelling, in the north chapel is also a plain niche with piscina. The font is a plain octagon.

OTHAM.

ST. NICHOLAS.

This church consists of a nave with north aisle, a chancel with north chapel, and a tower on the south side; the latter is of plain Early English work, with small narrow and obtuse apertures, and a stair turret; it is crowned by a wooden spire. Most of the windows are square-headed with Decorated tracery, but some are modern.* In the chancel they are Perpendicular. A north doorway is fine Perpendicular, its arch has good mouldings and shafts, the spandrels are filled with quatrefoils, and above is a course of elegant panelling, the whole included within a square compartment. The aisle is very narrow, and has one large pointed arch opening to the nave and another to the chancel on octagonal pillars. The font is octagonal upon a shaft of like form, beneath the basin are heads of animals and other ornaments. There are two monumental slabs of marble let into the east wall, one to Bishop Horne.

MARDEN.

ST. MICHAEL.

This church consists of a western tower, a nave, and chancel, with side aisles and a south porch. The tower in its lower portion is Early English, with a plain lancet, and a projecting turret at the north-west, but the belfry-storey is of wood with a

* Otham Church was nicely restored in 1873.

pointed top. The south porch is large, with a parvise over it, and an octagonal stair turret at the north-west corner. The outer arch has mouldings springing straight from the wall; the inner doorway has shafts. The parvise is lighted by a trefoil lancet. The south aisle has a moulded parapet, the north has none; there is no clerestory, but the roof of the nave is light and tiled, covering the side aisles. The aisles of the chancel have separate tiled roofs. The prevailing features are Decorated and Perpendicular. The nave is divided from each aisle by three pointed arches; those on the south have fine mouldings with dripstones upon heads and half figures; the piers are octagonal, one having a foliated, the other a moulded, capital. The northern arches are plainer, but large; the piers alternately octagonal and circular, the responds half octagonal piers. The roof is of waggon form, boarded, with ugly tie beams and king-posts. In the north arch are two very elegant Decorated windows of three lights with varying tracery, and at the west end of it one of two lights, in which are portions of stained glass. The windows of the south aisle have been vilely mutilated, and some dormer ones inserted in the roof. There are ugly deal high pews, and a west gallery with a barrel organ. The chancel arch is plain and pointed, rising on impost mouldings. The north aisle opens to that of the nave by a pointed arch on half octagonal capitals; the southern by a pointed arch on corbels. The chancel to each aisle by two pointed arches on octagonal pillars, lower than those of the nave. The north chapel has good Perpendicular windows of two lights, and the eastern of three; part of this chapel is used as a vestry. The chancel roof resembles that of the nave. The east windows of the chancel and of the south chancel are both bad modern works. The north pillar of the chancel is more finished than the southern. The south chapel is narrower, in its south wall is the remnant of a monumental arch with feathering and mutilated canopy. In the south wall of the chancel beyond the aisle, is a trefoil lancet with dripstone and corbel, closed up. The pulpit is ugly. The font, now in the north aisle of the chancel, is a plain octagon, painted brown on a stem of like shape, with a good cover of wood of the seventeenth century.

STAPLEHURST.
ALL SAINTS.

This church has a west tower, a nave and a chancel, each with a south aisle. There are portions of the three later styles; the tower is Perpendicular embattled, with a turret all up the south side of square form, terminating in an octagon; the belfry window is square-headed of two lights, the second stage has a cinquefoiled opening. On the west side is a doorway with label, upon corbels of crowned heads, and shafts, the spandrels are panelled with shields charged with arms. Above the door is a window of three lights. The tower is of stone, and other parts of the church are chiefly of the same material, but with flints intermixed. The roof is covered partly with shingles, partly with slates. The east end is chiefly stuccoed.* The nave is long; on the north side of it are several square-headed Perpendicular windows, and one Decorated of two lights. In the south aisle is one three-light Decorated window, and one of two lights at the west end, the others are late and square-headed. The nave is divided from the aisle by five wide pointed arches, of which the most eastern is widest, and rather depressed. The pillars are alternately circular and octagonal, with moulded capitals, the eastern pier being formed of two half octagonal shafts, back to back. On one of the piers is a bracket, probably for an image. The roof of the nave is coved. The chancel arch has been removed, and is replaced by an ugly Italian one of wood.†

* The church has been restored externally, and reseated throughout, the western gallery removed, and the lower arch opened. The organ has been placed on the north side of the church. H.

† The wooden arch, as well as the high pews, the west gallery, and the wainscot panels, disappeared when the church was restored. R.

SOUTH DOOR OF STAPLEHURST CHURCH.

Staplehurst.

The door that opened to the roodloft is seen on the south side. The pews are highbacked. A west gallery contains an organ, played either by keys or barrels.

The chancel is large and is divided from its south aisle by three pointed arches on circular pillars of Early English character, with moulded capitals and bases raised on square plinths. The east end has a fine early Decorated window of five lights with some pieces of stained glass. On the north side of the chancel is one singular window of a transition style from Decorated to Perpendicular, and one single light with foils and tracery in the head of similar character. Another window on the north is entirely Perpendicular. The altar is neat, the reredos and adjoining portions are of modern wainscot. The chancel has a coved roof with tie beams and king-post. The south chapel is Perpendicular, its east window of four lights, the others of two lights, all Late. The ceiling has some wood panelling, nearly flat, and painted with representations of crowns, &c.

The font is an octagonal mass attached to one of the western piers.

The altar picture represents the Descent from the Cross.

HARRIETSHAM.
ST. JOHN THE BAPTIST.

This is rather an interesting church, externally resembling many of the other Kentish churches, but having several remarkable features. It consists of a west tower, a nave with side aisles, south porch and chancel with chapels to the north and south, the former not now open to the chancel. The tower of Kentish stone is good Perpendicular, with an embattled parapet and octagonal stair turret, projecting along the whole of the south side, and rising above the parapet. The west doorway has a label and quatrefoiled circles in the spandrels; above it is a three-light window. The belfry windows are double and square-headed. The walls of the body and chancel are mostly of flints. The aisles are embattled. There are octagonal turrets with staircases both in the north and south aisle towards the east. The chancel has a tiled roof. The porch has a timber roof; the south doorway, has good arch mouldings. Most of the windows in the side aisles are late and square-headed. The roof of the nave has the usual plain tie beam and king-posts; the ceiling of the aisles is modern. The nave is divided from each aisle by three wide pointed arches upon octagonal columns with moulded capitals. One of the northern columns has a very high base, and to it is attached the font, which is an early one, in form a circular cup with the band of cable moulding upon a circular shaft having two courses of chevron work, and set on a raised square base. The tower arch is lofty, and springs from circular shafts with octagonal capitals. The chancel arch is pointed, springing from the wall without shafts. At the east end of the north aisle is a portion of an earlier building, ranging partly beyond the chancel arch, and now separated and enclosed as a vestry in its lower part; but what is particularly remarkable is that it has an upper storey above the vestry rising almost into a tower. The lower part has Norman features, and there is half of a semicircular arch in chalk in the wall, dividing it from the chancel, which is strengthened with large buttresses. The arch which divides it from the north aisle of the nave is of stone, vaulted with strong ribs which is rather remarkable, and the roof is groined in stone, with plain but bold crossing ribs without any boss; but on the west side springing from shafts. The upper part includes a chamber with a fireplace, and is approached by the staircase in the north turret, having also a small door opening on one side of the chancel arch, which must have led to the roodloft. Whether this was a priest's room, or not, it is difficult to say, but it probably was so. It is evidently of later date than the storey below, and is built of different stone, and covered with a pointed tiled roof, the external appearance of which is very strange.

Within the chancel arch is a good Perpendicular wood-screen, with five bays on each side. Above the chancel arch is a circular window now closed.

The chancel has a good east window of three unequal Early English lancets, partly hidden by a modern reredos. On the north side of the chancel is one lancet much splayed, and one Perpendicular square-headed window of three lights inserted and containing some stained glass. The original Early English string course runs below the windows on both sides. The south aisle is divided from the chancel by two plain ugly pointed arches without mouldings, having a square pier chamfered at the angles, with moulded capital. The south windows are late Perpendicular but the eastern one is Decorated of two lights, closed, however, by a monument. In this chapel are tombs of the Stedes; one is under a depressed arch, flanked by pinnacles, and surmounted by an ogee canopy with trefoil between the canopy and the arch. There is also an altar tomb to Sir William Stede, obt. 1574; and there is a late brass to Susan, wife of Edward Partheriche, who died 1603, with figures of two daughters, one in swaddling clothes, and one son. There are in the chancel some rather faded encaustic tiles, and the trace of a brass now gone. The tiles abound in the steps of the altar and within the rails. There is good woodwork in the door of the stair turret on the south.

SEVINGTON.

ST. MARY. 1843.

This small church has a west tower crowned by a shingled spire, a nave with small south aisle and south porch, and a chancel with chapel to the south of it. The tower is low and massive, of two stages with very small apertures and a single lancet on the west side; the buttresses small; the spire heavy and blackened. The walls are chiefly of stone, but mixed with brick and plaster. The south doorway has a plainly moulded arch. The nave opens to its little low aisle by two rather rude pointed arches; the western arch is very wide and straight-sided, upon impost mouldings; between the arches is a very considerable interval of stone wall. The tower arch is pointed, and to the chancel there is none. On the north side is one lancet and one labelled Perpendicular window of two lights; also one two-light Perpendicular window is set high up and beneath it there is an arch in the wall. The chancel has an east window of two lancets, which have the interior arches moulded and springing from corbels. On the north side of the chancel are some wide single lancets much splayed. The south chapel is loftier than the chancel and is evidently a later addition; in the wall between the chancel and the chapel is a low moulded arch of good form, beneath which there was probably a tomb, the wall of the chapel encroaching a little upon it. The windows of the south chapel are Late and square-headed; in its south wall is a square recess and an appearance of a piscina, also two brackets. The roof of this chapel is open. There are several prints of monumental brasses now gone, one in the chancel was of large size. The porch is mostly of wood. The font is an octagonal basin upon five shafts without capitals, the central one being the smallest, and the whole on an octagonal basement.

NEWINGTON (by Hythe).
ST. NICHOLAS.

This church is homely in its external appearance, and consists of a nave and chancel, with a north aisle to each, with a wooden belfry over the west end of the nave. On the south side of the nave is one lancet, and some Perpendicular windows. The north aisle has two very narrow lancets now closed. The nave is divided from the north aisle by three very plain pointed arches set at rather wide intervals, the piers being large and plain, with flat faces and merely an impost moulding. The aisle itself is very narrow and low. The chancel arch is semicircular, rising from impost mouldings. In one of the arches of the nave a

gallery pew is inserted for the family of Brockman. The chancel is neat within: it has two trefoil lancets on the south side, and at the east end two lancets, now closed up by the insertion of a modern reredos. The north chapel of the chancel has an east window, which seems to be a bad imitation of Decorated tracery. This chapel opens to the chancel by a plain pointed arch upon imposts, and to the aisle by a three-quarter arch. On its north side are two lancet windows. The east end of the chapel is raised for an altar. In it is a brass representing a man wrapt in a shroud, a woman, and a group of three children below. The legend "Hic jacet Thomas Chylton qui obiit X° die Augusti A° dni M°V° primo, ac pro bono statu Thomasine uxoris eius." Other brasses in the nave commemorate some of the family of Brockman. One with figures of three women and one man has this legend, "Pray for the soules of Rychard Kynge, Alys, Johan, and Kateryn his wyfs, the whyche Rychard decessed the first day of September in the yere of our lord God M°V°XXV. on whose soules Jhū have mercy, Amen." One of later date has figures in good costume of a man and woman, groups of five daughters and two sons, and armorial bearings, with this legend, "Here lyeth Henry Brokeman of Bechbrough esquire, Lord of this manor, who departed this mortall life upon the XXVII of March, 1630." There is another half figure of a lady in brass.*
The font is octagonal, entirely cased in wood, but the cover is elegant with beautiful wooden tabernacle work.

LYMINGE.

ST. MARY AND ST. EADBURGA.

This church consists of a west tower, nave with north aisle, chancel, and a south porch. The material is a mixture of flints and stone, and the whole appears to be Perpendicular. The

---

* Hain , "Manual of Monumental Brasses," p. 118, says of this "*circa* 1180." On p. 18 he describes another brass here as that of a vicar, John Clerk, who died 1501. E.

tower is low and massive, with large buttresses, an embattled parapet, and a pointed roof of wood. On the north side a very large octagonal turret. The belfry windows of two lights. On the west side a good doorway with shafts and spandrels panelled with shields. The south porch is of wood framework, open at the sides. The parapets of the church have plain mouldings, and the roof is of lead. At the south-east angle of the chancel is a curious large flying buttress, as at Rye, without any apparent use. The tower opens to the nave by a fine moulded arch upon shafts, much hidden by an ugly singing gallery. The nave is divided from the aisle by three well-formed Tudor arches, having good mouldings continued down the piers, which are attached shafts with octagonal capitals. The windows are in the nave, chiefly square-headed, and some have lost their tracery. The east window is of three lights, and has the Archiepiscopal arms in stained glass.

The chancel arch is very wide, with good mouldings and without shafts. The roof of both nave and chancel is open, with tie beams and king-posts. In the south wall of the nave, near the chancel arch, is a small arched recess, and over the porch is a small window, now closed, which may perhaps have opened into it. In the east wall of the north aisle is a stone bracket. There are some bits of ancient carved stalls, but the church is for the most part obstructed by high pews. The font is modern.

1862.

The church of Lyminge is now in a far more satisfactory and interesting condition than formerly. The interior has been cleared, the gallery taken down, and the pews replaced by open seats. There has been much scraping of the walls both within and without which has made the discovery that the masonry on the south of the nave is wholly of a very early character, like what is often called Saxon, with much mixture of ancient bricks. On the south side near to the chancel arch is, high in the wall, a straight-sided small window turned in brick, also one with semicircular arch likewise turned in brick, and above it a square-headed opening set obliquely.

The chancel is probably wholly of Early work, and has much early brick work in its walls. Early round-headed windows turned in brick have been discovered north and south, but some of the masonry externally is later. There are some curious horizontal courses in brick. On the north of the chancel appears a rude arch, open to the interior but closed externally.

There is an organ in the north aisle and six bells.

On the south side near to the church wall recent excavations have brought to light the foundations of a small building of very early character, with apsidal east termination, probably a chapel, but there is much difference of opinion as to what it was.

The church is probably built of the materials of a Roman villa.

The north aisle is a late Perpendicular addition. The tower is Perpendicular, and in the spandrels of the west door appear the arms of Archbishop Courtenay.

ELHAM.

ST. MARY.

This is rather a good church, consisting of a west tower, with a timber spire, leaded, a nave with side aisles, north porch,* and a large chancel. The walls are chiefly of rough flints. The tower is Early English and massive, divided into three stages, with large buttresses and an embattled parapet. There are double lancets in the belfry storey, and a single one in the stage below it. On the west side a doorway with continuous arch mouldings and dripstone returned, over which is a three-light window, the tracery of which is a transition from Decorated to Perpendicular. At the north-east angle of the tower is a polygonal turret. The parapets of the body are without battle-ment, the nave has a clerestory, which is very uncommon in Kent. Throughout, the church is a mixture of Early English,

* The north porch is most frequently used, but there is a south porch also. R.

Decorated and Perpendicular styles, except in the chancel, where are two Early English lancets on the south side. The nave is divided from each aisle by four pointed arches, with plain soffits, but tolerably good outer mouldings, springing from plain square piers having horizontal impost mouldings. The clere-

ST. MARY'S CHURCH, ELHAM.

story windows are square-headed, with two lights and labels. The west window of each aisle is a trefoiled lancet. The other windows on the north aisle are mostly Decorated, of two lights; of the south aisle Perpendicular, with depressed arches.

The roof of the side aisles has the beams forming an arch, with spandrels resting on head corbels set against the piers of the nave. The chancel arch is pointed, and a similar arch, upon half octagonal shafts, opens from the chancel to the north chapel. The chancel has a high tiled roof; on the south side a square-headed window of two light seems to be Decorated. There is one lancet window also on the south side, continued down very low, and two others nearer the east end. The east window is Perpendicular, of five lights, with transom

and depressed arch. The north chapel of the chancel has
very late square-headed windows. In the north wall of the
chancel beyond the aisle appears a pointed arch in the wall,
and a shallow kind of stall. The west end of the south aisle is
enclosed and contains a small library. The font is octagonal
and cased in wood.*

BUCKLAND (by Dover).

ST. ANDREW.

This small church has a nave, north aisle, and chancel with
south aisle, a south porch, and a wooden belfry over the
west end. The walls of rude flints contain a good deal of
curious work of good character. The roof is tiled. At the
west end of the nave are three lancets, over which an arch is
thrown from one buttress to another. To the south of this,
in the west front, is a single lancet, and at the west end of the
north aisle, a small Norman window closed. The aisle of the
nave is very narrow; there are some small lancet windows and
some modern ones on both sides of the nave. The aisle is
divided from the nave by three plain Early English arches,
one of which is circular, the piers octagonal with invected
capitals. The chancel arch is pointed with Early English
mouldings, and springs from half shafts of octagonal form.

The chancel has a south aisle or chapel from which it is
divided by two very dissimilar arches that seem to have been
opened in the original wall. The chapel was probably added
in the fourteenth century, as it has windows of Decorated
character which have lately been restored. The western arch
has its spring very low, its mouldings are fine and rest on corbel
heads; a dripstone over it is continued in the wall and stopped
by the other arch. The eastern arch is of very different shape,

* This casing was removed and many other improvements made, when the
church was restored.—R.

having its spring very high upon half octagonal shafts; in this arch is a low stone partition wherein there seems to have been a stall or sedile; in the space eastward of this arch is a moulded niche *trefoiled*, having a dripstone and containing a shelf and piscina; also another arched recess walled up. The east window is Decorated and on the north of the chancel is a low side trefoil lancet. The south chapel is included under the same roof as the chancel. In the north wall is a square aumbry.* The situation is pleasing and the churchyard beneath a chalk hill is planted with shrubs and evergreens.

EAST LANGDON.
ST. AUGUSTINE.

This small church of unprepossessing exterior consists of a nave with south aisle, north porch and chancel, with a small steeple surmounted by wooden belfry at the west end. The walls are as usual of rough flints and the roof tiled. The aisle extends along part of the chancel, but is very narrow. It was separated from the nave originally by two rude Early English arches having entirely plain soffits, but these two have of late been thrown into one by removing the central pier for the sake of giving more room; the responds are half circular shafts having square capitals invected. The chancel arch is a very curious Norman one, having the impost moulding enriched with a kind of chain ornament and shafts inserted in the angles, some parts of the work have unluckily been cut away, and the whole clogged both with lampblack and whitewash. North of the chancel arch is a rude small arch, perhaps a hagioscope. The south porch is of brick, apparently of the seventeenth century; within it is a narrow doorway, perhaps originally Norman, but altered. Most of the windows in the south aisle are modern and wretched. The chancel opens to the aisle by a plain round

* The church has been well restored.—H.

arch with modern keystone. The east window is Perpendicular of two lights. On the north side is an acute trefoil lancet. On the south (and nearer to the east end) a more obtuse one, below which is a rude obtuse-headed recess in the wall, perhaps a credence, being set too high for a sedile. Opposite to it on the north side is an oblong recess in the wall, rather shallow, which perhaps was an aumbry. The font has an octagonal bowl, moulded and contracting towards the base which is surrounded by a band of foliage, the shaft octagonal and plain. The pulpit cloth is a remarkable feature in this church, it seems to be a part of the priests' vestments, and is of crimson velvet richly embroidered with a representation of the Annunciation of the Virgin Mary with the lily pot and scrolls, and other elegant devices and cyphers. The scrolls are inscribed: "*Ave grā plena . . . Ecce ancilla dñi . . . fiat michi secundum, &c.* The colour of the velvet is well preserved considering its age. The cushion of the pulpit is also of a similar material. In the north wall near the pulpit is a rude arched recess. The altar is a chest. In the belfry are four bells, and there is a west gallery and hideous pews.

RINGWOULD.

ST. NICHOLAS.

This church has a tower, nave (31 feet long) with north aisle, south porch and chancel 25 ft. 10 in. long, by 15 ft. 10 in. broad. The tower is an ugly erection of flint and brick. The walls of the church are chiefly of flints with some stones intermixed, and for the most part stuccoed. The porch is plain. The nave is divided from the aisle by three pointed arches springing from octagonal pillars, the eastern respond being a square impost. The chancel arch seems to be Early English, with no soffit mouldings and resting on plain imposts. The windows of the nave and aisle are mostly late Perpendicular with square heads; but there

is one rather large lancet near the pulpit on the south side; also a small obtuse one on the same side and one at the west end of the north aisle. The chancel has three lancet windows on each side, whereof the two western are trefoiled, the eastern ones wider. On the south of the altar are two unequal sedilia, the western one with plain pointed arch, the eastern with rudely formed trefoil head, and between them an octagonal pier with moulded capital. The east window is Perpendicular lately restored. The pews are as usual high and ugly, and there is a west gallery with a barrel organ.* The font is a small octagonal bowl on a large base, which does not seem originally to belong to it. In the nave are three brasses: (1) A legend half broken without a figure and clearly of Protestant period:—" Here lieth Elizabeth, wyffe of Robert .... unt, who lyved vertuously, and dyed in chyldbed, very godly, y^c xx of September, 1589." †
(2) Three figures of which one is entirely gone; one man remains in good preservation, and of the lady only half, and there is a group of five children.‡ Legend:—" Of your charyte pray for the soulles of Willm Abere, Alys, and Anne hys wyfes, which Willm decessed the x day of October the yere of our lord thousand ccccc et v. On whose soullis Jħu have mercy. Amen." (3) A small and rather coarsely executed figure with this legend:—" Of your charityc pray for the sowle of Johñ Upton wch dyed the yere of our Lord m^o. v^c. xxx." In the north aisle is a slab § on which is a plain cross. The walls are inscribed with several texts mostly in lozenge compartments.

* This church has been restored and reseated.—H.
† "On a brass plate, under three figures in brass, out of the mouth of the middlemost of which proceeds a label or scroll, with this sentence: 'Jħu Merci, Lady help.' and under them a group of five small figures, all fixed to a flat stone." Bryan-Faussett's Collecta.—H.
‡ Bryan-Faussett's Collecta.—H.
§ "Very ancient." Bryan-Faussett's Collecta.—H.

DEAL.

ST. LEONARD.

The parish church in Upper Deal has undergone many injudicious and tasteless alterations. There is an ugly west tower of brick built in 1684; a large modern addition has been made on the north side of the nave, not one original window remains, and but very little of the ancient flint walls. The nave is divided from each aisle by three obtusely pointed arches, springing from circular columns with square capitals and invected moulding. The responds have rude foliage. These pillars are hideously painted in imitation of marble. The chancel arch is pointed and very plain. There are numerous galleries and a most horrible gallery pew erected between the nave and chancel. In the northern added wing is the organ. The chancel still retains some interesting ancient features. On the south side are two ascending sedilia, the western of which is pointed with excellent mouldings, the eastern trefoiled also with fine mouldings: the shafts are detached, of marble, with moulded capitals. Eastward of these is a curious piscina beneath a pointed niche, formed by what resembles a Norman cushion capital upon an octagonal shaft, which is moulded with chevron work, the basin itself is square and sloping to the orifice. In the north wall of the chancel is an arched recess either for a credence or an ambry. At the east end of the south aisle is a green marble tablet inlaid with the brass figure of a knight kneeling at a desk, with an inscription:—" Thomas Boys, Esquier, son to John Boys of Fredfield in the parish of Nonnington . . . . Captain of Deale Castle, made so by Edward VI., 1551; buried February 13, 1562, whose sowle resteth with God."

"Houche Thomas Boys lys corpse in grave bereded doth lye
Yet Boys a Boys sayth to him he shall never dye."

On a scroll " Tousjours prest " The font is modern and ugly.

MONGEHAM.
ST. MARTIN.

July 1865. K.a.

This church has a lofty west tower, a nave with north aisle, a south porch, and chancel, with large chapels both on the north and the south.

The tower is Perpendicular, built of flint and stone, with an octagonal turret at the north-east corner; the parapet embattled, the belfry window on each side of two lights, somewhat mutilated. On the west side a good doorway with label and panelled spandrels, containing shields and quatrefoils. Over the door a three-light window, set in one compartment with the door. It appears that there was once a south aisle, now destroyed, and there is an Early English column and capital built into part of the porch, which is an addition constructed of brick. The southern windows are of a wretched description,* those of the north aisle are square-headed with Perpendicular tracery, which has in some instances been restored. There is a clerestory on both sides; that on the south has two trefoiled lancets and one Decorated window of two lights; that on the north is similar, but is hidden from the exterior by the roof of the aisle. The nave is divided from the north aisle by three very plain Early English arches with square, plain piers having impost mouldings, and the angles chamfered. The tower opens to the nave by a high and good pointed arch, with fine mouldings and shafts. The chancel arch is similar in character to those dividing the aisle, but has small shafts. The whole interior is whitewashed to a very glaring extent. The chapels north and south of the chancel have separate roofs; that on the north has small Norman windows, that on the south has obtuse lancets; but both are separated from the chancel, and the south one appears to be used only for rubbish.ˣ The east window of the chancel is modernized.† The font is a plain, rude, octagonal block,

---

* This church has been well restored.—H.
† The whitewash has all been removed, and the east window restored.—H.

ˣ *now occupied by the organ — contains a small niche, supposed to be a leper's window.*

attached to one of the piers of the nave. The steeple and some other portions of this church are mantled with ivy in a picturesque manner. In the chancel arch is a wood screen, and the door to the rood-loft is seen on the north.

now in the Tower arch.

NORTHBOURNE. *Aug. 1818.*

ST. AUGUSTINE.

This is an interesting cruciform church without aisles, and presenting some excellent specimens of Norman and Early English work, often mixed together in a curious manner. The tower is in the centre, and surmounted by a pointed roof of tiles. The roofs of every part of the church are high pitched and tiled, and the gables high. The belfry windows are small single lancets. The materials are chiefly rough flints, with some admixture of stone; part of the south side of the nave has been rebuilt, and has buttresses of brick. The west window is a single lancet. On the north side of the nave are two Norman windows set high in the wall, and one of Early English character. On the south side is one Norman window placed in the same manner, but partly destroyed by the modern wall. At the west end is a pointed doorway with hood moulding. The north door, which is closed, is early Norman, without mouldings or shafts, having a horizontal stone transom; the south door, similar in shape, is included within an arch with chevron mouldings and shafts. The east end has a high gable, two single lancet windows, one above the other, and a moulded circle near the point. The tower rises upon four arches opening to the nave, transepts, and chancel. The western arch is pointed, with plain single soffit, and the outer moulding chevroned upon an impost; the inner moulding has shafts at the angles with inverted capitals. The three other arches of the tower are semicircular, with cylindrical mouldings, and shafts. In all these arches there is a curious mixture of both styles. The end of the north transept has two plain lancets, on the east side one. The south transept end has a double lancet within a general arch and a dripstone; in the apex a lozenge. On the east side of this transept are lancets. The nave is fitted up with deal pews, but the avenue in the centre is tolerably wide. The chancel has three lancet windows on each side, which are surmounted internally by trefoil rude openings in the thickness of the wall. Of the two lancets at the east end the lowest is long, the upper one is smaller and obtuse. In the east wall is a pointed Early English arch, with foliated capitals of shafts, which have disappeared. This looks like a communication with a sanctum now destroyed. On the south side of the chancel is a wide flattish arch, which perhaps may have been a sedile sufficient for three priests, but undivided. Eastward of this is a curious straight-sided arch upon shafts, much clogged with whitewash, within which is a small, round-headed recess. The font is octagonal and modern Gothic. The tower contains five bells. The walls are inscribed with texts.

EASTRY. *July. 1885. B.Q.S.*
ST. MARY.

A large and handsome church, presenting a beautiful specimen of nearly unmixed Early English style, in some points singular. It consists of a large west tower, a long nave with side aisles, and a spacious chancel. There are also chapels adjoining the tower on the north and south. The walls are chiefly of rough flints, but some stone is intermixed, in the tower; the parapets of the body and chancel are plain, and in some part repaired with brick. The tower is of considerable size, and has a curious mixture of Norman and Early English work. The west door is Norman, and rather small; the moulding has the cylinder, the shafts cushion capitals and abacus. There is a horizontal stone transom above the door, and the tympanum filled with stonework in form of hollowed squares. Above this door is a horizontal moulding with three corbels. The middle story on the west side has three lancet windows, set within elegant arches with trefoil feathering, and shafts having moulded capitals; in the intermediate spaces of the arches are heads, rather an uncommon feature; the buttresses are flat faced; the belfry windows single lancets; the parapet plain, with a corbel table below it. One of the tower buttresses was originally pierced by an arch; the stages of the tower are unequally divided by string courses. Near the tower door is a benatura. The small chapels north and south of the tower are more like sheds, and closed up. They are divided from the tower by pointed arches pierced in the solid masonry, and from the aisles by half arches upon clustered shafts. The tower opens to the nave by a pointed arch rising from half columns upon large bases. In the north-east angle, within the tower, is the termination of a staircase on a curious kind of bracket, having two moulded corbel tables, and ending in a strongly formed trefoil arch, with good mouldings. The nave is wide, but the aisles rather narrow, the interior solemn and grand. The nave has on each side five rather plain Early English arches, with simple soffits and hood mouldings; the eastern arch on each side very narrow; the piers are all circular, with moulded capitals and bases, except the second from the west end on the south side, which is octagonal, and has a kind of four-leaved flower on the capital. The eastern responds are moulded circular brackets, the western are shafts. The clerestory has a single lancet window in each compartment; those next the west end are trefoiled on the south side, as are all on the north side; the dripstone is continued. The windows of the side aisles are chiefly Early Decorated, of three trefoiled lights within a rather depressed arch. Some of them have been mutilated. At the east end of the aisles are Perpendicular square-headed windows; that of the south aisle has in the jamb a little elegant panelled bracket, for a statue, surmounted by a small battlemented cornice. There is also a small niche and drain at the east end of the same aisle. The chancel arch is moulded, and rises on octagonal brackets brought to a point, the southern having a piece of foliage; and on each side of this arch, facing the nave, is a small, square bracket, ending in curling foliage. In the spandrels of this arch, facing the nave, are two pierced quatrefoils, and corresponding with them on the east side two moulded trefoil arches—a very curious arrangement.˟ The chancel has on each side five lancet windows, with dripstones returned and continued, and string underneath; but those on the south are shockingly encroached on by modern monuments. The most eastern window on the south is set higher, has a flattened hood moulding, and is divided into two lights of Early Decorated character. There is modern wainscoting at the east end of the chancel,* so that it cannot be seen whether there are sedilia. There is a priest's door on the south, the string going over it in a depressed arch. The northern lancets are free from encroachment. In the north wall, near the altar, is an elegant moulded arch, which seems to have been once divided in two by a central shaft, and has tracery in the head, in which are the heads of two pointed arches, and a *vesica piscis* between them. This seems to have been an aumbry, and is both singular and elegant, but much clogged with whitewash.

There are prints of several brasses now gone. One that remains has figures of a knight and lady, "Thomas Nevynson of Estry ob^t 1590, Provost Marshall and Scout Master of ye Est parts of Kent, and Ann his wife, daughter of Rychard Tebolde, Esquier." There are texts on the walls. The font is an octagonal bowl with shields and roses, and a moulded band below it with square flowers. The shaft octagonal on a plinth of like form.

The south porch is ugly. The east window of the chancel had originally three lancets, but the central one has been altered into a square-headed light with late tracery. The east gable is high. The chancel, finely mantled with ivy, is 46 ft. 3 in. long, by 16 ft. wide. The total length of the nave (81 feet) and tower space is 101 ft. 10 in.

* The church has been restored, whitewash removed, &c.—H.

˟ *above these are seven frescoes.*

STAPLE.

ST. JAMES.

This church has a west tower, a nave with north aisle and chancel, the aisle not beginning quite at the west, but continued along part of the chancel. There is a mixture of Decorated and Perpendicular work, but none earlier. The walls are all of flint and the exterior is plain. Within the south porch is a pointed door with small shafts. The north aisle has a moulded parapet, the rest has none but tiled roofs. The tower is embattled and plain, rather of small size; the west door has arch mouldings and small shafts; the buttresses are not carried up high; the belfry windows are small and single. The tower arch to the nave is pointed and plain, but there is in the wall a trace of a Norman capital, the remains of an earlier building. There are four bells.

The interior is not inelegant though plain, but far too glaring from coarse whitewash.* The roof has tie beams on foliated spandrels and king-posts. Many of the original open seats are perceptible, but on some of them modern pews have been exalted. There are three pointed arches of Perpendicular character opening to the north aisle, with good piers of lozenge form having four shafts and mouldings. The nave seems rather of transition character from Decorated to Perpendicular; the southern windows of two and three lights have odd tracery of that sort. On the north are some square-headed windows of three lights. There is no chancel arch, and the chancel is nearly as long as the nave. The east window is large, of five lights, each trefoiled within a large general arch; the style is Decorated and rather early; the dripstone rests on head corbels. The side windows of the chancel are Decorated of two lights, in many of which are fragments of fine painted glass. On the south side of the chancel is a trefoil niche with drain, and in the south wall near

* The church has been restored; whitewash removed, and open seats reinstated. H

the entrance to the chancel is an odd arched recess. The chancel opens to the north chapel by a plain and low pointed arch; this chapel, belonging to the Lynches, was fitted up and adorned in the bad style of the end of the sixteenth century; the roof of painted stucco, and the east window bad. There are several ugly modern monuments, a brass of a merchant, and prints of two other brasses, one with one figure, another with three. Between the north aisle and this chapel is a wooden screen of Perpendicular character.

The font is perhaps the most conspicuous feature in this church, the bowl octagonal of large size, enriched with figures of angels bearing shields containing the cross and emblems of the Passion, the insignia of four Evangelists with inscribed scrolls, also a representation of the Trinity, the Three Divine Persons being all signified. The lower part of the bowl has monsters with extended wings and a flowered band; the shaft is surrounded by grotesque beasts, both large and small, and elevated on two high octagonal steps. The style is probably Perpendicular.

WINGHAM.

ST. MARY.

This church is spacious, comprising a west tower with wooden spire, a nave with south aisle, a chancel with both north and south aisles; the latter, however, is divided off and used as a school, by which means it has experienced much ill-treatment.*
The walls are of flints with admixture of stone. The south porch is embattled, of two heights, but without floors; the walls on the north are of rougher material than those on the south. The tower is embattled, with buttresses not at the angles, and an octagonal turret at the north-west; the belfry window is of two

---

* The church has been thoroughly restored throughout.—H.

lights; the west window is Perpendicular of three lights, and below it is a moulded doorway. The spire is leaded and of pretty good proportion. The roofs are tiled, and separate in each portion of the church. The church has both Decorated and Perpendicular features. The length is considerable; but the arches which at present divide the nave from the south aisle are quite modern. The tower arch is pointed, rising from half octagonal columns, having the four-leafed flower in the capitals. The windows in the nave are plain Perpendicular of three lights. The chancel arch is pointed, rising from shafts with moulded capitals which appear to be Early English. The roof is plain, in the style very common in Kent.

There is some stained glass in one of the southern windows of the nave inscribed " Edwarde Warham Gentell . . . . . of makinge this wyndowe . . . . A°. . . . . ." The chancel and its aisles are chiefly Decorated, of which style they contain fine specimens, especially the windows. On the south side are two very fine windows of three lights with most elegant geometrical tracery. The east window is closed, but appears to have had originally three lancets. The chancel is long, extending beyond the side chapels, and is approached from the nave by a wood screen of the style of the 17th century with twisted columns. In the chancel are all the original stalls in good preservation with misereres. There are three steps to the altar. Between the chancel and the north chapel is a very fine arch having extremely deep mouldings of Early Decorated character springing from clustered shafts, having well moulded capitals, but not reaching all down the pier, and each terminating in a kind of point. The corresponding arch on the south is similar, and there is also a pointed and moulded door on each side. The space enclosed for the altar is very large; the east window is hidden by an ugly modern reredos; and on the north side within the rails is a huge monument to one of the Palmer family, 1627. The south chapel belongs to the Oxenden family, and opens to the south aisle of the nave by a narrow pointed arch. It has a superb Decorated window on the south side of five lights, the interior arch of which is beautifully moulded, rising from shafts with foliated capitals. The east window is of three lights, resembling those of the chancel, but curiously set in a kind of bay or recess. It has shafts, as also have those of the chancel. In the Oxenden chapel is a vast pagan monument of marble of pyramidal form, with Cupids, &c., 1696. In the south wall of the nave is a flat arch partly hidden, under which there must have been a tomb. There are several texts inscribed on the walls ; a seraphine in the chancel is played by the incumbent's lady. The north chapel, now used as a school is, as might be expected, in a wretchedly dirty and mutilated state. The font is an ugly modern one. There are the traces of several brasses in the chancel, all unhappily destroyed, but they must have been of large size and rare beauty.

ST. STEPHEN'S (near Canterbury).

This church is cruciform but without aisles, and has at the west end a very massive but low tower with tiled penthouse roof surmounted by a short wooden spire. The lower parts of this steeple are Norman, verging to the next style. On the west side is a very fine doorway slightly pointed, but with Norman ornaments ; two courses of double chevrons and two shafts on each side, the capitals and bases of which present much variety of moulding, the billet, cable, rude foliage, and cushion, the shafts all set on square plinths. On the south side of the tower is a Norman window ; those of the belfry are square-headed and late Perpendicular. There is a Perpendicular south porch, within which is a fine Norman doorway, the shafts have cushion capitals, with abacus and horizontal band above the door-case ; the head of the arch is moulded with the hollowed squares. The tower is so wide as to equal the breadth of the nave. On each side of the nave are some lancet windows, a few obtuse. There is a plain round arch opening to the south transept, an obtuse one to the north transept, and a pointed one to the chancel with mouldings and shafts. In the south transept is a Decorated window of two lights, and one lancet closed. The north transept has a curious Decorated window of three lights, without dripstone, the upper part having three spherical triangles trefoiled, its east window is late and bad Perpendicular. The chancel has a Perpendicular east window, with good tracery, of five lights; the windows on the sides of the chancel are of two lights with very elegant tracery, of a transition character from Decorated to Perpendicular, the heads containing four quatrefoiled circles, and vertical lines rising from the apex of each light which is trefoiled. The interior arch of each of these windows is moulded and springs from shafts with moulded capitals. There is in them a little painted glass. The roofs are tiled.

HAWKINGE.

ST. MICHAEL.

A small mean church consisting only of nave and chancel with south porch, and a wooden cage for a bell over the west end. The walls of rough flints, the roofs tiled. At the west end is a door with obtuse arch, now closed. The porch has a ruinous wood roof. There is a descent of three steps from the entrance into the church, and the interior is dirty and out of condition. At the west end is an obtuse lancet, now closed. There are some small lancet windows on the south, of the plainest character, and two with plain trefoil heads. Some others are single but apparently very late. On the north the windows are all closed. At the west end under the belfry is a kind of raised daïs, and the font, which is on a raised square plinth, has a small octagonal bowl on a shaft of like form. The door within the porch has a contracted arch. There is no chancel arch. The roof of the nave is ribbed and open, that of the chancel ceiled, but the tie beams and framework are seen, being quite different from the roof of the nave. The east end has two lancets included beneath a general arch, the centre pier is buttressed externally, and within bears a pedestal for a statue. There is an ugly, debased square window on the south side of the chancel, below the sill of which is a kind of extension, something in the form of a stall, but too high in the wall for a seat. It may perhaps have been a credence. The lower part has a projecting slab. Near it in the south wall is a very rude piscina, with pointed arch, the basin projecting. On the north side of the altar is a plain arch in the wall encroached on by a modern marble monument. There are hideous high pews in the chancel especially offensive in so small a church.*

LANGLEY.

ST. MARY.

A small church in a woody churchyard adjoining the road from Maidstone to Tenterden.† The plan—chancel, short nave with north aisle, south porch and west tower, which latter is apparently modern, the lower part of stone, the upper of brick and crowned by a shingled spire. The walls of the church are chiefly of the Kentish rag, and the roofs are tiled. The porch is very plain. The nave is short and confined, and still further impaired by the presence of high pews, and a hideous gallery at the west end encroaching on almost the whole of one of the two arches. There are some plain Perpendicular windows of two lights; that at the east of the aisle having an obtuse arch, and that at the west a trefoil lancet. There are two brackets at the east end of the aisle. The two arches dividing the nave and aisle are extremely plain and rude but pointed,

---

* The church has been restored and reseated.—H.
† This church has been subsequently rebuilt [by the rector].

the pier is square without any capital. The chancel arch is similar. On the north side of the chancel is a single lancet, on the south a square-headed Perpendicular one with label. The east window has three lancet lights within a general pointed arch. The exterior of the chancel is stuccoed.

The chancel is wainscoted within, so that the sedilia, &c., if any, are completely hidden. The font has an octangular bowl panelled with shields, beneath which is a slope ; the stem is octagonal and ribbed at the angles.

HEADCORN.
ST. PETER AND ST. PAUL.

A handsome Perpendicular church close to the Dover Railroad, situated within a very large cemetery. Plan—west tower, nave and chancel, each with south aisle, a south porch and vestry north of the chancel, the whole of Kentish rag, and the exterior well finished. The tower not very lofty, is three stages in height, and has a good battlement and octagonal turret at the north east. The west door has good mouldings with small shafts, a label and panelled spandrels. Just over the door is a square tablet, containing a shield within a quatrefoil ; on the shield is a " bend engrailed." Above is a window of three lights which has tracery of apparently Decorated character, the hood moulding on head corbels, but it is probably coëval with the rest of the church, which is wholly Perpendicular and of uniform character. The belfry windows vary, some of two, some of three lights, all square-headed ; the intermediate stage has a single opening. The aisle and the porch have a good battlement, the buttresses set at equal distances ; the south side of the church has windows of two lights with labels, and one of three lights ; those on the north are of better design ; in some are good pieces of stained glass, in which figures of saints beneath canopies, with inscribed scrolls may be seen. The porch is large, with a parvise, and in the angle is an octagonal stair turret, the door has good mouldings, the windows are square-headed. The length of the church is considerable, and the interior fine and spacious, though the arches and walls are glaring with the coarsest whitewash.* The tower arch has bold and deep mouldings, the inner member springing from shafts. On each side are strong buttresses supporting the east wall of the tower. There are eight bells. There are five pointed arches between the nave and aisle, springing from light octagonal columns. The chancel has a tiled roof. The chancel arch is lofty, and is carried from one of the octagon piers to the opposite wall; and another very wide arch is thrown across the aisle, separating that of the chancel which must have been a chantry chapel. Between this and the chancel are two plainer pointed arches, springing from an ill-shaped pier, a polygon with unequal sides, having a squared capital. Some stones seem to have been taken from this pier. The east window of the chancel is of three lights, with a transom; on the north of the chancel is a two-light window with some good stained glass. The south chantry has the east window of five lights, with flattened arch, and in the south wall is a long square recess, containing a piscina. This part of the church is very damp and full of green mould. There is a small door under one of the windows in this chantry, which is raised one step above the aisle of the nave. Its ceiling is flat, panelled in wood with foliated bosses. There is beneath one of the south windows a fine Perpendicular tomb in the wall (probably of the founder, one of the Cole-peppers) rising above the window sill, and having an embattled cornice. The arched canopy has bold rich double feathering with foliage at the points, and panelling with shields in the spandrels.† The effigy is concealed by a pier. There are also

---

* The whitewash has been all removed, as well as the paint from the rood-loft screen. The church is about to be reseated, &c., 1876.—H.

† " The arms of the Culpeper family are cut in the stones at each corner . . . Tradition says that the founder of the church, who was a Culpeper, was buried underneath the above mentioned stone."—" a gravestone, six feet and a half in

prints of destroyed brasses, but one still remaining is of late date, and represents a child kneeling at a faldstool, with a legend: "Here lyeth the body of John Byrd, the sonne of William Byrd of this parish of Headcorne, who was borne the 10 of May, 1629, and in the time of his sickness delivered many godly exhortations to his parents takinge his leave of them with such unexpected expressions as are not common in so younge a child. He departed this life the 31 of Jan^y, An. D. 1636." The nave roof has the timbers arched and an embattled cornice. The aisle roof is out of order, and supported upon additional framework lately added. The lower part of the rood-loft screen remains; it has an elegant cornice and panelling, but is hideously painted white. The font has an octagonal bowl, its faces are ornamented with shields, angels bearing scrolls, the Holy Lamb and the rose. The stem is octagonal, with buttresses at the angles, and raised upon two steps.

PLUCKLEY.

1844.

The church is well situated on an eminence commanding a fine view. Plan: West tower with shingled spire, nave and chancel each with south aisle. The tower, of a rude mixture of flint and stone, has a Perpendicular west door and window, the former has label and spandrels, enriched with quatrefoiled circles, the window is of two lights, labelled. The other windows are single apertures. There is no parapet to the tower, and the shingled spire, squared at the base, is undergoing repair.

In the nave is the brass of a Knight of the Malmaine family [Richard Malemayns, Esquire, 1440] with dog at his feet, the legend much worn. There are also three brasses of smaller size,

length, raised above ground a foot or more, without any date or inscription." "The same arms are cut in a stone on the outside of the church over the belfry door." Parsons' "Monuments," p. 367.—H.

1. A lady with this legend. "Off y^r charyte pray for the sowlle of Julyen Deryng gentyl woman, whyche decessed, 1526."
2. A Knight with a dog under his feet, legend destroyed.
3. A still smaller figure of a Knight beneath an arched canopy; apparently a child.

The south porch has a parvise, and the entrance arch on shafts. The body is chiefly of Kentish rag, but much of it is stuccoed, and the aisle has a moulded parapet. On the south side there is the usual projection resembling a large buttress, corresponding with the chancel arch. The prevailing features are Decorated and Perpendicular, the southern windows are late Perpendicular, flat arched of three lights; on the north are two of Decorated character, of three lights, one of which has three trefoiled lights, without tracery in the head. The nave is lofty and wide, the roof has tie-beams with king-posts, branching into two. There are four pointed arches, dividing the nave and aisle, of which the western one is more acute and lower than the others with a square plain pier, evidently Early English, and the only specimen of this style in the church. The other three arches are wide and lofty, and spring from slender octagonal columns with moulded capitals. There is no chancel arch, the pier between the centre arch of the nave and that opening from the chancel to its south chapel is square. The arch is rather acute, and springs from brackets. On the corbels supporting this arch are the arms of Dering. The chancel windows are Perpendicular, the eastern of three lights. On the north the windows are late and square-headed, and just by the altar, or to the north and south, are single-light windows, which seem to be of the same date. On the south side of the altar are two sedilia, divided by a low kind of stone elbow, and included within a general pointed arch. Eastward is a trefoil niche with piscina on a bracket which is carried to a point. All these are of green marble. On the north side, opposite to these, is a trefoiled niche, with a projecting ledge, which seems to have been a credence. The south chapel belongs to the Dering family,

and is enclosed with wooden screens; it abounds with monuments
to the family, and is now occupied as their pew. It is divided
from the aisle of the nave by a pointed arch. The windows of
this chapel contain modern painted glass. It is fitted up with
stalls, better than is often found, but still too much of the
parlour pew. The monuments which it contains are mostly
mural marble tablets of uniform kind, and free from the objection-
able devices generally seen. The screen facing the chancel is
elegant, with vine cornice and Tudor flowers; that in the
western arch is of later date and mixed style. On the screen in
the western arch is this inscription, " Hanc capellam Ric. Dering
Armiger fundatam A° Dnī 1475 reparavit et ornavit Anno Dnī
1634. Dilexi domum Domini Dei." The font is Perpendicular,
the bowl octagonal, panelled with quatrefoils containing roses
and shields, in which occur the arms of the Malmaines and
of the Derings. The shaft of the font has buttresses at the
angles, and is set upon four wide steps of Bethersden marble ;
the whole is covered unfortunately with colouring. At the west
end of the church is a double gallery.

WALMER.

This church in its present state is but an unsightly object.
It originally consisted only of a tower, nave, and chancel of
small dimensions, but the tower has fallen down ; a mean bell-
turret has been erected over the west end, and a huge brick
excrescence added on the north, filled with pews and galleries,
and making the church quite shapeless. The original walls are
of rough flint, partly stuccoed. The south porch seems to have
been rebuilt, and its outer door of Norman character with
enriched mouldings and shafts. Within the porch is an original
Norman doorway, lofty and good ; the mouldings have varied
kinds of chevron ornament and billets ; the shafts with cushion
capitals and abaci, which are continued horizontally on each

side. The chancel arch is also Norman, and presents towards the nave a much richer appearance than to the east, and in its general features closely resembling the south door, with impost continued on each side. Towards the east the soffit is plain, and the imposts have a kind of nail-head ornament. The chancel is small, and has Early English features; the east window and one on the south are single lancets, and there is a lychnoscope on the south much spoiled. On the north side of the chancel is a bracket for a statue; on the south a niche of a flattened trefoil form. Most of the nave windows have been altered. One square-headed one still retains its label, with head corbels. There is some ivy on the west end. The pulpit fronts the north, in order to face the congregation, who occupy the north wing or excrescence. There is an organ. The font has a plain and small octagonal bowl. A vestry is added adjoining the south porch.

RIPPLE.
ST. MARY.

A neat small church, but of good height, consisting only of a nave and chancel, and over the west end a wooden turret and small spire.* The church is chiefly of Norman character, with a little of the later styles. The west window has good plain mouldings and shafts; those on the sides of the nave are set very high, and are perhaps early Norman, resembling those at Guston, narrow and plain, having externally a kind of long and short course, the stones laid in different ways, and immediately beneath the arch forming *quasi* imposts. There is a north porch of wood and plaster; the south door, which is closed, has an embattled moulding on the imposts. There is no chancel arch, but a large buttress projecting on the south side marks where the chancel begins; the walls are of rough flints, the roofs

* This church has been rebuilt.—H.

tiled. The chancel has a boarded roof within; the nave is ceiled. The east window is early Decorated, of three lights, and seems to have been curtailed of its original proportions. On the south of the chancel are two trefoil lancets. The interior is neat, but has high pews. In the chancel are quasi wooden stalls. The reredos of mediocre modern Gothic design. The pulpit rather neatly carved, temp. James I. In the north wall of the nave is a plain arched recess, and a bracket. The font ugly and poor, with the date 1663, has a small octagonal bowl on round shaft. In the chancel is a brass to one Edward Warren, 1591, the figure gone. There are two bells, and in the chancel a small finger organ. The situation is lonely, but pleasing. Near the church is a fine yew tree.

CHERITON (near Folkestone).

ST. MARTIN. 1841.

This church is in a lonely situation, but is an interesting building, consisting of a nave with south aisle, north porch, and transept, and chancel, with a small plain tower at the west end. There are several good Early English features, especially in the chancel. The tower has no divisions by string-courses; the belfry window and another on the west side are single lancets. There is a plain pointed west door. The walls are chiefly of a rough admixture of flint and stone. There are separate tiled roofs to the nave and aisle; the windows of the south aisle are poor modern ones, except that at the east end, which is Decorated of three lights, but rather peculiar in its tracery.

The nave is divided from the south aisle by three pointed arches springing from octagonal pillars; and the north chapel, or transept, opens to the nave by a plain pointed arch rising on imposts. In this chapel is a two-light Decorated window in the east wall, having no hood moulding, but containing a fragment of stained glass in which is seen the Crucifixion.

There is one window on the north side with a single trefoil light; the others are modern and bad. The north porch with its doorways is quite plain. At the east end of the south aisle are two sedilia of rather curious arrangement and Decorated character.

Just without the north porch is a slab charged with a cross flory. In the south aisle is a monumental arch in the wall, beneath which is an effigy. The chancel arch is pointed, very plain, rising upon imposts. The chancel is large, and of much superior character to the rest of the church. It has on each side three lancet windows, having fine arch mouldings internally and a string-course beneath; at the east end are two lancets set at some distance from each other with a vesica piscis above them in the gable and now closed. These lancets have mouldings and shafts internally. Under the windows on each side of the chancel are six fine Early English niches or stalls, having very fine mouldings and shafts of Purbeck marble with moulded capitals: the shafts at the extremities are clustered. There is an arch in the north chancel wall for a door now closed, and one lower one. There are several stone brackets. The pulpit has tolerable wood carving of Perpendicular character. The chancel is placed on a steep bank, and there is a sudden fall from the east end.

GILLINGHAM.*
ST. MARY.

Aug: 1884.
July. 1886 K. a. S.
1811.

A large Kentish church; the nave has aisles and a clerestory (which last is not common in Kent), and the chancel has a large chapel on either side, exceeding in width the aisles of the nave. There is a north porch and a western tower. The tower is chiefly of Kentish rag stone; but much of the walls of the body are of flints. The aisles have battlements; but the

* Formerly a Peculiar of Canterbury; now in the diocese of Rochester.—H.

chapels of the chancel have separate tiled roofs and no parapets. The external appearance is chiefly Third Pointed, but the porch is modern. The tower is rather plain, has a battlement and a circular stair turret at the north-east angle. The buttresses extend to the second story. The belfry windows square-headed, of two lights, with label; on the west side a small window and a door with continuous mouldings, over which is a niche. Within, the lower story of the tower has stone groining and forms now the principal entrance. The windows of the aisles of the nave are Third Pointed of two lights, some square-headed; those of the clerestory are square-headed of two lights. The nave is divided from each aisle by four arches of pointed form, of which the two western on each side are lower and wider than the others; the first pier from the west is circular, with octagonal capital; the second on each side is square, having a moulded capital. The two eastern arches are acute, and have piers as the first mentioned. They all appear to be First Pointed, but not of the same date. The roof of the nave has plain timbers with spandrels on stone corbels with angel figures. The chancel arch is pointed, on half octagonal shafts. The chancel is divided from each of its large lateral chapels by three pointed arches, lower than the eastern ones of the nave, with octagonal pillars having plain moulded caps. The responds consist of three early clustered shafts set in recesses having square abaci, and one on the north side has quite a Norman character, scolloped. The chancel roof is coved, with king-posts, &c. The east window is Third Pointed of five lights, filled with poor modern painted glass. The sacrarium is paved with marble. The north chapel has a three-light east window of curious Third Pointed tracery and two others of two lights. In this chapel is a mutilated piscina with trefoiled head and triangular canopy. The south chapel is partly disfigured with high pews, partly in a wretched state of dirt and neglect. Its roof is open, and coved with plain frame-work. Its windows resemble those of the north chapel, and it contains some screen-work ; a piscina and two sedilia (the third having been cut off by a modern wall) rising eastward with ogee canopies, cinque-foiled feathering, and good mouldings springing from marble columns with moulded capitals and bases, and early Middle Pointed character. There are remains of magnificent brasses in the chancel—one large of two figures, one smaller of three. In the north chapel is the trace of one representing a knight and lady, with fine canopy. In the chancel a small one remains, inscribed : " Hic jacet dñs Johēs Pegge Vicarius de Gyllyngham cui^s aiē ppiciet'-deus. Amen."

The font is Norman, the bowl cylindrical, moulded round the rim, and surrounded by an arcade of round arches springing from circular columns with zigzag mouldings, square capitals and round bases.

At the west end a double gallery and an organ.

GODMERSHAM.
ST. LAWRENCE.

Plan. Nave with south transeptal chapel, chancel and tower on the north side of the nave. The south side of the nave and the south transept are chiefly of brick and modernised. On the north of the nave are two plain Romanesque windows (one closed) and one Third Pointed of three lights. The west window of four lights is Middle Pointed, not of a very common character. The tower is of early character without buttresses, contracting in width towards the upper part ; against its east wall is a most singular semicircular apse with some small Romanesque windows. The windows of the tower are small and round-headed. The chancel is built of flints, and has a good triple lancet east window with shafts and good mouldings internally. On its south side is one closed lancet, and two early Middle Pointed windows of two lights, having in the head the double feathered quatrefoil found not unfrequently in Kent. The western one has the sill extended as for a "lychnoscope." On the north of the chancel is a pointed door within a porch, one lancet and one two-light Middle Pointed window. On the south side of the chancel under a window is a sedile with trefoil head springing from First Pointed shafts with moulded capital; also a piscina under a feathered trefoil canopy of Middle Pointed character. The roofs are tiled; that of the nave has tie-beams with king-posts and pierced spandrels. There is no chancel arch. An aristocratic pew occupies the south transept. In the church-yard is a fine yew.

WYE.

ST. MARTIN AND ST. GREGORY. 1845.

A church of curious appearance, imposing at a distance, but having little or nothing of architectural elegance.

Plan. Nave with aisles and clerestory; south porch; modern chancel, and tower situated on its south side.*

The external character is mostly Third Pointed, except what is modern. The clerestory is very lofty, and has a sloping tiled roof. The aisles are embattled, some part of the north side is chequered in flint and stone. The west door has mouldings and shafts which are somewhat of a First Pointed character. The north door has a pointed arch and plain mouldings. The south porch is mostly modern; the tower seems to be wholly so, and is massive and low, not rising much above the clerestory, the parapet is embattled and four very large pinnacles occupy the angles. It is wholly of stone and contains eight bells. The chancel has some indications of ancient flint walls, but is

---

* "This church was formerly a very large building, consisting of three aisles and three chancels, with a tower steeple in the centre, supported by four pillars, which (on the 21st of March, 1685), giving way, the steeple fell down, and, by its fall, destroyed all the chancels. The parish has since built a small but very neat chancel, and a very strong though low tower on the south side of the chancel, with eight very musical bells in it." Bryan Faussett's "Collecta."—H.

essentially modern, and in a very poor style with a kind of apse. Within, it is fitted up with wainscoting.

The nave is very lofty, and has an arcade on each side of four fine moulded arches, springing from clustered piers; four shafts set at intervals upon each with moulded capitals and bases, the base of the main pier is somewhat stilted. These have something of a First Pointed appearance, but may very possibly be later. A fifth arch on the north with octagonal pier now opens to the vestry, which is modern. The roof has tie-beams and carved brackets with figures of animals, &c. The windows both of aisles and clerestory are generally of three lights, and Third Pointed, and at the west of the aisles of two lights. The west window a bad modern one.* There is a west gallery with an organ and a south gallery. The font is Third Pointed, has an octagonal bowl panelled with quatrefoils containing roses; the stem octagonal also. There is a brass of a female between two civilians, with a group of children.

> "John Andrew justus, Thomas Palmerq. venustus.
> Consors et similem imitatur Alicia cladem.
> Exempti seclo, claudantur marmore duro.
> Ut vivant Christo, non immemor. te precor. esto." †

BOUGHTON ALUPH.

ALL SAINTS.   1845.

Aug. 1853. B.A.S.

A handsome church. Plan cruciform, the nave having aisles, and the chancel a large north aisle. Transepts lofty, but not extending beyond the line of the aisles. Tower in centre, low and massive. The buttresses are very strong; the material is a mixture of flint and stone. The principal features good Third Pointed, but with some later windows, &c., and some earlier indications. The transepts have very high-tiled roofs. The

---

* The mullions of this window have been restored.—H.
† See Parsons' "Monuments," p. 3.—H.

tower, very heavy but low, has a large square stair turret at the south-east angle encroaching on the transept. The belfry windows single, with trefoil heads and the parapet embattled. The west window of the nave is a very elegant Middle Pointed one of four lights; and beneath it is a door with continued mouldings. The western windows of the aisles are of two lights; the others in the aisles, of three, are much mutilated. The nave has two arcades, each of four fine pointed arches rising from octagonal pillars with capitals and bases. Three arches from the aisles to the transepts, and four very fine ones under the tower with octagonal shafts. Over the western one is seen a small door open to the interior. The north transept has a large window like that at the west of the nave, both containing some fine pieces of stained glass. That of the south transept is mutilated, but on the east side is a two-light Third Pointed window, and a trefoil lancet lighting the tower staircase. The chancel is lower than the nave, and is separated from the north aisle by two low pointed arches, rising from a central circular column with moulded capitals, apparently First Pointed. One of these arches is closed, and seems to have been so at an early period, there being within it a raised stone ledge. The east window of the chancel is early Third Pointed, or transition, of five lights, containing some brown and yellow glass, with figures of a king and queen, and some legends. Near the east window is a circular moulded bracket, and on the south a single sedile with good mouldings, and one stilted shaft; near it a piscina, with crocketed canopy trefoiled. The north chapel, according to the fashion of Kent, is very wide, extending beyond the line of the transept, but now desolate and disused. It has a four-light east window of Third Pointed character, beneath which there seems to have been a reredos; on the north two lancets and two Middle Pointed windows of two lights. The arch opening to this aisle or chapel from the transept is very acute. It contains a plain piscina and the bracket of a niche in the east wall, exhibiting an angel figure. There are some prints of brasses, and a marble recumbent effigy of a lady, A.D. 1631. The pews are deal, and very ugly; some bright red may be distinguished on one of the southern piers of the nave. The font has an octagonal bowl, with shields on a base of like form; not of good work. The south door is closed, and the north porch is modern.

WORTH (by Sandwich).
ST. PETER AND ST. PAUL. 1846.

This church is rather a mean structure; the plan, a nave with south aisle, north chapel, and chancel; a modern north porch, and steeple at the west end, which seems also modern, having a short spire. The north doorway is Romanesque, the arch on the outside somewhat of horseshoe form, and has two orders of mouldings, the tympanum of the arch filled with stone, so that the door itself has a flat top and a horizontal kind of transom over it. The arch springs from shafts with sculptured capitals and abaci, projecting much. There is a benatura near the north door. The walls are of rough flints, and the roofs are tiled and carried over the aisle nearly to the ground. The aisle is very narrow, and its western portion much lower than the eastern. The nave is divided from the aisle by six plain pointed arches, with low circular columns; the western bay of the aisle is enclosed as a vestry; and the first pillar is massive, of decidedly Romanesque character, with abacus and square base, having the tongue-like wedges at the angles. There is a north aisle, a chapel, opening by two pointed arches with a light octagonal pillar, upon a high base. Its two windows are wide trefoil-headed lancets, much splayed. The chancel appears to be wholly modern; but built into the east wall is a curious stone, with sculpture of leaves and heads, evidently of First Pointed character. The western part of the south aisle is very low, its eastern portion has a cinquefoiled lancet, which is probably late. The font is modern.

ASH (by Sandwich).

Aug: 1885.
1816.

ST. NICHOLAS.

A fine large church, cruciform in its plan, with a central tower surmounted by a leaded spire. The nave and chancel have each a north aisle, and there was once a chapel to the south of the nave, which opened to it by two arches now seen in the wall. On the north of the nave is a large porch with parvise. The walls are chiefly of flints, with stone dressings, and there is some admixture of the three Pointed styles. Over the west window in the gable is a quatrefoil circle. Several bad windows have been introduced, but there has been considerable improvement going on for some years, and it is to be hoped that a gradual restoration will in time be effected.* The arcade of the nave has four First Pointed arches, with hood mouldings; two of the piers are circular, with octagonal capitals, one of the piers being very slender, on a high base. The western arch springs straight from the wall without pillar or capital. The west window is a fine Middle Pointed one, lately filled with glass of flowered quarries, and having four lights. Under it is a door with plain mouldings. Between the north aisle and the north transept is a plainer First Pointed arch upon imposts. In the south wall of the nave are two First Pointed arches with capital, once opening to the destroyed chapel. On the south of the nave are some Third Pointed windows. The tower rises upon four very lofty pointed arches, having continuous outer mouldings and large circular shafts: these, with the whole of the tower, are Third Pointed. The tower has two stages above the roof of the church with two-light windows and an embattled parapet, with a stair turret at the south-west angle, octagonal above and round below. The spire is covered with lead, and is a conspicuous object in the surrounding low country. The western portion of the north aisle is occupied by a vestry.ˣ In the transept are some Third Pointed windows. The nave is very

* This has been accomplished.—H.

ˣ *vestry now over north porch.*

wide: the chancel very clearly is not in a line with it, but inclines to the south. The chancel has on the south-east a lancet window; on the south side one two-light Middle Pointed one, and one Third Pointed one. The east window is Third Pointed.✗ On the south side under the lancet window is a piscina of First Pointed character; the arch trefoiled on shafts with capitals of curiously entwined foliage. There is a solid wall between the chancel and north chapel, in which is pierced one rather straight-sided arch of plain character, and a pointed door, eastward of which, let into the wall, is a very fine Middle Pointed tomb. There is another tomb within the straight-sided arch, with the effigy of a cross-legged knight, once painted and gilt, and a lion at his feet. In the sides of the arch are large iron hinges, the position of which is somewhat singular and difficult to explain, and below the figures a cornice of four-leaved flowers. Beneath this effigy, another of black marble has been inserted, probably of a later date, and representing a female in a wimple, but not of the best execution.* The other tomb, before mentioned, has a fine canopy of ogee form, with crockets and finial, panelled with a four-foiled circle and three-foiled loops, but no feathering to the arch. The effigies are of a knight and lady, of alabaster, very fresh and well preserved, and of excellent workmanship. The knight has a lion at his feet : † the lady with mantilla head

---

* On the shield of the man has been painted his coat armour ; on the femme side, I, with much ado, made out the arms of Septvans, alias Harfleet . . . but the baron side was quite effaced. Philpot says the tomb is in memory of Sir John Goshall, a worthy knight who lived in the reigns of Edw. 3 and Rich. 2, and that his arms, viz., a lion rampant, within semée. . . . Arg. He thinks the figure underneath was designed for his skeleton. Fol. 50. But I am sure it was done for a woman. The motto to the arms of Septvans was " Dissipabo, inimicos regis mei ut paleam," alluding to the coat, viz., three thrashers' vans, or fans. See App. to Somner's " Canterbury," edit. Battely, fol. 32. Bryan Faussett's " Collecta." The monument is lithographed in the History of Ash (" A Corner of Kent "), by Planché, 1864.—H.

† " In complete armour, and a collar of SS." "All the brasses are torn off except a small one fixed to the top of the arch, which bears the following coat, Septvans impaling a fess between three fleurs-de-lys in chief, and three fishes naiant in base, given by Philpot as the arms of Kirton." Bryan Faussett's

✗ *Modern window put in, in 1855.*

dress and muffled neck. The angel figures at the heads are much
mutilated. The chapel is of late Middle Pointed work, verging to
Third Pointed, has an east window of four lights, and one on the
north which seems Third Pointed. The arch opening to the chapel
presents a contracted form, and the effigies are seen through.
There is a large brass of a man and woman to Christopher
Septvans of Moland, obt. 1602;* another bears the date 1620.
There are also brasses in the chancel, one of a female in a reli-
gious habit, under an ogee crocketed canopy; another smaller one
also representing a female, Jane Keriell, with lunar headdress.†
Some others are much later, 1525 and 1606.‡

BARHAM.

ST. JOHN. 1846.

A cruciform church, with a western steeple, the nave having
a south aisle. The walls, as usual, are chiefly of flints with chalk
and rubble intermixed, with tiled roofs, and the features chiefly
Middle Pointed, with portions of First and Third Pointed. The
tower has a shingled spire; its west door and window are Third
Pointed; the belfry windows are single and trefoiled. At the west
of the south aisle is a lancet; the windows of the south aisle are
debased; those on the north of the nave Middle Pointed of two
lights. The nave is divided from the aisle by three pointed
arches, with light octagonal pillars having high bases. There
are no arches to either chancel or transepts, but between the
south aisle and south transept is a pointed arch on a small
foliated bracket. The roof of the nave has tie-beams and king-
posts, with pierced spandrels. The chancel is Middle Pointed;

"Collecta," and Planché, p. 222. This monument is also lithographed in
Planché's History, pp. 185 and 218. H.
* Engraved in Planché, see p. 225. H.
† Engraved in Planché, see p. 207. –H.
‡ These and other monuments are fully described, and the principal of them
engraved, in Planché's History, pp. 203—218.– H.

the east window of five lights, the side ones of two lights. There is a piscina, trefoiled, with mouldings. The south transept has one lancet closed, and a triple lancet within a containing arch. This transept belongs to the Oxenden family. The font has an octagonal bowl, upon a central stem and four corner shafts.

KINGSTONE.
ST. GILES. 1846.

A small church, having only a chancel and nave, with low western tower; the whole with flint walls, in the usual style of a Kentish village church. In the north porch is a benatura with label. The tower is plain Third Pointed. The roof is much like that at Barham. Some windows are mutilated, others are Third Pointed and square-headed. Those at the south of the chancel are single. There is no division between the nave and chancel. On the south side of the latter is an arched recess for a seat, and a piscina with wooden shelf. The font is of wood.

BISHOPSBOURNE.
ST. MARY. 1846.

A small church, which may be called cruciform, though the transepts partake more of the nature of short aisles, each being divided from the nave by two arches. The nave has no aisles, but there is a chapel on the south of the chancel, and a vestry on the north. At the west end of the nave is a low Third Pointed tower, with plain parapet and three stages; the west window of three lights and a door below it. There are buttresses, and a staircase turret of octagonal form. The walls are as usual of flints, and the high sloped roofs tiled. On the north side is a First Pointed door, with imposts, and near it a benatura.

There are several Third Pointed windows, but those in the chancel are Middle Pointed; the eastern one of five lights resembles that at Barham; the others are of two lights, and contain some good modern stained glass. There is no chancel arch, and the roof resembles that at Barham. In the north chapel are some obtuse single windows, trefoiled, containing stained glass. The north chapel opens to the nave by two pointed arches, with an octagonal column; the south transept has two plain pointed arches with slender circular pillar, having a square capital with the angles cut off. There is a rood door on the south. The chancel opens to its south chapel by a low arch. The south chapel is partly of brick. There is a neat organ, and the tower arch is open.

BRIDGE.
ST. PETER.   1846.

This church has a nave with small aisles, chancel, and tower with shingled spire placed at the west end of the south aisle. The tower has obtuse narrow windows; the spire has been rebuilt. The south aisle is in a great measure rebuilt in brick and flints.* The walls are of the usual flints. The tower in its lower portion is of Romanesque origin, and opens to the nave and aisle by very rude semicircular arches. It has also a small window of similar character. The chancel has much of Romanesque character. On its north side are two windows closed; on the south a fine doorway and two windows, now closed; the former has fine chevron mouldings. The west door is also late Romanesque, of excellent style, having the embattled ornament mixed with the rope and toothed ornaments and shafts. There is a small window of the same style at the east end of the south aisle. At the west end of the north aisle is a lancet. The north aisle is very low and narrow, divided from the nave by

* 1860. This church has been extensively repaired and partially rebuilt [by the late Mrs. Gregory, of Bridge Hill.—H].

three rude pointed arches with large wall piers having no capitals or impost mouldings. The arcade on the south of the nave has been removed. The north transeptal chapel has two lancets, and on its east side an entrance formed by a passage. The chancel arch is First Pointed, with mouldings and shafts very much worn. On its north side is a hagioscope with two square apertures. In the north wall of the chancel internally is the tympanum of an arch filled with ancient sculpture in two ranges of compartments, representing various subjects: those in the lower range may be clearly made out, representing (1) Adam and Eve expelled from Paradise by the Angel; (2) Adam and Eve by the forbidden fruit; (3) Cain's offering; (4) Abel's offering; (5) Abel slain by Cain. With these, inscriptions are intermixed. In the same wall, within a recess, is a recumbent effigy of a man in robes, in low relief, the figure divided in two parts by a central pier. The east window is poor Middle Pointed; the western one Third Pointed.

CHILHAM.

ST. MARY. 1846.

A good ordinary village church of Kent, surrounded by beautiful lime trees. The material mostly flint. There are aisles to the nave, a north and south transept, and chancel with chapels of modern date on its north and south sides; a west tower and south porch. The aisles are embattled, and the nave has a clerestory with plain parapet. The south porch has a parvise and battlement, and single trefoil-headed windows. Its outer doorway is Third Pointed, and has quatrefoil panelling in the spandrels. The transepts and chancel are tiled. The tower is Third Pointed, of very common kind in Kent, with battlement and large octagonal turret on the south side, but not quite at the angle. The west window is mutilated; the door has a label and spandrels. The tower is chequered in flint and stone. The interior is spacious, and well proportioned. There is an arcade on each side of the nave of four pointed arches, with octagonal pillars, reaching to the chancel, and including the transept. There is a modern flat ceiling in the nave, but some of the original spandrels may yet be seen. The aisles have two-light windows of Third Pointed character, with some pieces of stained glass; the clerestory windows are of the same character. The chancel arch springs straight from the wall without corbels. The east window is debased, of five lights. On the north of the chancel is a First Pointed arch in the wall; the original chapel on the north is replaced by one of Italian character, of circular form, with a high dome and coloured glass, containing monumental tablets to the Colebrooke family. This domical chapel, built 1755, under the direction of Sir Robert Taylor, as the mausoleum of the Colebrooke family, has been much admired for its gorgeous though incongruous character. In an arched recess on the north of the chancel is a large gorgeous monument, with flattering inscriptions to Margaret Lady Palmer, sister of Sir Dudley Digges, obt. 1619. The north rotunda is of brick. On the south side is another monumental chapel of Italian design, built temp. James I. by Sir Dudley Digges. This is highly enriched, and contains a large elaborate tomb, full of urns, emblematic figures, &c., with a pompous inscription commemorating Sir D. Digges, and his lady, obt. 1638. There are traces of brasses of late date and a bit of the rood screen in the vestry. The north transept has Middle Pointed windows, and in its north wall is a large pointed recess. The south transept has a roof with king-posts, and a window of three plain five-foiled lights within a containing arch. On the south is the rood door. The tower arch is pointed, with plain octagonal piers. The font has a square bowl, all cased in wood, on an octagonal stem and four circular shafts, set upon a square plinth.

There is a small adjunct on the north of the transept, with shed-like appearance.

ST. PAUL IN CANTERBURY. 1846.

The plan is a nave and chancel with south aisle coextensive, and a low tower at the west end.* The arcade has four First Pointed arches, with light circular columns having moulded capitals. The two east windows have fine Middle Pointed character; that of the south aisle is of four lights, and very good geometrical; that of the chancel is of three lights. There are Third Pointed windows of two lights on the north, and others modern. The south aisle is wider than the nave. The font has a square bowl panelled, with three-foiled arches, on a square pedestal with the angles cut off. In the west gallery is an organ.

SWALECLIFFE.
ST. JOHN. 1846.

A small mean church without aisles, having a small belfry and spire over the west end.† The roofs are tiled, and the walls mostly rough-cast. Both east and west ends have been partially rebuilt. There is no chancel arch, but on the south-west of the chancel is a kind of pointed "lychnoscopic" window, with shutter and grating. The north-east window has the sill extended, but it is doubtful whether this is original. There are a few lancets, and some ordinary windows, which may be either Middle or Third Pointed. In some the tracery has disappeared. The font has an octagonal bowl, on four shafts and octagonal plinth.

* The church has been greatly enlarged by the addition of a south aisle to the nave and chancel, and has been restored throughout.—II.
† This church has been entirely rebuilt, 1876.—II.

WHITSTABLE.

ALL SAINTS. 1846.

This church, in rather a dilapidated state,* is on an elevated spot away from the town. It consists of a nave and chancel, with a north aisle continued to the east end, and a large tower placed on the south side of the west end. The latter is Third Pointed, and opens by a pointed arch to the aisle; the parapet has no battlement; the belfry windows have two trefoiled lights within a square, and on the north is a single narrow window. The tower buttresses are large, and it is whitewashed in order to make a conspicuous sea mark.† The north aisle is embattled; the roof tiled. A north porch is plain. The nave is wide, and has an arcade of four pointed arches, with large octagonal piers, and a large space of wall beyond the eastern arch. The chancel has two narrower pointed arches (with an octagonal column) which incline, though the chancel itself does not deviate from the line of the nave. There is no chancel arch. On the south side of the entrance of the chancel are traces of the rood door and steps, and a closed "lychnoscope." The walls are very thick. The east window is Third Pointed of three lights; on the south of the chancel is one of Middle Pointed tracery of two lights. On the north side are some windows of two lights, rather of transition from Middle to Third Pointed; at the west end, one of three lights has lost its tracery. There are traces of several brasses now destroyed. The font has a plain octagonal bowl on plain pedestal and plinth. There is one brass to Thomas Braude, A.D. 1440. The pews are most unsightly, and many are coloured light blue; they are, however, about to be removed, and a general repair effected.‡ There are

---

* This church has been thoroughly repaired, the chancel lengthened, with a vestry added on the north side, 1876.—H.

† The whitewash has been removed, and the tower restored. H.

‡ This design has been completely carried out. 1876. H.

six bells. The pulpit is a sort of "flying" one, apparently supported on air, and approached by a singularly ugly staircase and passage.*

MINSTER IN SHEPPEY.
ST. MARY AND ST. SEXBURGA. 1846.

This curious church, which is but a fragment of the original conventual church, comprises a wide nave and chancel, each with north aisle; at the west end of the north aisle is a low tower, surmounted by a heavy wooden *quasi* spire. There is also a south porch, which, as well as the tower, is Third Pointed. The latter is unfinished but massive; it has a four-light west window, and a door which has panelled spandrels and shafts with octagonal capitals and a label. The material of the church is a mixture of Kentish rag and flints. The doorway within the porch is First Pointed with mouldings and shafts; the church has considerable First Pointed features, and some later, but there is much mutilation. It seems probable that the northern of the two divisions formed the original nave and chancel, though the southern is now so applied, and the northern chancel walled off in order to form a school. The arcade of the nave is of three chamfered arches, which seem First Pointed, with one circular and one octagonal column. The south (or present) chancel is open to the aisle; the north opens to the nave by a tall First Pointed arch; there is also one between the chancel and its aisle, with good mouldings and octagonal shafts with foliated capitals. In this arch is a Third Pointed screen. The south aisle is wider than the north, though probably not the original nave and chancel. The northern has the original open roof. There is a wood screen across the entrance to the chancel. The east window of the south chancel was originally a First Pointed triplet with shafts,

* A new pulpit has been erected. H.

now terribly mauled by a recent insertion. The west window also had three lancets, with a circle over them. On the south

MINSTER CHURCH AND ABBEY GATE-HOUSE.

side are a few lancets; but most of the windows are Third Pointed. The northern division, or original chancel, which ends abruptly, perhaps once extended farther to the east. It is now miserably treated, and divided by a floor into two stories. The monumental remains are of great interest. In the south wall is a Middle Pointed tomb under a fine canopy with double feathering, and a beautiful finial of oak foliage, with the well-executed effigy of a knight cross-legged and lying on his side, having a small armed figure at his feet. On the sides of the tomb is a range of cinquefoiled arches. This commemorates Sir Robert de Shurland, created a banneret by Edward I.

* In the pavement of the chancel is a very fine brass of a knight and lady, Sir Roger de Northwood and Joan his wife, circ. 1330, supposed to be of French execution, from the lady's attire. The knight is cross-legged. The tower arch is lofty and Third Pointed, with good mouldings and shafts. There is a late Third Pointed tomb in the north chancel. The font is a plain octagon. There is a rough unfinished look about this church. A fine Third Pointed gateway tower † remains in chequered flint and stonework ; the north side is scarcely accessible.

COLDRED.

A very mean small church, consisting only of a chancel and nave.

SIBERTSWOLD.

This church has only a chancel and nave, and no steeple, but is not devoid of interesting features.

1863. The church has been rebuilt.

LYDDEN.

Comprises a chancel and nave, with low western tower.

---

* This early and beautiful specimen is noticed in the " Manual of Ancient Brasses," p. 45. [It is minutely described by Mr. J. G. Waller, in " Archaeologia Cantiana," IX. 149.—R.]

† Of the Abbey of St. Sexburga.—R.

EWELL.

ST. MARY AND ST. PETER. 1847.

This small church, mean in its exterior, consists of nave and chancel, with north chapel running along the latter and part of the former. At the west end a mean steeple, being a tower of rough flints without buttress or battlement, has a Sussex-tiled roof and square-headed belfry window. The tower arch to the nave is pointed, straight from the wall; the west window is Middle Pointed of two lights. There is a small Norman window on the north side of the nave. The north door is very fine Norman, with shafts; it has a billeted hood and excellent mouldings, one cylindrical, one embattled and the inner member on imposts. The north chapel is separated from the church and used as a school.* The chancel arch is First Pointed springing from imposts. Between the chancel and the north chapel is a plain pointed arch on imposts walled up, and eastward of it an oblong recess in the wall. There is a First Pointed plain arch between the chapel and the nave, on imposts. On the western impost is a round piece of stone, sculptured with a wheel. There are some square-headed windows on the south side—some Third Pointed and one Middle Pointed. The east window is of the latter kind, and on each side of it is a plain bracket. On the south of the chancel is another oblong recess and a splayed lancet, also a lychnoscope with two small square-headed lights. In the north chapel is a large obtuse arch in the wall. There are wretched blue communion rails, and pews in the chancel also painted blue. Those in the nave are of deal.† The Font is modern, but the old one is remembered. In the churchyard is a stone cross on three steps.

* This chapel has been restored to the church.—H.
† The church has been thoroughly rearranged within.—H.

ALKHAM.
ST. ANTHONY. 1847.

An interesting village church of considerable size, in a very picturesque commanding situation, amidst the varied scenery often found near the Kentish coast, in which open downs, woody dells, and rural village dwellings form a part. The material is, as usual, rough flint, and the external features plain; though there appears internally much of ornamental work. There is a western tower, a nave with south aisle and porch, a chancel with a spacious northern chapel, which is continued along part of the nave. The sloping lean-to roof of tiles is carried over the south aisle. The tower is low and rude, without a parapet, and has a pointed roof of tiles; the lower storey is of larger dimensions than the upper part. There are traces of lancet windows and a First Pointed string-course in the belfry storey. The west doorway is rude, and has a double arch, an obtuse one within a pointed one; and a huge modern buttress has been added on the north-west. The nave opens to the south aisle by an arcade of four First Pointed arches, with light circular columns, over which is a clerestory of small circular windows. There is also the same clerestory on the north of the nave, westward of the beginning of the aisle or chapel, whence it seems probable that a narrow aisle on the north resembling the present southern one, formed part of the original plan. The present large aisle, extending along the whole chancel, as well as part of the nave, is, however, of First Pointed character, and is divided from the nave and chancel by three pointed arches, the eastern of which, open to the chancel, is much the widest, and springs from octagonal half shafts; the other two have no mouldings and the columns are First Pointed, as on the south. The north chapel is the finest and most interesting portion of the church. It has at its western end two fine lancets of plain work with a circle above them. The north chapel is wide and lofty, with a separate tiled roof. On its north side is a range of single lancet windows with very elegant mouldings, and shafts of black marble, under which, internally, is a range of nine stalls or seats, having excellent mouldings, trefoil heads, and springing from shafts of Purbeck marble with moulded capitals. The lancets are plain externally, but set on a string. At the east end of the same chapel are two lancets also, with very fine mouldings and marble shafts. The chancel is not divided from the nave, and the roof is plain. There are some remains of wood stalls in the chancel, and in its south wall three ascending sedilia, having trefoil heads with hood mouldings. The eastern sedile is widest, and divided from the others by a wall-piece; between the two others is a shaft. Eastward of them is a piscina of similar form and character. The east window is Middle Pointed of four lights, without tracery, save a quatrefoil in the head, the four lights being merely trefoiled. In it is a little stained glass. The reredos is of wood, imitating First Pointed work, the altar rails are of iron. There are some lancets in the western portion of the nave on the north. The south aisle has some square-headed windows apparently Middle Pointed, and some of later date. On the south side of the chancel is a square-headed window of three lights which seems to be Middle Pointed. The porch has on its sides small trefoil-headed lancets.

The font has a plain octagonal bowl on a stem of the same form. On the south side of the chancel is an ancient tomb with a marble slab, on which appears an inscription not very easy to decipher.* It is probably of the fourteenth century.

* "On the verge, or edge, of a very ancient marble, shaped like a coffin, and raised about a foot from the ground, close to the south wall, in very old characters—

✠ Hic jacet Herbertus, Simonis Proles, vir opertus,
Ad Bona Spe certus, Fidei Sermoni disertus."
Bryan Faussett's "Collecta."—H.

HOUGHAM.
ST. LAWRENCE. 1847.

A church of mean exterior, but in some respects curious. The walls are chiefly of rough flints, but with some admixture of stone. The nave has a north aisle, and a south porch, eastward of which is a chapel. The chancel has had a south aisle, now destroyed. The tower, if it can be so termed, is at the west end, but does not rise above the nave, and is covered with a pointed roof of tiles, and a wooden belfry. On the west side of the tower is a lancet window; and beneath it a semi-Norman door, having good mouldings and shafts with abaci. The tower is of large dimensions, and has somewhat the appearance of a narthex. The porch has a pointed outer doorway. The south chapel is divided from the nave by a plain semi-circular arch on imposts without mouldings. The arcade between the nave and north aisle has two wide pointed arches, with a central column of circular form with octagonal capital, which overhangs and exceeds the width of the arch, whence it seems probable that some alteration has been made. There is a rood door in the east pier on this side. The windows of the north aisle are lancets, with elegant mouldings internally; that at the east end of this aisle is a triple lancet of extremely good work, with fine mouldings, and shafts of a kind rarely found in the aisle of a small church. There is no west window to the aisle. The roof is very plain; there is no chancel arch; the chancel has some lancets on the north, and in its south wall appear two rude pointed arches with impost moulding to the intermediate pier. In these lancet windows are inserted; possibly the aisle was never completed, as the windows look contemporaneous. Between them a huge buttress is added. The east window is closed; it has three lancets within a containing arch. The font is modern; the pews high and ugly. The churchyard unusually large.

BOUGHTON MALHERBE.
ST. NICHOLAS. 1847.

A small church, with nave and chancel, each having a south aisle, a south porch, and a low west tower.* The architectural features are rather ordinary, but there are some rather pretty Middle Pointed two-light windows in the nave of the Kentish sort, one on the south with an octo-foil in the head, one at the west end of the aisle has the kind of star sometimes seen. There is also one Middle Pointed two-light window on the north of the chancel, but all the others are Third Pointed. The nave has two wide plain pointed arches dividing it from the aisle, with an octagonal pier. The chancel arch is plain pointed and straight from the wall, and there is a considerable ascent to the chancel. Between the south aisle of the nave and that of the chancel is another small pointed arch on octagonal shafts. Between the chancel and the chapel is a plain arch on imposts, which appears to be First Pointed, and eastward of it in the wall is a sepulchral arch with very fine double feathering. In the south chancel aisle are some very good encaustic tiles, with lozenge pattern and some legends. Also the effigy of a knight; and in the chancel is the brass of a knight and lady, A.D. 1520. "Here lyeth buried the bodie of Edward Wollenshaw." Also a small one, A.D. 1499, with figures of a man and woman, and children kneeling. The nave has tie-beams with carved spandrels. There are some plain open benches, and the pulpit has the linen pattern. The tower arch is plain, without mouldings, and springs straight from the wall. The tower has a battlement but no buttresses, and is of three stages, with single belfry windows, apparently late and poor Third Pointed. The porch has a flat wooden ribbed ceiling, and within it is a benatura. The font has a plain octagonal bowl, upon a stem of like shape. The roofs are tiled.

* This church has since been partly reconstructed, and much embellished, at great expense [1848].

CHISLET.

ST. MARY. 1848.

This church is chiefly First Pointed with some Norman features. The plan is a nave with aisles, a chancel, and a massive tower situated between the nave and chancel. The nave has a high tiled roof and a closed clerestory. The chancel has a similar roof; the aisles have moulded parapets. The tower is large and low, having a Norman character, with two stages of windows of that style, and one small square aperture just under the roof. It is surmounted by a large heavy slated belfry with flat top. At the south-west angle is a large square stair turret, not extending the whole way up the tower. The nave is wide, and has on each side a very plain First Pointed arcade of three arches. Those on the north are entirely plain and rude, without the least chamfering, with large square wall piers, having impost mouldings. The southern arches do not correspond; the western is closed to form a vestry; the next is low; the third very wide; and all the piers entirely plain. The walls are of flint, with stone buttresses; the roof has tie-beams, and the aisles are rather narrow. In the north aisle are Middle Pointed windows of two lights; those on the south are bad modern ones. At the west of the nave is a three-light Third Pointed one, and at the west of the aisles single ones with trefoil feathering and returned hood. There is a modern west porch and a plain pointed south door. There are north and west galleries; in the latter a small organ. The tower has very thick walls; its western arch (to the nave) is rude and plain First Pointed; the eastern (to the chancel) is Norman; its western face having two orders, one cylindrical and chevroned; and the abacus of the shaft is continued as a string-course. The east face is plain.

The chancel is a fine First Pointed one, having an eastern unequal triplet, much splayed, with shafts to the interior mouldings. On the north and south sides are three single and large lancets, without shafts, but having, internally, hoods upon corbel heads, and beneath them a string which is carried over the priest's door in a square form. On the north side is a door beneath the string; the north-east window is closed by an ugly pagan monument. Under the south-east window are three shallow Third Pointed sedilia with cinquefoiled arches and trefoiled spandrels, surmounted by a battlemented cornice; eastward of which is a trefoiled piscina now filled with dirt. All the lancets are externally plain. The sedilia are partly hidden by wainscoting; and there is an ugly reredos and quasi stalls of modern work. The walls are whitewashed, and the floor of brick. The font appears to be modern; the bowl octagonal with some panelling. Over the west arch of the tower are three First Pointed brackets.

HADLOW.

ST. MARY. 1861.

A large church, which seems to have been recently to a great extent rebuilt, but on the whole in tolerable style, and preserving the Kentish character. Over the west door is the date 1637. The plan comprises a wide nave with north and south aisles; a large chancel, and western tower surmounted by a heavy shingled spire. There were originally no aisles, so that great enlargement was effected in 1839, when the chancel was rebuilt. The arcades of course are new, and the walls of the aisles. The tower seems to be original, and has a pointed west doorway and two tiers of lancets north and south; the belfry windows Perpendicular; the buttresses at the angles and the whole stuccoed. The spire is four-sided, and has more the character of a high pointed roof.

The walls of the church are Kentish rag; the roofs are high pitched and tiled, and there is a north porch of timber with tiled roof. The roofs are wholly new. The nave has on each side an arcade of four wide pointed arches, on pillars alternately circular and octagonal. The aisle windows are Decorated in general, but one is Perpendicular.

The chancel arch is a large pointed one, on octagonal piers. The chancel has an eastern triplet and Decorated two light windows north and south. The chancel is stalled. The nave has low regular pews, and a gallery at the west end containing an organ. The font is new.

There is a new vestry on the north of the chancel.

LULLINGSTONE.

ST. BOTOLPH. 1859.

A small church, close to Lullingstone Castle, consisting only of a nave and chancel, the latter having a north aisle or chapel; a wooden bell cot is over the west end. The windows are mostly Decorated, of good plain character, and of two lights, but the east window has three. The interior is much modernised, but on the whole handsomely fitted up with oak pews, marble pavement, and stuccoed ceiling; and the many monuments which it contains are costly and well preserved. Between the nave and chancel is a pointed arch modernised with stucco, &c., and a rood screen which seems post-Reformation, with debased Gothic tracery and groining. The north chapel is late Gothic of the sixteenth century; has three-light windows, and between it and the chancel is a very fine canopied tomb to Sir John Peche, having a Tudor arch with panelled spandrels and open sides, and a very fine monumental effigy. There is in the north chapel a very large altar-tomb of alabaster to Sir Geo. Hart and family, with effigies of him in armour and his lady with joined hands, and four figures at the angles of the tomb; all the countenances are very fine. He died in 1587. There is a kind of screen in stucco at the west end of the chapel with inscription commemorating Percyval Hart, Esq., the repairer and beautifier of the church, who died in 1738. On the south of the altar is the splendid tomb of Sir Percyval Hart and his lady, obt. 1580.—" Chief Server and Knight Harbinger to four sovereigns." There is also in the chancel a brass to Sir William Peche, obt. 1487. There are several other sepulchral effigies. There is a memorial to Elizabeth Huldynohe, gentlewoman to the Lady Mary, Queen. The chancel is stalled, and the windows are full of stained glass, some of late character with armorial shields, some representing saints.

HAM.
ST. GEORGE. 1861.

This small church is in course of restoration and to receive new roofs. It consists of nave and chancel only, built of rough flints, with a wooden bell cot. The north side is of particularly rude masonry; in the west end some stone is intermixed with the flints. The east window, a modern one of two lights, will probably be replaced by something better. On the south of the chancel are two lancets now restored, set internally within rude pointed arches upon slight square shafts chamfered at the angles—a singular feature. On the north of the chancel is a pointed aumbry with the hinges. The windows of the nave have been smashed, and will probably be restored. That at the west is a single lancet, wide and trefoiled. There is no chancel arch, but a poor modern screen. The south doorway is pointed, with Perpendicular mouldings and shafts. A new porch will be added.

SUTTON-AT-HONE.
ST. JOHN. 1816.

A fair Kentish church, comprising a nave with south aisle, chancel, western tower, and south porch. The walls are chiefly of flints stuccoed; the roofs are high, separate, and tiled. The

tower is very rude, without door or string-courses, but having a
battlement and corner buttresses; it has a two-light west window
of Third Pointed character, the other openings are plain slits.
At the south-east angle is a circular stair-turret. The porch
is large, and there is a north door with mouldings and hood.
Most of the windows are Middle Pointed, of which character is the
principal part of the church. The east and west windows of the
aisle are of three lights reticulated; two others on the south
have segmental heads, one being of two, the other of three lights.
On the north is one of two lights, somewhat Flamboyant, and
one Third Pointed. The chancel has a good east window (now
closed) of three lights, with tracery somewhat Flamboyant but
of much elegance. There are two-light windows on the north
and south of the chancel which have very decided Flamboyant
tracery. The interior is neat and well cared for. The arcade
has four Middle Pointed arches, two of the piers being clustered
of four shafts with moulded caps and square bases, the
other pier is octagonal. The eastern arch is smaller than the
others; and the next to it is inferior in mouldings. The nave
and aisle have tie-beam roofs, with pierced spandrels. The
tower arch is a tall pointed one, chamfered, upon octagonal
shafts. The pews have Jacobian wood-work with the linen
pattern, and the pulpit is of the same character. The chancel
seems to have an inclination from the line of the nave. The
chancel arch dies into the walls. In its south pier is a hagioscope, formed by a rude slit; and on each pier is a kind of
stone ledge, which must have been connected with the rood
loft. The east window is closed by an ugly reredos. The
sacrarium is laid with a marble pavement. The south-east
window sill is extended for a sedile, and near it is a piscina of
transition character from Middle Pointed to Third Pointed,
set deep in the wall, having an ogee arch without foliation, with
pierced trefoils in the spandrels, the whole being contained in a
square head with label. It has a shelf at the back. The
chancel has a coved roof. In the aisle is an ugly monument,

A.D. 1625, to Sir Thomas Smith. The west window of the aisle has been restored with shafts to the rear arch, and filled with modern stained glass, with figures of SS. Peter, James, and John, as a memorial of Jane Chapman, by her sister Ann Eleanor Mumford. There is also a new Third Pointed font. The situation is retired, at a distance from the village.

BEXLEY.

ST. MARY.

1846.

The plan of the church is a nave and chancel with a north aisle, and a western tower with clumsy, shingled spire. The styles are mixed; the walls seem to be chiefly of flints stuccoed, and there is a hideous modern porch. The roofs, as usual, are tiled, without coping. The tower seems to be First Pointed, is without buttress, and has a lancet window on the south, and two on the west side. It opens to the nave by a pointed door only. The spire is composed of an octagonal shingled extinguisher, set upon a quadrangular one which fits the square of the tower. A north doorway is First Pointed, with shafts and moulded capitals, and there is one lancet in the north aisle. Some other windows of the nave and aisle are Middle Pointed, of two lights, some square-headed of Third Pointed character. That at the west end of the aisle is of three lights, it may be either Middle or Third Pointed. There is no architectural division of chancel, but the chancel probably includes the eastern bay of the aisle. The arcade is irregular, but apparently all First Pointed. One of the arches is so very wide as to appear to be two arches thrown together. The west arch is a very low one, the second higher and wider; the eastern very wide; the two western piers are circular columns, with moulded capitals, the other octagonal with spring of the arch low. The reredos entirely blocks the east window. There are lancet windows north and south of the chancel, and one Middle Pointed one, of two lights. On the south side are three sedilia ascending eastward, the mouldings dying into the wall without shafts, and partially encroached on by a modern monument. Eastward of them is a very plain pointed piscina. The chancel roof is coved, with ribs forming an arch. That of the roof has a higher pitched arch with king-posts, struts and tie-beams. There are frightful pews, and a gallery at the west end with a good organ. It is written on a pew,

"These three pews were built at the charge of the Parish, 1765."

The churchyard is entered by a lych gate.

CHELSFIELD.

ST. MARY. 1818.

The church is built chiefly of flints, partially stuccoed. It is essentially a First Pointed church, and consists of a wide nave, with chapel on the south; a chancel; a tower on the north side of the nave, terminated by a shingled spire; and a south porch. There is a triple lancet at the east end, with shafts internally, and some Norman windows set high in the walls, but there are several later windows. The tower is of decidedly First Pointed style, with lancets, and opens by a plain arch to the nave. The south chapel is divided from the nave by two low pointed arches of dissimilar character, that on the east springing from a circular shaft attached to the pier. Over the west window is a small circular one, now closed.

In the chancel are several monumental remains. There is a brass of Robert de Brun (Priest), A.D. 1417, with a crucifix and figures of SS. Mary and John. On the north of the altar is a tomb in dos d'âne form below an arch in the wall of late Third Pointed character. There are on the south of the altar tombs of three successive rectors, father, son, and grandson, by name Smith, and a brass of Alice Bray.

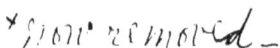

ORPINGTON.

ALL SAINTS. 1848.

This church has a nave without aisles, a tower on the north side, and a chancel with north chapel. There is a west porch, and the west doorway is semi-Norman, the pointed arch having chevron ornament as well as toothed, with two orders of shafts. Most of the windows are Third Pointed, the roof is tiled, without parapet, the usual Kentish arrangement. The tower arch is Norman, and the tower is vaulted in its lower portion. The tower, at present, scarcely rises above the roof of the nave, the upper part with a shingled spire having been destroyed by a storm. The lower part seems to be First Pointed. There is a First Pointed chancel arch and a wooden rood-screen. In the chancel is a slab with brass to Thomas Wilkinson, Prebendary of Ripon and Rector of Orpington, A.D. 1511.

There is a west gallery and organ.

LEIGH.

ST. MARY. 1847.

This church has a nave and chancel, each with south aisle, a south transeptal chapel, south porch, and an unfinished western steeple. The nave is very wide, the aisle narrow with lean-to roof, and the chapel is much like a shed. The material is mixed stone and flint, the roof partly tiled, partly shingled. The porch is a nice rustic-looking one of wood with feathering, and open roof with tie-beam. Within it is a First Pointed doorway; the outer arch is segmental upon shafts, the inner one springs at once from the jambs. The arcade of the nave has three good lofty First Pointed arches upon circular columns with moulded capitals; a First Pointed arch also opens to the transept upon circular shafts. The windows of the nave and aisle are Third Pointed, as are those in the transeptal chapel, except one on the east side which is Middle Pointed with a nice bit of stained glass, in which is the figure of the Virgin Mary. The chancel arch is also First Pointed on circular shafts. The chancel has two low pointed arches, with clumsy octagonal pillar with cap, dividing it from its aisle. There is a small square recess (as if for oil) in the pier of the chancel arcade on the east side. The east window of the chancel is a tall one, of two lights, with circle above and included in an arch, with hood having buckles, of transitional character from First to Middle Pointed. On the north side are three wide lancets, much splayed. Between the aisle of the nave and that of the chancel is a very acute First Pointed arch set crooked, having on the north side a foliated corbel. This chapel is pewed, and in its shed-like roof is a dormer window. There is an altar picture representing the Man of Sorrows. Within the sacrarium is a small brass representing a corpse in a tomb, the angel blowing the trumpet, and a woman watching, inscribed

> " Beholde, O Lord, I come wyllyngly—
> Farewell all ye
> Till you come to me."

The pulpit has the hour-glass stand remaining. The font has a panelled octagonal bowl with quatrefoils, of Third Pointed style, on panelled octagonal stem. The nave has a plain tie-beam roof. The tower is unfinished, but opens to the nave by a pointed arch on circular shafts. It has a Third Pointed west door, large buttresses, and the beginning of a stair turret at the south-east. The superstructure is of timber, and like a dove-cot, the whole scarcely rising above the roof of the nave. It contains five bells. There is a west gallery and barrel organ. Some part is pewed, some fitted with open benches.

Leigh church underwent a laudable restoration in 1861, when the former apology for a tower was replaced by a fair new one of Perpendicular character, having the octagonal corner turret so common in Kent. The new seats are all open, and the gallery has been removed. Several windows are filled with stained glass. There is a questionable and conspicuous turret added to the south chapel of the chancel, containing a staircase which seems wholly unnecessary.

EAST MALLING.
ST. JAMES. 1850.

A large church, comprising a nave with aisles, chancel, west tower, and south porch; the chancel lower than the nave, and the whole embattled. Both aisles begin some way from the west end of the nave. The material is the Kentish rag. There are features of Middle and Third Pointed character, with faint indications of earlier work. The nave is very wide. The arcades are irregular; the arches all pointed, three on each side, those next the east have better mouldings and are larger. One pier is octagonal, the other a large wall pier, forming a break, with octagonal shafts attached. The church had evidently no aisles originally. There is a clerestory to the nave, as well as chancel of poor Third Pointed character. The roof is a new panelled flat one. The chancel arch is pointed, on octagonal shafts. There is a rood door on the north, but westward of the entrance of the chancel. The windows vary, some are good and elegant Middle Pointed, especially in the north aisle, where are two of curious tracery, one at the east end, each of three lights, supermullioned with two-light tracery in the head. One of these contains some fine stained glass of beautiful colouring. In the south aisle are some Middle Pointed two light-windows, with the Star tracery, also one trefoil-headed lancet; at the west a Third Pointed one of three trefoiled lights, another similar, of two lights. That at the east of the south aisle is Third Pointed of three lights, and those north of the nave, to the west of the aisle, are of the same period, of two lights. There is an arched aperture in the wall over the square pier on each side. The east part of the north aisle has a flat wood panelled ceiling, with gilt stars, the rest is ceiled. The chancel is Perpendicular, has a clerestory and a late poor roof. The chancel has been rather mutilated. The east window modernised,* and the southern windows closed. On the north side is a vestry. The east end of the north aisle, which was a chantry, has a late panelled ceiling with bosses gilt, once the Twysden chapel.

The font has an octagonal bowl and stem. The cover is of wood, with rather elegant carving and friezed tracery.

The tower is Third Pointed in its upper part, having a plain battlement, and corner buttresses; the belfry windows are each of two lights, and under them is a string. In the stage below is a single light. The west door has tolerable mouldings. Over it is only a small single window, perhaps part of a large one mutilated. The lower part is rude and Norman, and the arch to the nave is of that date. There is a brass to Thos. Selby and his wife, 1489; she has a winged head-dress. Another of a Priest, 1522, and another "Hic jacet Ric. Adam qui Prebendarius magne misse in monasterio de West Malling, et Vicarius de Est Malling."

LEYBOURNE.
ST. PETER AND ST. PAUL.

July. 1891.
1847.

A small and rather mean looking church, comprising a nave and chancel, with north aisle to both, a south porch, and low ugly western tower which seems to be modern, as is also the porch. The aisle is very narrow. On the north side of the north aisle is a curious niche of transition from Early English to Decorated,† engraved in Hussey's "Churches of Kent, Surrey, and Sussex," (p. 92).

It has two trefoiled lights or arches, and a quatrefoiled circle in the head; the outer arches as well as the others are well

---

* The east window has been restored (1861).
† In an elaborate paper, by the late Rev. Lambert B. Larking, contained in the "Archaeologia Cantiana" (vol. V. p. 133—193), it is shewn that this is the heart-shrine of Sir Roger de Leyburne.—H.

moulded, and the central shaft has a moulded capital. The purpose of this is doubtful.

The walls are of mixed flint and Kentish rag; most of the windows on the south of the nave have been modernised, but on the north are some of Third Pointed character. The nave has two pointed arches with octagonal column, of large size; the chancel arch is similar, and there is one plain one between the chancel and north aisle. In the chancel on the south side are two wide lancets, one trefoiled. One window on the north, of Norman work, is filled up. The east window is Middle Pointed of three lights; that of the north aisle is Third Pointed, with square head. The aisle of the nave is galleried.

EGERTON.

ST. JAMES. 1854.

This church has lately had the benefit of a careful restoration, by which the interior has been placed in a condition of much beauty.

The plan comprises a chancel and nave, each with a north aisle, a large western tower, and a south porch. There are portions of various styles. The outer walls are now in excellent condition; the porch has a battlement and pinnacles, and a door with panelled spandrels. The inner doorway is continuous. The arcade of the nave has three good pointed arches, rising from light octagonal columns. The roof of the nave is of plain timbers with king-posts. The north aisle has three Decorated windows, varying in character, having shafts internally, and a single window with cinquefoiled feathering. All the Decorated windows in this church have shafts with capitals to the rear arches. At the west end of the aisle is a Perpendicular window of four lights. South of the nave are some late square-headed windows, and one lancet set higher in the wall. The east end of the north aisle has a Decorated window of three lights. The chancel arch springs straight from the wall. The chancel extends far beyond the aisle, to which it opens by one pointed arch on octagonal columns. The chancel roof is richly coloured, of a deep blue with gilt stars, and divided into panelled compartments, the effect of which is very fine. Across it is a beam on which is inscribed : " The Lord is in his holy temple." There is a screen separating the aisle from the chancel, and a brazen altar-rail. The chancel has on the south and north two Decorated windows of two lights, and at the east, one of three lights, the pattern of which is by no means elegant. The southeast window has some stained glass. The aisle has a coved, panelled roof. The sacrarium is laid with tiles; the altar set on a pace. On the south are three equal sedilia, with cinquefoil arches rising on *quasi* brackets, and octagonal shafts against the wall. Eastward of them is a piscina, also cinquefoiled, with shelf and an odd-shaped drain. East of this is an oblong recess, perhaps an aumbry. In the north chapel in its east wall is a flat ogee niche with piscina. The nave is fitted with very neat new oak benches, having flat-topped ends. The pulpit of similar character. The font has an octagonal bowl with roses, angels and gryphons, on an octagonal stem, having buttresses, set upon a step. The tower arch is a large one, lofty and quite open, springing from semi-octagonal shafts. The tower is very large and Perpendicular, of three stories divided by strings, embattled, having large buttresses, and an octagonal turret at the north-east, rising in the Kentish fashion above the parapet. The west window is of four lights, and below it is a labelled door with quatrefoiled spandrels. The belfry windows are of three lights. Within the tower are stone benches.

---

aug. 10:

CHART PARVA. 1854.
ST. MARY.

This church has nave with north aisle, chancel, south porch, and west tower. The latter Perpendicular, and of the usual Kentish fashion, resembling that of Egerton, but smaller. The porch has a door with panelled spandrels, and shafts on octagonal bases. The east window, Perpendicular pointed, is of three lights. The other windows are all Perpendicular, chiefly square-headed, of two lights. In some are pieces of stained glass. The roof has tie-beams. The tower arch is open, containing a curtain. The arcade of the nave has two wide pointed arches with octagonal pier having a capital. The chancel is undivided from the nave, and has one lancet window remaining on the north side. The aisle belongs to the Dayrell family, and is separated by screenwork within the arches. The rood door may be seen high up. The font is octagonal, plain and poor. In the north aisle are sepulchral memorials to the Dayrells. A brass of a man and woman. The effigy of a knight in alabaster with SS collar with crown for crest and lion at his feet, set on an altar-tomb. A brass plate against the wall, A.D. 1509 to Sir Jos. Darell.* Another slab has part of a border and plate in brass: "Hic jacet corpora Johanis Darell Amigeri Senescalli, Reverend. in Xpo. Archiep. Cantuar.† qui obiit XXV° die mens. Octobris a. dni. 1438, et dne. Florencie uxoris dni. Johis. que obiit —————— quorum animabus ppiciet. Deus.

Arms of Darell and Chicheley.

"Si vis deleri tua crimina die miserere
Miserere mei flectitur ira dei—
Miserere miserator quia vere sum peccator,
Unde vere licet reus
Miserere mei Deus."

There is a broken piscina in the south wall near the pulpit. Five bells.

CHARING.

ST. PETER AND ST. PAUL.   1851.

This church has a nave without aisles, north and south tran-septs, chancel with south chapel, west tower and south porch. The tower and porch are of good stone masonry, and fair

---

* The inscription is given in Parsons' "Monuments," p. 117.—H.
† Archbishop Chicheley.

Perpendicular character. The former a good specimen of the Kentish tower, not unlike that at Egerton, having a four-light west window, and labelled door with two orders of fine mouldings and shafts, corner buttresses, and tall octagonal turret at the south-east corner.

The porch has a battlement, and a good doorway like that of the tower, but the spandrels are enriched, and one moulding has vine foliage. The inner doorway is labelled, and there is a shaft in an angle as if for a stoup. The roof is groined, with moulded ribs which run down the side walls. Parts of the walls are of rough flint work; the roofs are tiled. The south transept is of brick, and bad. On the south side of the nave is a singular window, large and of square form, of four lights with tracery apparently transitional from Decorated to Perpendicular. The chancel has an Early English north wall, of rough flint masonry, in which appears one lancet window. There is also one lancet on the north of the nave, and one good early large Perpendicular window of four lights, subarcuated. In the spandrels of the west door are shields, with star and eagle. The east window of the chancel is very similar, and of very good sort, of four lights. The chancel arch is on clustered shafts, set upon grotesque corbels. To the transepts are large pointed arches opening from the nave, springing from octagonal pillars. The tower arch has two orders of shafts. In front of it is a gallery built 1733, containing an organ. The north transept has a square-headed reticulated Decorated window of three lights, on the east and west, and bad late windows at the transept ends. The chancel extends eastwards of its aisle or chapel, which is an addition of very late Perpendicular work. It has tolerable late windows, and good stone masonry, and is divided from the chancel by Tudor shaped arches with hollowed jambs. The roof bears the date 1620, and some ancient seats in the nave, 1592 and 1622. In the chancel are three plain rude sedilia, mis-shapen and obtuse. The font resembles that at Little Chart, plain and poor.

HINXHILL.

ST. MARY. 1861.

This church, in a pleasing rural spot, consists of nave and chancel, each with north aisle, western tower with shingled spire, and south porch. The walls are chiefly of Kentish rag, and the church is an average specimen of the East Kent village church. The usual arrangement of churches near Ashford is with one aisle to nave and chancel, sometimes north, sometimes south; very rarely two aisles. The roofs are of tiles, and that of the nave is carried down over the north aisle. The main features are Early English. The north aisle, which is very narrow, has a single lancet at the west end, and single trefoil-headed lancets on the north. The arcade of the nave is Early English, of three Pointed arches upon circular columns with octagonal capitals, the responds being octagonal. There is a square-headed three light Perpendicular window on the south of the nave. The tower arch is Early English, very rude and pointed, without mouldings. There is now no chancel arch; but there are indications of one. The roofs of both nave and chancel have tie-beams and king-posts. The chapel to the north of the chancel is loftier, and extends wider than the aisle of the nave; but the arch dividing it from the chancel, if it ever existed, has disappeared. The Decalogue is between the nave and chancel, written on plaster and supported on a beam.✗ The chancel has a single lancet at the east, on the south a two-light Decorated window, and near the east a single lancet. There is a Perpendicular piscina cinquefoiled and a single sedile with cylindrical moulding continued all down the arch. There is a handsome Elizabethan monument of the family of Edolph north of the altar, with recumbent effigies.* There is a small brass to one Gauley, 1518. The north chapel has a late and debased square-headed east window,✗ and on the north a two-light ogee-headed

---

* The inscriptions, with the escutcheons, are given in Parsons' "Monuments," pp. 49, 50. H.

✗ now removed.

window. In its east wall is a cinquefoiled ogee niche which seems not to have been a piscina. There is a little stained glass in a south window. The reading-desk is constructed out of some pretty good ancient screen work. The pews are ugly and painted white. The font has a square bowl on a central cylindrical stem and four detached legs, on a square plinth. The tower, low and rude, Early English, has corner buttresses, a slit-like belfry window, very few openings and no string. The spire is heavy and shingled.

*font removed.

LOOSE.
ALL SAINTS. 1850.

An uninteresting church, originally of chancel and nave only, with low south-western tower which has a slated belfry and a clumsy shingled spire. This tower is, rather curiously, at the south-west angle of the nave, and does not reach higher than the roof of the body, but projects beyond its west wall. The windows are rude slits much splayed, and it may possibly be of early character. There are three bells, and an organ in a west gallery; also a north gallery. The west door of the nave is Third Pointed, with continued mouldings. The west window is of three lights and has tracery, which may be Middle Pointed, but is not very good, and somewhat doubtful. A modern north aisle has been added, but without arcade. The south windows of the nave are Third Pointed, of two lights. The chancel arch is continuous, and probably late. The chancel, also Third Pointed, has an east window of three lights, on the south one of two lights, of late character, and one bad modern one. On the north of the chancel is a vestry. On the south is a piscina under a window, the arch trefoiled, with good outer moulding. The font has a plain octagonal bowl of small size and modern. The church is crowded with large pews.

BREDGAR.

ST. JOHN.   1850.

This church has a nave, chancel, aisles, west tower, and south porch; all are Third Pointed except the Norman door on the west side of the tower, which is the only trace of ancient work, and some windows of two lights which appear to be Middle Pointed. The material is a mixture of flint and stone, the nave and chancel have tiled roofs, the aisles are embattled. The nave has an arcade on each side of three pointed arches, with octagonal piers. The chancel is only of one bay, the arches springing from grouped octagonal shafts, three in each group. The chancel arch rises straight from octagonal piers. The windows, save the few Middle Pointed ones, are Third Pointed, varying in tracery. The eastern of each part of three lights, most others of two. The south aisle has a flat roof; the rest a plain one with tie-beams. There are some pieces of stained glass, and two brasses, one 1518.* At the east end is some ugly wainscoting and rails re-turned. At the east end of the north aisle is a plain pointed piscina. The south aisle is narrower than the north. On the south is an octagonal rood-turret with door. The south porch has a doorway with continuous mouldings. The font has a circular bowl on a cylindrical stem. The tower arch resembles those in the arcade. The tower is of flints, with stone corners, embattled with the Kentish octagonal turret at the south-east angle. It has three stages, belfry windows square-headed, of two lights, and a single labelled trefoiled-light below. The Norman doorway is a very fine one, with two orders of moulding and shafts. One moulding, a sort of studded chain, the other a chevroned cylinder. On the capital of one shaft are some animals.

* Thomas Coly, warden of the college of Holy Trinity.—H.

FRINSTEAD.*

ST. DUNSTAN.   1850.

This church has a nave and chancel, each with north aisle, west tower, and south porch. The walls are chiefly of rough flints, the roofs high and tiled, without eaves. The roof of the aisle is carried down very low. On the south side is one very narrow Norman window, and in the chancel a lancet closed; another window on this side is Middle Pointed of two lights, with ogee head, and another Third Pointed of two lights, and there is one square aperture in the wall now closed. At the west end of the aisle is a square-headed slit closed. There is no chancel arch, nor any architectural distinction of chancel. The arcade of the nave is First Pointed, of three plain arches with circular columns having round capitals. The responds are square pilasters. The aisle is very narrow, and shed-like. The chancel has a north chapel of a different character, wider and finer, apparently substituted for the original narrow aisle, as it opens by an arch resembling those of the nave, except that the capital has foliage. There is also a kind of dwarf pointed arch eastward of it, and the respond has a foliated capital. In the north chapel are some Flamboyant windows of two lights, probably of late character. This chapel has been recently put into good order, fitted with oak benches, and the roof renewed. In its north wall is a sepulchral ogee arch with finial and feathering. The roof of the chancel has tie-beams and king-posts. The tower arch is Third Pointed, on round shafts, with octagonal capitals. The tower, Third Pointed, has a coarse battlement, and octagonal turret at the south-east, and grouped buttresses, the whole patched with brick. There is a west door and a two-light window, and one string-course. The font is modern and bad. Between the two north aisles is a small narrow First Pointed arch. The east

---

* This church has been elaborately restored at the cost of the late Lord Kingsdown. The chancel and its aisle are fine examples of modern colouring. A carved screen of wood occupies the place of the chancel arch.—R.

window is Third Pointed of three lights. In the chancel is a cinquefoiled piscina, and in the north chapel some tolerable wood screen-work.

MILSTEAD.

ST. MARY AND HOLY CROSS. 1850.

The church has a nave and chancel; the latter being long in proportion and narrow—a north chapel adjoining the chancel, and a western tower.* On the south is a porch chiefly of wood, with feathering on the gable. There was once a chapel on the south of the chancel,† to which opened a First Pointed arch, seen in the wall. The tower and nave are Third Pointed. The tower resembles that of Frinstead—of coarse masonry, and without buttresses—having a turret of octagonal form at the north-east. The nave has the common roof of tie-beams and king-posts. The windows of the nave are square-headed, of two lights. The chancel arch is pointed, on octagonal shafts. The chancel and its chapel present some earlier features—and fair First Pointed work. On each side of the chancel are two double lancets—the lights rather wide. The east window has three trefoiled lights under one arch. The north chapel opens to the chancel by two small First Pointed arches, with plain soffits and a circular pier, having square capital with foliage. The respond on the east is a block corbel; on the west is one with a fleur-de-lis. The windows of this chapel are very small lancets set in pairs. The chancel extends from eastward of this chapel, and is nearly equal in length to the nave. The font is a plain octagonal bowl set in a pointed recess on the south of the chancel. The material of the walls is almost wholly flints.

* The north chapel has been enlarged, and the whole church thoroughly restored and re-seated. H.

† A new south chapel has recently been added.—R.

ST. PETER AND ST. PAUL. 1850.

A large church, consisting of a nave and chancel, each with aisles; western tower and south porch. The south side, including the porch, is embattled; the roof is tiled; the chancel very large; and the three eastern gables, following the usual Kentish arrangement, are wide and equal. The material of the tower is a mixture of flint and stone, the rest of the church chiefly rough flints, and the north side patched with brick. There is an octagonal rood-turret on the south side, rising high, lighted by slits. The tower is very massive, and without buttress or battlement; it has only one string-course; two belfry windows, one on each side, are square-headed, of two lights; the rest are square-headed slits. There is a projecting square-turret at the north-west angle, reaching partly up the tower. The west door is Norman, of late character, with fine rich mouldings. The hood is scolloped; one course of moulding has studded chevron; the next is cylindrical with beaded spiral. There are three orders of shafts. The west window of the tower is Third Pointed of three lights, and on the north side appears a little one of Norman appearance. On the north side are three Middle Pointed windows of two lights, like those at Frinstead; most of the other windows are Third Pointed. The east window of the chancel is mutilated; those east of the aisles are debased pointed. In the south chancel-aisle is a lancet window, set high in the wall, presenting internally a shafted arch. The interior is rather irregular, and the nave very short in proportion to the chancel. The tower arch is a fine Norman one, much hidden by the organ,* having shafts and chevron mouldings. The nave has only two bays; the arcades are dissimilar; on the north the arches are First Pointed with light circular pier; the pier on the south is octagonal, with foliated capital. There

* This fine arch was completely uncovered when the church was restored, and the font now stands upon the floor of the tower.—R.

is no chancel arch; a large square pier intervenes between the
arcade of the nave and that of the chancel. The aisles are very
wide. The chancel arcades differ. There are but two bays, and
the north arcade of the chancel is not in a line with that of the
nave. The arches are pointed; but those on the north have no
chamfer. The north pier is circular; the southern octagonal.
In the south chancel-aisle is a piscina,* with moulded trefoil-
arch and the hole quite at the back. The roof of the nave has
tie-beams and king-posts. The south chancel aisle has a late
boarded roof in form of a flat arch, with panels and cornice of
Tudor flowers. Several windows contain some very poor modern
painted-glass. The font is curious, from being a specimen of
1723. The bowl is octagonal, on a similar stem. The cover is of
Gothic wood-work upon iron, with pulley and inscription giving
the above date. There is also a cock to drain off the water.
There are eight bells.

TUNSTALL.
ST. JOHN. 1850.

A nice church, comprising nave, with aisles, and chancel
with south aisle, south porch and low west tower. The material
is chiefly of flint; in some part on the south quite smooth.
The nave has a high tiled roof, and the south aisle is embattled.
There are portions of the three Pointed styles; the tower has
a moulded parapet, and no buttresses; the belfry-window is
single and trefoil-headed. The west door has an ogee head,
with elegant foliated mouldings. At the north-east is a
stair turret; the west window is Third Pointed of two lights.
The tower arch is pointed, on large octagonal shafts. The
windows on the south side of the nave are Middle Pointed, of
two lights, having ogee heads mutilated, but the finials remain,
the mullions are mostly replaced by wood.† The northern

* There is also a remarkable piscina, of the Norman or Transition period, in
the high chancel. It is wrought in the engaged pier of the south arcade. E.
† Thoroughly restored in stone in 1851. E.

windows are somewhat less mutilated, some are Middle Pointed; they contain portions of stained glass. In the eastern part of the north wall the windows are Third Pointed, of three lights, each trefoiled, without tracery. Each of the arcades is of four pointed arches, on octagonal pillars. The chancel arch rests on octagonal corbels. The nave roof is ribbed; that of the chancel is coved, and panelled with bosses and cornice. There is part of a rood screen. The chancel is large and stalled in oak; the floor laid with tiles. On the north are three lancets, with some stained glass. The east window is Third Pointed, of five lights, without tracery; filled with stained glass by Ward and Nixon. The lancet windows contain figures of the Prophets. The south-east window is a lancet, also with stained glass, opening into the south chapel, which is a much later addition, of brickwork and late Third Pointed. Under this lancet is an odd double piscina; the two heads are trefoiled, containing rather flat arches below them. The pier between them is octagonal and detached; the drain quatrefoiled. On the north of the sacrarium is a flat arched aumbry with hinges and shelf. The chancel opens to the south chapel by two dissimilar arches; one apparently connected with a tomb. Between the south chapel and the south aisle of the nave is a pointed arch. The font seems early, the bowl is cylindrical, with trefoil niches moulded, on shafts of rather Romanesque appearance. In the south chapel are three-light late windows. It contains several sepulchral memorials; an alabaster tomb without inscription; a brass* to Margaret, wife of John Rycyls, 1496; two of later date 1590, and 1654, and some others of little note. The south porch has a pretty doorway with fine mouldings, and small stilted shafts, the hood terminates in crowned heads; the door has an iron grating and peep-holes.

The situation is pretty and retired; the churchyard shaded with fine trees; the chancel has lately been much improved.

* There is in the nave a brass to Ralph Wulf, rector, obiit 1525.—R.

HUCKING.

ST. MARGARET. 1850.

A small church, of mean appearance, yet not without interest.* It has a nave with short low aisles, a chancel, with north chapel, north porch, and a wooden belfry over the west end. The porch is of wood and flints, bearing the date 1617. The walls are of rough flints. The west windows of nave and aisles are lancets; that of the south aisle a double one; the others rather obtuse. In the south aisle are two others now closed. The tiled roof extends shed-like over the aisles. Between the nave and each aisle are two very plain round arches, not quite similar, with huge piers between them. The chancel is large in proportion to the rest, but does not open by an arch to the nave; nor yet to its aisle or chapel, from which it is divided by some wood-work. There is also part of the base of the rood-screen remaining. The east window is of three lights, and pointed, but the upper part is mutilated. On each side of the chancel are rude windows,† at the east end of the south chapel is a double lancet, on its side two small ones. The roof has tie-beams and king-posts; the spandrels on uprights. There is a rood door up high in the angle of the north aisle. The font‡ has a cylindrical bowl banded at the top, the lower part being attached to a pier. In the porch is a small benatura.

LITTLEBOURNE.

ST. VINCENT. 1851.

A respectable church, having nave with aisles, large chancel, and western tower with short shingled spire. There are portions of all the Pointed styles, especially the First. The walls are of

---

* This church has been restored since 1850.— R.
† The tracery had disappeared. The mutilated form of these windows has unfortunately been reproduced in the restoration. R.
‡ Replaced by a new font of red marble.— R.

flints; the chancel is lofty, with a good high tiled roof. The tower has on the west side a door and lancet window; the spire is heavy and low. The north arcade of the nave is modern, with light piers. On the south are three very plain pointed arches, with oblong wall piers; in the eastern respond appears the rood door. In the south aisle are some single lancets and one Middle Pointed window of two lights at its east end, also one of Third Pointed character. The north aisle does not extend quite to the west end of the nave; its windows are Third Pointed of two lights. The chancel arch is modernised. The chancel is fine First Pointed. The east window is a triple lancet, and there are four single lancets on the north and south. The south door, within a brick porch, is First Pointed with shafts. The font is modern; there are ugly pews,[*] and an organ in the west gallery.

THANINGTON.
ST. NICHOLAS. 1851.

This church is in a lone situation near the high road, not more than one mile from Canterbury. The plan may be called cruciform, without aisles, there being a transeptal chapel on the south, and a tower corresponding on the north; but the chapel is perhaps rather more like an aisle than a transept. The tower is low and plain, of First Pointed character, with a pointed tiled roof; the belfry windows are lancets, as are some others below; and one has a flattened trefoil head. There are no windows on the north of the nave. On the south is a lancet. The roofs are all tiled. The south chapel has no arcade, but there is a wood screen between it and the nave. Its east and west windows are lancets filled with Powell's floriated quarries. The tower arch is a coarse continuous First Pointed one. The roof is plain, with tie-beams. The chancel has two lancets at the east end; on the south is a small Norman window, splayed, and set

[*] The church has been reseated.—H.

high up; there is a similar one on the north. On the south of the sacrarium is a plain arched recess. In front of the altar on a slab is a fine brass of a knight. The west window is a late one of two lights. The interior of the church has been recently much improved; the seats all open; the pulpit low, and a small organ in the south chapel. There is a south porch.* The font is octagonal.

HARBLEDOWN.

ST. MICHAEL.   1851.

This church deserves but little notice. It consisted originally only of a nave and chancel, but a large excrescence is added on the north in brickwork. In fact the whole church underwent a renovation in very poor style in 1829, and nothing ancient now remains but the north wall of the chancel, in which are two plain lancets; and the construction is of rough flints. The east window may be debased or modern of two lights. The chancel arch is altered, and the chancel wainscoted. There is a gallery and an organ, and a wooden belfry at the west end.

BETTESHANGER.

ST. MARY.   1851.

A very small church † within the park, comprising a nave and chancel, with added sepulchral chapel on the north. Over the west end is a modern wooden belfry with small spire. There are Norman doorways north and south of the nave, the doors having square heads; their arches are tall and chevroned. In the tympanum of that on the south is a vesica containing a representation of Our Lord giving his blessing. There is a late square-headed window at the west end, but most of the windows

---

* A lych gate has been erected as a memorial to a late rector, the Rev. W. Pearson. H.

† Said to be greatly improved since 1851.

of the nave have a modernised look. There is no chancel arch. In the chancel are lancets north and south; at the east end a small square-headed window. In the north wall of the nave appears a large trefoiled niche, with its arch on moulded capitals; but this cannot be in its original place, being much too large. It may have been part of a sedile, or credence, or Easter Sepulchre, removed from the chancel.* The north chapel is modern and of brick; it contains a huge monument by Schumaker, with naval subjects. The font is a small modern Gothic one.

*Now replaced on the south side of the chancel.

ULCOMB.*
ALL SAINTS.   1850.

An interesting church, of fair dimensions. The plan, nave and chancel with south aisle throughout, north aisle along the the chancel and only part of the nave. South porch and west tower. There are portions of all three Pointed styles. The walls are mostly of Kentish rag. The tower is Third Pointed, of a common Kentish type, embattled, with octagonal turret at the south-east angle. The belfry windows are square-headed. The west door is continuous, and over it is a three-light window. On the south side of the tower is a small shed-like building, with tiled lean-to roof, and trefoil-headed lancet window. Whether this was a chapel, or what was its purpose, is doubtful. The south porch has a labelled outer door with spandrels; the inner one is continuous. The south arcade of the nave is rude First Pointed, of three plain arches, without mouldings, and square piers of large size, having imposts. The nave is ceiled. There is one arch similar to those on the south, opening to that part of the north aisle, which ranges with the nave. The tower arch to the nave is a fine one, on shafts with octagonal capitals. The chancel arch is similar, but loftier. There is also a First Pointed arcade of two bays between the chancel and the south

* This church has been completely restored since 1850. Frescoes upon the south arcade of the nave have been uncovered.—R.

aisle, with arches much like the others; the pier cylindrical, of Norman look, with square capital, chamfered at the angles and indented, and set upon a high square base. The third bay (next the east), both on the north and south, is arched and has mouldings, with a square pier having imposts, but the arches are walled and in them are inserted windows of three lights, of a somewhat doubtful Middle Pointed character, perhaps modern. The east window of the chancel has three fine lancets with excellent mouldings, filled with a course of roses, and large marble shafts with bands and bases. The north chapel of the chancel is Third Pointed, and is divided from the chancel by two Tudor arches with light piers of four shafts, with stilted bases. The windows of the whole of the north aisle are Third Pointed, square-headed, except that at the east end, which is of three lights. Between the south aisle of the nave and that of the chancel is a pointed arch on octagonal shafts. There are some tolerable Third Pointed wood screens in the chancel and some stalls. The nave has two Middle Pointed windows on the north of two lights, in its south aisle are two early Middle Pointed ones of three lights and rather elegant character, and there are also two of Middle Pointed, reticulated, in the south aisle of the chancel. In this aisle are two brackets, one on each side of the east window. In the floor of the chancel may be seen the altar stone, with its five crosses. In the north chapel are some sepulchral remains. On a marble altar-tomb is a fine brass of a knight under a canopy, inscribed "Hic jacet Wills Maydeston Armig qui obiit VIII. die mensis Aprilis anno Dni Millmo CCCC. decimo nono anno ætatis, [cujus]—aie misereatur Deus. Amen."* "Credo quod Redemptor &c.," round the border.

In the nave are two later brasses; one of a knight and lady, Ralph Sentleger and Ann his wife, A.D. 1470, the lady in butter-fly head-dress.

The font has a square bowl, chamfered, on a large stem

* See Parsons' "Monuments," p. 392. H.

surrounded by four shafts. The cover bears the date 1759, and is drawn up by a pulley with ornamental iron-work.

RAINHAM.
ST. MARGARET. 1852.

This church, of a common Kentish form, has a nave and chancel, each with north aisle, a west tower, and north and south porches. The nave is wider than the chancel as it projects on the south side, with some indication of its having been rebuilt on an extended scale. The walls are chiefly of flints, with tiled roofs. There are portions of all the Pointed styles. The tower is Perpendicular, of a frequent Kentish type, chiefly of Kentish rag stone, with flints intermixed. It is of three stages, divided by strings, the central being the widest; it has a battlement, corner buttresses, and an octagonal stair turret rising high at the north-east. The west window is of three lights, those of the belfry are square-headed and labelled. The north porch is chiefly of brick, and has a good continuous doorway. The east gable of the nave is boarded, which seems to have been done when the nave was extended on the south. Most of the windows of the nave are Decorated of two lights, but many are mutilated.* Some are Perpendicular, and there is one lancet on the north. Inserted in the roof are several modern dormers.* The interior has rather an irregular appearance, and the junction of the nave and chancel is awkward, without an arch, the original one having probably been removed. The arcade of the nave has in its western part three pointed arches, with octagonal piers having capitals, the western respond being semicircular; then follows a very wide wall-pier, having a large octagonal pillar attached to it. There is a pointed arch between the north aisle of the nave and that of the chancel; the arcade of the chancel is more irregular than that of the nave; the eastern arch is

---
* There has been considerable restoration of windows, &c., effected, and the church has been reseated throughout.—H.

× now flocked up in 1890.

pointed, but extremely rude, and without mouldings, the adjacent pier being quite plain, and having attached on the east a circular shaft; the second column is circular with moulded capital. The central arch of this arcade is much smaller than the other two. There is a late altar-tomb inserted in the eastern arch. The south wall of the chancel has an arcade with octagonal slender shafts, each arch inclosing a window, one is Decorated of two lights, lately renewed, another is an original lancet. The shafts are set on a stone bench against the wall. There are three sedilia south of the altar which have trefoil heads under triangular canopies: there is a trefoiled piscina. Over the rood-loft's place the roof is boarded and rudely painted.* The rest of the roof is plain, with tie-beams and king-posts. The base of the rood-screen remains, and there is an indication of a projection on the north corresponding with it, lighted by slits for the rood-stairs. The tower arch to the nave is a fair Perpendicular one. The north chapel of the chancel seems to be Perpendicular, and has late flat-arched windows of two lights. It has a crypt beneath, the burying-place of the Earls of Thanet, to whom it contains several monuments, and there is a screen in the arcade. The font has an octagonal bowl with Decorated tracery, but seems to be new. There is a bad organ. The churchyard is unusually spacious.†

HARTLIP.

ST. MICHAEL.

An interesting church, comprising nave and chancel, each with aisles, a western tower, and south porch. The nave and aisles are contained under one tiled roof; the chancel and its chapels or aisles have separate roofs. The walls are chiefly of flints. Against the tower on the north is a small shed-like

* The painting in each compartment represents a "rose en soleil," the badge of King Edward IV.—R.

† In the chancel there are seven monumental brasses, and a handsomely carved chest of the 14th century. R.

building, tiled, and lighted by small slits. The tower is low and Perpendicular, with plain parapet and two-light belfry windows of square form and labelled, there is an octagonal turret at the southwest and a large chequered buttress on the north-west. The inner door of the south porch has continuous mouldings, and a hood upon corbel heads. The tower arch opening to the nave is a plain pointed one. The west window of the south aisle is Decorated of two lights, the other windows of the nave are Perpendicular and square-headed, of three lights. The arcades of the nave have each three pointed arches, with octagonal columns having moulded capitals. The chancel arch is a plain pointed one, upon moulded imposts. The chancel is Early English, and much the best portion of the church. It is divided from each aisle or chapel by a wide plain pointed arch, upon moulded imposts. To the eastward of the aisles, the chancel exhibits a curious irregular arcade, of Early English character, consisting of three arches, of dissimilar shape and size and the spring of a fourth. The first, from the east, is stilted, and contains a lancet window, resting at the west end on a shaft with square capital and abacus, from which springs a second arch of unequal sides, the spring being so much higher on the west side. The next arch on the west is wider; both these are well moulded and spring from shafts, with early capitals, but not quite alike; both shafts are jointed, but not in the same place. In the corner under the lancet window is a piscina of Early English character, the arch springing from a large shaft with plain capital. The piscina opens on two sides by arches. The bases of the shafts are square. At the east end is an odd spring of an arch with mouldings and octagonal shafts, as if connected with the original Early English window which has been replaced by one of odd and not very elegant design, perhaps debased, yet possibly transitional from Decorated to Perpendicular, of three lights, with flowing tracery in the head and rather depressed arch. The south chapel is now used as a vestry, has the not uncommon Kentish arcade on the wall of two plain pointed arches, springing from a central pilaster with imposts, and within each arch is a lancet window, one trefoiled and one cinquefoiled. The east window of this chapel is Perpendicular, of two lights.

The north chapel is entirely Early English, its east window is a double lancet, the rear arches spring from elegant marble shafts with foliated capitals, and the extremities rise from corbels. Between this chapel and the north aisle is a low moulded Early English arch, and a smaller one over it as the chapel is higher than the aisle. Its windows are single lancets, lately restored. There are two brasses of late date; one of 1551, in Latin to Johana Northampton, one English and Protestant to John Osbourne, A.D. 1577. The font is new; a very good imitation of the fine Decorated font of Swaton in Lincolnshire.

UPCHURCH.

ST. MARY.

An interesting church. Plan: Nave and chancel, each with aisles, north and south porches, and west tower, in which are five bells surmounted by a heavy shingled spire, square below and octagonal above. There is a great deal of good Decorated work and some Early English in the chancel verging to Decorated. The walls are almost wholly of flints; the tower has no buttresses, but a square projecting turret in its lower stage. The openings are small and slit-like, its arch opening to the nave is a plain pointed one. The west gable of the south aisle is of brick. The porches are odd, and have a kind of shed-like projection, and small round windows on the sides. The south door has a continuous chamfer, and hood on corbels. The windows of the aisles of the nave are Decorated, of two lights, set somewhat irregularly, and all having externally ogee heads. The west window of the north aisle is Decorated, of three lights. Some on the north are closed. The north aisle is narrower than the south aisle. The interior is in good condition and has recently been much improved.* The nave arcades are Decorated, three arches on each side, with octagonal columns having moulded caps and bases set on plinths. The responds end in octagonal brackets on the north and corbel heads on the south. Along the south aisle runs a stone bench. Beneath the windows† of the south aisle is a range of three compartments of Decorated arched panelling somewhat shallow, but having good foliation and trefoiled spandrels. There is a rood door in the pier eastward of the southern arcade, with part of the stone steps remaining. The roof has plain tie-beams and king-posts. The chancel arch ‡ has finer moulding than the arcades and springs from bold octagonal shafts. Between the south aisle and the south chapel of the chancel is a kind of stilted arch, within which is another upon corbel heads. There are three steps to the chancel.

The chancel is full of interest, and is superior to the nave. It has on each side two good pointed arches with excellent mouldings, rising from a transitional pier, clustered of four marble shafts alternating with mouldings. The shafts have capitals of fine foliage (quite Decorated) and separate octagonal bases set on plinths. The responds are corbel heads. The pier on the south is more highly stilted; one of the southern arches is closed. The ascent to the Sacrarium is by four steps, on the ascent are three sedilia in the south wall, ascending eastwards, without canopies, and merely divided by elbows, and eastward of these in the Sacrarium is a piscina, with trefoiled canopy having a projecting octagonal basin. A portion of a moulded arch is seen in the wall on this side, stopped by the masonry in which the piscina is inserted, and thus marking a change of plan. Opposite, on the north, is a similar Early English arch with good mould-

* This church was completely restored in 1876.—R.
† Above these windows an early English wall painting is now visible.—R.
‡ The plinths of the piers of a Norman chancel arch were uncovered during the restoration, and are still visible *in situ*.—R.

ings, on circular shafts with moulded capitals. The eastern part of the chancel has a ribbed roof. The east window is a pretty Decorated one of three lights, having a six-foiled wheel in the tracery, and remains of stained glass. In the east wall are two double aumbryes of square form, deep and moulded. Under the east window is a string. In the pavement of the sacrarium are several encaustic tiles. The east end of the north aisle forms a vestry, and contains a round trefoil-headed piscina. Its east window is of three lights reticulated. The other windows of this chapel have been mutilated. In it is a sepulchral monument, with ogee finialed canopy, and broken feathering, flanked by small crocketed pinnacles. There is also a monumental brass.* The arch between this chapel and the north aisle of the nave is pointed and very plain.

The south aisle of the chancel has a Perpendicular east window of three lights, and some Decorated ones of two; also part of a fine wood screen. The altar pace remains, on the north side of which is an elegant ogee recess, crocketed, having fine shafts with foliated capitals much mutilated, and in the east wall a trefoil-headed piscina. There is a stone-bench against the wall. In the pier between the two north aisles is a trefoil-headed piscina, and there is another in the south aisle of the nave. The south chapel is unfortunately used as a school,† and a horrid brick chimney added.

The floor of the nave has been laid with nice new tiles, red, black, and white, in patterns, and a fine new font erected of Decorated character, with ball-flower ornament.

TEYNHAM.
ST. MARY. 1852.

A fine church, cruciform in plan, with aisles to the nave, and western tower which is engaged in the west end, there being on each side of it a small shed-like building, extending beyond the

* Of the 14th century. R.   † Not so now.—R.

line of the aisles. The aisles are under the same sloping tiled roof as the nave, and the transepts and chancel have also tiled roofs. The church is perfectly uniform, the transepts are equal, but perhaps disproportionate to the nave from their large and almost spreading dimensions. The walls are chiefly of flints. The tower is plain, with Perpendicular battlement and two-light belfry windows, but there is an earlier lancet window below and a continuous west door. The tower has large buttresses. There is a single lancet at the west end of each aisle. The aisles are rather low and narrow. The north aisle windows are Perpendicular, squareheaded, those of the south aisle are also Perpendicular. The two chambers north and south of the tower are used, one as a vestry, the other as an approach to the gallery. The nave is divided from each aisle by two wide pointed arches, quite plain and without moulding, with octagonal columns, eastward of which is a break in the arcade, and then a third plain, and very wide arch, upon impost mouldings, opening to each transept, rather lower than the other arches. The transepts and chancel are of good plain Early English. The former have two lancets on the west, and at the two ends also two lancets, with a circle above them quatre-foiled. On the east sides of the transepts are Perpendicular windows. There are plain pointed arches between the transepts and the aisles. The chancel arch is lofty, on octagonal shafts with moulded capitals. There are rood doors up high, on each side of the chancel arch. The chancel is large, and has on each side three lancets, with string under them. The east window is Perpendicular of five lights. The font has an octagonal bowl on cylindrical stem. The pulpit is Jacobean. The roofs have plain tie-beams and king-posts. There is a west gallery and a large barrel-organ.

QUEENBOROUGH.

HOLY TRINITY. 1852.

A bad church, of late character, and tastelessly disfigured, consisting of one undivided space, with no distinction of chancel; a west tower and south porch. The walls are chiefly of stone, and have plain buttresses. The roof is tiled, coved within and painted blue, to represent sky, with gilt stars. The tower, containing three bells, is low and plain, embattled with large polygonal turret at the south-east, square-headed labelled belfry windows, and no string-courses; a bad west window and door. It opens to the nave by a plain pointed arch. The windows are nearly all modernised and square-headed. The porch has a coarse obtuse door. The north door also has a depressed arch. The interior is full of high pews. The altar rails are of iron, the sacrarium laid with marble, there is a credence table of wood, and a lectern within the sacrarium containing the Homilies and a book of sermons. A west gallery contains a seraphine. The font is of late character, and has a small octagonal bowl on banded stem.

COWDEN. *July, 1893. K. A. S*

ST. MARY. 1853.

This church has a nave and chancel undivided, and a modern aisle added on the north side of the nave. Over the west end of the nave rises a shingled turret and spire, set on in an unusual, but rather picturesque manner, not upon the gable, but at a little distance from it, on the slope of the roof. The east window is Decorated of three lights, the rear arch is moulded and on shafts with moulded capitals and bases. Some other windows are Decorated, with square heads, and some are Perpendicular. In the nave on the north side, near the rood-screen, is a trefoil-headed piscina. There is also another on the south. The roof has tie-beams and king-posts. The rood-screen is modern Gothic. The pulpit has Caroline wood-work, and there is the iron stand of an hour-glass. On the south of the altar is an ogee crocketed piscina, with cinquefoil feathering. There are no arches nor piers. The screen is set a little eastward of the entrance to the chancel. There are single trefoiled windows north and south of the west end of the nave. The west door is Perpendicular, with plain continued moulding. The south porch is large and Perpendicular, the outer door continuous, the inner with spandrels. Over the door a two-light window. The aisle is probably occupying the place of a more ancient one. The roof of the chancel was ceiled in 1740, with money found in custody of S. Wickenden, a pauper. In 1726 R. Still gave 20s. for tolling the bell every day at 5 a.m. and 8 p.m. The font is Perpendicular, the bowl octagonal and panelled. In the east window is some modern painted glass, with subjects in small medallions.

ASHURST.

ST. —— 1853.

A small mean church, with chancel and nave undivided, a south porch and a wooden pointed belfry over the west end. The gable itself is boarded. At the west end is a continuous doorway, now glazed, with hood moulding. The east window is Decorated of three lights. Some windows are single with ogee head and trefoiled. On the north and south of the chancel are square-headed Perpendicular windows. At the north-east corner of the chancel is another arch in the wall. The chancel is coved and boarded with panelling and ribs with bosses. The font has a square bowl, on a cylindrical stem, surrounded by four shafts at the angles. The porch has the date 1621. The roofs are tiled.

GROOMBRIDGE. 1853.

ST. JOHN.

A chapelry to Speldhurst; rebuilt in 1625, as appears by an inscription on a tablet over the south door.

> D. O. M.
> WILLIAM CRANFIELD,
> OB FELICISSA CAROL.
> PRINCIPIS EX
> HISPANIIS REDITU
> SACELLUM HOC.
> 16.   D. D.   25.

It is of brick in a kind of debased Gothic style. The east and west windows of five lights, but the latter closed. The side windows of three lights and of large size. There is no aisle, the whole forms one space and is fitted with open seats. There is a south porch and a small belfry.

CANTERBURY.

ST. MARY BREDIN CHURCH. 1861.

This small church is in a neat condition, having recently been restored and partially rebuilt, but it is to be lamented that the interior should have been treated with so little regard to ecclesiastical propriety.* It has a body with north aisle, which last appears to be a recent addition to the original plan, and there is no distinction of chancel and no arcade; the whole space is pewed, and there is a gallery with an organ at the west end. There is a bell-cot over the west end. On the south side are some single and double lancets with shafts, either restored or, more probably, entirely new insertions, and at the east end

---

* 1868. St. Mary Bredin has been rebuilt on a larger scale, in flints and in Gothic style, lofty and pretentious, but open to criticism.

a triplet; the new northern windows are square-headed, and east of the north aisle is an early Decorated one of two lights. On the south of the altar are three plain Early English sedilia with shafts. Near the south door is a stoup. There is an Elizabethan monument and a modern font. The situation is pretty and quiet, near the Dane John walks.

ST. MARY'S CHURCH, NORTHGATE. 1861.

This church has been for the most part rebuilt in brick in a very poor meagre style, with a tower at the west end and an east end facing the street, but the original north wall remains, though somewhat concealed. It is of rough flint work, with a trace of a Norman window and one square-headed Perpendicular one. The east end of this church was formerly over the north gate, which is now destroyed.

ST. ALPHAGE'S CHURCH. 1861.

This church consists of two equal aisles with a low tower at the west end of the northern, the chancel occupying the east end of the southern, but not marked by any architectural distinction. The walls are mostly of rough flints patched occasionally with brick. The tower, apparently unfinished, is without buttresses, but has a labelled Perpendicular north doorway. It opens to the nave by a very plain pointed arch. The aisles are divided by an arcade of five moulded pointed arches upon octagonal pillars with rather concave capitals. There is a late labelled niche on one of the piers of the arcade. The roof has tie-beams and king-posts. The windows are mostly Perpendicular of two and three lights, some square-headed and labelled; but on the south of the chancel is one good Kentish Decorated window of two lights. The east window of the chancel has been entirely mutilated. The east wall is not at right angles with the other walls. The west window is a large Perpendicular one. Some windows contain fair pieces of ancient stained glass.* There is a western gallery with an organ; the pews, old and ugly, are full of green baize. The font is Perpendicular, the bowl octagonal, with roses and shields; the stem octagonal with shafts.

ST. MARTIN'S CHURCH.   1859.

This church has obtained a reputation for antiquity far beyond what anything in the architectural features of the present church would warrant. The features are almost wholly Early English, with a few indications of Norman.

The plan is a nave and chancel, with small chapel on the north of the latter, and a western tower. The outer walls are chiefly of rough flints, with a mixture of what looks like Roman brick. The chancel arch is acute and plain Early English upon imposts. The chancel has an east window of triple lancets with marble shafts, which may possibly have been added in the late restoration, on the south are single lancets with an arcade, on the north is one lancet. There is an arcade of round arches under the east window.† In the nave the windows are mostly plain lancets with trefoil heads, and at the south-east corner of the nave is a round-headed niche like a piscina. Many of the windows have stained glass, the church has recently been very fairly restored, and is in a very good condition. In the north wall of the chancel is what is said to be Queen Bertha's ‡ coffin stone. The font, though it can hardly have been of Saxon period, is a very fine one, of cylindrical form, and surrounded with sculpture: around the upper part is a range of interesting arches with beaded mouldings; below, is a series of interlacing scroll work, also beaded.§ The work is rude and shallow, and the font is constructed of a great many different stones, ill put together. There is an organ.

* See Parsons, p. 278.—H.
† Inserted when the church was restored.—H.
‡ There is no doubt that Queen Bertha was buried, not in St. Martin's Church, but in the "porticus," or chapel of St. Martin, in the church of St. Peter and St. Paul (St. Augustine's Abbey). H.   § Font engraved in Simpson's Fonts.

MILTON, JUXTA CANTERBURY.
ST. NICHOLAS. 1861.

This small church has but little to deserve notice, but has been put in good condition and is kept very neat. The outer walls are of flints, and the plan comprises only a small nave and chancel, with a bell-cot over the west end, which is graduated, and has one open arch for a bell. It has been so much renovated, that it is difficult to distinguish the original features. The bell-cot and font are entirely new; as also is the roof. The chancel arch is pointed and well finished, on brackets. The west window is Decorated, of two lights; the west doorway has continuous mouldings. The other windows are lancets, some on the south trefoil-headed, and the east window is a double lancet with shafts. The roof is of arched timbers, not bad; the nave has open seats; the chancel is stalled, and there is a good deal of stained glass.

NACKINGTON.
ST. MARY. 1859.

This church has a nave and chancel undivided, and a south chapel to the latter, with low west tower and north porch; the walls are of flint, with tiled high roof, some brick courses being intermixed with the flint. There are two Norman windows in the nave. The chancel has two lancets on the north and a modern east window; it is divided from the south chapel by a pointed arch; on the south of the chancel is a small arched recess; on the north is another, more straight sided, which has hinges and must have been an aumbry. The roof has tie-beams and king-posts. The south chapel has monuments to the Millers and two small pointed recesses in the wall, one having a piscina. The font is modern, and there is an organ. The tower is very poor and low, with tiled roof. The lower part, of flints, has a splayed lancet on the west, and no buttresses.

PEMBURY.
ST. PETER.   1868.

The parish church consists of nave and chancel only, with a south porch, and western tower crowned by a low shingled spire. The nave is very wide, and has an excellent plain roof, with tie-beam and king-post, supported on brackets pierced with quatrefoils. There is a small Norman window on the south of the nave, set high over the porch. The other windows of the nave seem to be Perpendicular, one square-headed, of three lights; others single, with trefoil and cinquefoil feathering. There is a plain piscina at the south-east of the nave. The tower arch is pointed, on octagonal shafts, with capitals. The chancel arch is of considerable width and of like character. The chancel has a new roof, coved and panelled. The east window is new, Decorated, of three lights, with shafts; on the north of the chancel is a trefoil-headed lancet filled with obituary coloured glass, and at the north-east a Decorated window, of two lights. On the south is one Decorated window, of two lights, one cinquefoiled single light window, and another similar one set as a lychnoscope, and having a label externally, the north-west window is also labelled. The buttress on the south of the chancel has heraldic shields. The interior is in excellent condition, well restored, with nice new open seats, and the galleries are gone. The chancel is laid with new tiles, and fitted with seats stallwise. On the south are two new sedilia, and the reredos of alabaster is very elegant. The font is new. A vestry is added on the north of the chancel. The porch has the original timber roof. The south doorway within the porch has an obtuse arch. The porch is Perpendicular. The tower, containing two bells, is low and squat, with corner buttresses, but without string-courses. On the west is a doorway with continuous arch mouldings, and above it an ogee trefoliated window. The belfry story has circular lights quatrefoiled. The spire is of broach form, shingled, short, and heavy. The walls are of stone, which has much of iron colour, they are wholly divested of stucco. The churchyard is quiet and picturesque.

CAPEL.

ST. THOMAS À BECKET. 1863.

A small church partially modernised, consisting of nave and chancel, with western tower. A large portion of the wall of the nave has been rebuilt in very poor style, in brick, especially on the south side; but there is a small Norman window much splayed, on the north of the nave, also one single light window with ogee head trefoliated; and on the south near the west is a two-light, labelled Perpendicular one. The nave has the original open roof, with tie-beams upon strong brackets and king-posts. The chancel arch is pointed, on octagonal shafts. The east window is a wretched one. The nave is filled with hideous pews.* The altar and rails bear the date 1682. The font has a very plain octagonal bowl, on a circular stem. The tower is low, and of plain Perpendicular character, with battlement and pointed roof of tiles, it has corner buttresses, and a west doorway with obtuse arch over which is a window of two ogee lights; the belfry is lighted by slit lights. There is one bell.

KNOWLTON.

ST. CLEMENT. 1870.

A small church, close to the mansion house, in neat order, having undergone much improvement, yet not up to the mark of the present day. It has a single nave and chancel, without aisles, with high pitched tiled roof, which seems to have been wholly renovated, and a bell-cot over the west end. The features are mostly Perpendicular; there are good windows of three lights on the north, south, and west of the nave, and fair

* The pews have been removed, and open seats substituted.—H.

doorways north and south, which have flat arches labelled. The east window of the chancel is of three lights, and appears to be Decorated: on each side of it, internally, is a canopied niche having good base mouldings. There are some single light windows south of the chancel, rather wide and with slightly ogee heads. The chancel arch is pointed, on corbels. On the south of the chancel is a cinquefoiled piscina. The interior is small, and abounds with sumptuous marble monuments to the D'Aeth family, and the windows have much modern coloured glass. The font has a panelled octagonal bowl, but seems to be modern.

The walls are of flint, but much renovated.

CHILLENDEN.
ALL SAINTS. 1870.

A small church, having only nave and chancel, with a bell-cot over the north-west corner of the nave. The north and south doorways are Norman: the former has two orders with chevron and billet ornaments. The latter is closed, but has good recessed arch mouldings. The north porch has wood framework. There is no chancel arch; the roof is original, and has tie-beams and king-posts. The windows are Perpendicular, some square-headed, of two lights; the eastern is of two lights and pointed. On the south side of the chancel is an ogee piscina, cinquefoiled, and Perpendicular in character. There is a little ancient coloured glass. The pews are high, and old-fashioned. The bell-cot rises upon strong woodwork, with cross timbers within the nave. The font has a plain octagonal bowl. The walls are of rough flints.

NONINGTON.
ST. MARY. 1870.

A large church, consisting of two long aisles, of which the southern ends in the chancel, and a tower at the west end of the northern aisle or body. There is much of Early English work. The nave has an arcade of three wide-pointed arches of two orders, upon light circular columns with capitals, having undercut mouldings, clearly Early English. Eastward of these is a break in the arcade with octagonal corbels attached to the pier, and in the chancel the arcade has two arches quite similar to those in the nave. There are pointed arches dividing the chancel, and also the north aisle of the chancel from the western portions, each arch rising upon corbels. The southern aisle is the widest; the roofs, as usual hereabouts, have tie-beams and king-posts. In the nave the windows are mostly square-headed, of three lights, and Perpendicular. At the west end of the nave is a pointed doorway and three-light pointed window. The chancel has at the east a fine Early English triplet, on the south side of it are four windows closely set, two are single lancets, the others are early Decorated, of two lights. The north chancel has at the east end a four-light window, without foliation, having rather a debased look; on its north side is one single Early English lancet, and one square-headed three-light Perpendicular window with label. The priests' door on the north is closed. The tower arch to the nave is Early English, with plain soffit on impost moulding. The font has an octagonal bowl of doubtful character. The walls are of flint, partly plastered. The porch on the south is of brick, but within it is a fine Early English doorway, with excellent arch mouldings, and one order of shafts, the other moulding is continuous. The tower is plain, and seems to be Early English, divided by one string-course, has no buttresses originally, the windows of the belfry and lower stage single lancets.

WOMENSWOLD.

ST. MARGARET. 1870.

This church has nave and chancel without aisles, a small north transeptal chapel, a south porch, and west tower. The original work is chiefly Early English; there has been a recent restoration, and the church is in very satisfactory condition. The roofs seem to be new, but on the old model, with tie-beams and king-posts. There are no windows open on the north side of the nave; on the south they are late and almost debased, square-headed, of two lights, unfoliated. The tower arch to the nave is Early English, with plain soffit, on impost mouldings. There is a similar small pointed arch opening to the north chapel. The transept is small and shallow, has a single lancet much splayed, and two stone brackets. The chancel arch is coarse and obtuse, without imposts. The chancel is long, and of excellent Early English character. The east window a triplet, and on the north and south are three single lancets, with excellent mouldings to the rear arches, set on a string carried round the east end. There is a priest's door on the south. In both north and south walls of the chancel is a pointed sepulchral arch, and on the south an oblong aumbry and three sedilia and a piscina. The sedilia ascend eastward; they have trefoil heads surmounted by straight-sided hoods, and spring from shafts. The piscina is similar, the mouldings of the arches and of the capitals being excellent. There is a piscina at the south-east of the nave with a round basin.

The nave has good new open benches.

The tower has no buttresses, a plain parapet, and single lancet openings. The west door looks new. The font has an octagonal bowl on a circular stem. The roofs are covered with new tiles.

SUTTON, NEXT RIPPLE.

ST. PETER AND ST. PAUL. 1870.

A small church which has undergone a recent restoration and partial rebuilding. It has only nave and chancel, the latter terminating in a semicircular apse, and a new bell-cot over the west end, which is rather too much perched up. There is a

new north porch of wood covered with tiles. The south porch
is made into a vestry. The original features are Norman;
some of the masonry may be original, but some is new. The
original form and features have been generally maintained, but
some windows are inserted in the nave, which seem too large for
so small a church, being of two round-headed lights on a
central shaft contained within a large arch, but other windows
on the north and south of the nave seem original and are small,
much splayed, and set high in the wall. At the west end are
two Norman windows. The south doorway is a plain Norman
one, but that on the north is a fine and enriched one of the
same date, having two orders of moulding; the outer has
lozenge ornamentation, and the inner a variation of lozenge
ornament with the cylinder. The outer member is continuous,
with plain jamb, the other has shafts with finely sculptured
capitals and abaci, in which are seen the star and billet ornaments, and the necks have rope ornament. The lintel of the
door is square, and the tympanum covered with the hollow
square ornament with beads. There is a Norman chancel arch,
and another between the chancel and apse, very similar in
character, with plain soffit, the arch upon imposts, which have
a kind of billet ornament. The apse has three Norman
windows, and under them an arcade of semicircular arches,
having shafts with sculptured capitals set upon a ledge. Encaustic tiles have been laid in the sacrarium, and at the back of
the arcade is some ornament in terra-cotta. The chancel is
stalled. The pulpit is Jacobean. The font may be new, it has
a square bowl scolloped, on a circular stem.

BOBBING.

ST. BARTHOLOMEW. 1871.

The church has nave and chancel, each with north aisle, a
western tower and south porch. The walls are chiefly of flint. The
nave has an arcade of three-pointed arches, on octagonal pillars.

The windows of the nave are of flowing Decorated, of two lights, of which character the church mainly consists. The chancel arch is a wide pointed one on octagonal shafts, as also that between the chancel and north aisle. The chancel has an east window of three lights, with reticulated tracery; on the south is a trefoiled lancet and one mutilated window. There are three equal sedilia, of which the arches have trefoil feathering and marble detached shafts, with good capitals and bases; a piscina, with octofoil orifice of plainer character; also a square recess. One shaft of the piscina is formed from a piece of Norman sculpture with lozenge and chevron ornament, and figures of a bishop and monk. The north aisle or chapel has windows of flowing Decorated tracery, of three lights at the east; the others of two. It contains also a piscina, with trefoiled ogee arch and two stone brackets. The organ is in this north aisle. The roofs have the usual tie-beams and king-posts. The tower arch to the nave is pointed and very plain. The tower has no buttresses, but an embattled parapet; one string-course; Decorated west window of two lights; single belfry windows and a plain west doorway. There is an oblong opening on the south near the east end of the nave, now built up. The font has a plain octagonal bowl, on stem of like form. In the north chancel is a mural monument, with two busts of some of the Tuftons, 1657. There also is a mutilated brass, inscribed "Hic jacet Arnaldus Savage, filius Arnaldi qui obiit in festo nativitatis beatæ Mariæ virginis Millmo CCCC. vicesimo;" part of the ogee feathered canopy remains.

In the chancel is a large brass of a man and woman. "Orate specialiter p. aiabs dñi. Arnaldi Savage, militis, qui obiit in vigil. Sci. Andree, Apli. anno dñi. M'CCCC decimo, et dñe. Johane quondam ux. eius q' aiabs ppiciet. de., Amen." These are clearly the parents of the other Arnold Savage. The nave has open benches, and the whole church is neat. The porch has pointed doorways with continuous arch-mouldings.

IWADE.

ALL SAINTS. 1871.

A small church of rather rude character; has nave and chancel, with south aisle, south porch, and low western tower. The tiled roof of the nave is carried over the aisle, almost to the ground, the aisle being so remarkably low and shed-like. The aisle does not begin quite from the west end of the nave; westward of it is a rude sort of shed-like building with overlapping roof. The nave is wide and has an arcade of two very wide Tudor-shaped arches on octagonal pillars, and not entirely in a straight line. The features which have any character are mostly Perpendicular, of which style are the east windows of the chancel and aisle, both of three lights; other windows are square-headed, with mullions simply cinquefoiled. The square-headed windows on the south have labels. On the north is one Decorated window of two lights, and a single light trefoiled. The walls lean very much; the roof has the usual tie-beams and king-post. There is no arch or division between the chancel and nave. The rood-screen is now made to enclose the east end of the south aisle so as to form a vestry, and has fair Perpendicular tracery and cornice. There is a small plain niche with piscina on the south of the chancel, and another with trefoil head in the south aisle, encroached upon by a fire-place. Near the south door is a stoup. The font has an octagonal bowl, on stem of like form. There is a brass to Symon Snellyng and Joknosa his wife, of the fifteenth century. The porch is of wood, with plain boarding. The doorways have plain pointed arches. The tower opens to the nave only by a small pointed doorway. The exterior is rude and patched. The walls of the chancel have much brick, and the south wall of the nave has been strengthened by brickwork, but the original work is chiefly flints. The tower is very low, and has no architectural character; it has some plain slit-like openings and no buttresses, and is covered with a pointed tiled roof.

DAVINGTON.

ST. MARY MAGDALEN. 1871.

A curious church, the remains of a church of a Benedictine nunnery; for a long time in ruins, but now nicely restored. The present church comprises the nave, the east end of which forms now the chancel; there is a north aisle to the whole, but only a short aisle or chapel on the south, on which side the conventual buildings closely adjoined. The present tower is engaged at the west end of the south aisle, and there seems to have been once a corresponding tower at the west of the north aisle. The outer walls are of flint; the nave has a high-pitched tiled roof. There is a wooden porch on the north which seems to be new. The nave is mainly Norman; the north arcade has five plain semicircular arches, with square piers having imposts. There is also a Norman clerestory both north and south, having long windows with semicircular heads. The roof is coved and has tie-beams and king-posts. On the south two similar arches open to the short aisle where now is the organ. There is a pointed arch at the west of the north arcade, which seems to mark that another tower once existed there. The tower opens to the nave and aisle by pointed arches, and in its lower part forms a baptistry, in which is a new font. The west doorway of the nave is a very fine late Norman one, having three orders of mouldings and shafts with abaci and foliaged capitals; one shaft is jointed; the mouldings present the cylinder with toothed or flowered ornament, quite Early English. Above this door are three equal Norman windows, filled with new coloured glass. On the south side of the south aisle is another Norman doorway, which seems to have opened to the nun's cloister. The south clerestory windows are closed. The east window is an Early English triplet, below which is a reredos. The eastern bay of the north aisle forms now a vestry, opening by a pointed doorway, and contains a small niche or piscina, and a single-lancet window. There are two doors at the east end of the church as occasionally are seen, opening perhaps once to a reredos or room behind.* The windows of the north aisle are single lancets. In the north wall appears part of a sepulchral arch; and one pillar has been scooped out by a rude niche. The aisle has a leaded roof. The tower has double Norman belfry windows, and a tiled pointed roof. This church was restored by the late Mr. Willement, who purchased the property and restored the church to divine worship. The coloured glass and illuminations are probably from his designs.

OARE.
ST. PETER. 1871.

The church has only chancel and nave, with a wooden bellcot over the west end. The south porch is a new one of wood. There is a trefoil-headed lancet on the north of the nave; on the south are some Perpendicular windows, square-headed of two and three lights, but with arch over the square head. There is no arch to the chancel, or any division beyond a slight variation in the walls. The roofs have tie-beams and king-posts. The nave is neatly fitted with open seats. The chancel has Perpendicular windows; the eastern of three lights, the others square-headed of two cinquefoiled lights. The south-east window has the cill extended for a sedile, and near it is a piscina with plain pointed arch. In the north wall is a square recess with ledge, perhaps a credence. The font is large and Norman: a square marble bowl on cylindrical stem surrounded by four legs on square bases, but with no capitals. The walls are of flint, with stone dressings as the labels of the windows. There is a plain priest's door, and at the west end of the nave a pointed doorway with hood, over which is an original circular window, viz., a circle containing a quartrefoil. The roofs are tiled and the whole is buttressed.

* The e doors led from the parish church into the nuns' private portion of the sacred edifice

NORTON.

ST. MARY. 1871.

This church is of rough flint, with high roofs covered with tiles, and consists of nave and chancel with western tower. The chancel has on each side three lancets with trefoil heads, wide and slightly ogeed. The east window is a triplet, the central one being highest. There is no chancel arch. The roof has tie-beams and king-posts; the chancel is wainscoted.* There is an odd-shaped north doorway, with very flat arch on moulded imposts, of doubtful character. The south-west window of the chancel is set a little lower down. The south doorway has a plain pointed arch. The church is full of modern monuments. The tower has neither string nor buttress, and is patched with brick-work; has plain battlement and rude slit-like openings.

LUDDENHAM.

ST. MARY. 1871.

This church has only nave and chancel, undivided save by a slight distinction in the roof. There is a south porch of wood, very plain and poor, and a wretched little tower of brick in the south-west angle of the nave, modern and evidently a clumsy addition. The walls are of flint, mostly covered with plaster. The west doorway is Norman, having a bold course of chevron ornament, with imposts bearing foliage much worn. The chancel is good Early English; it has north and south two single lancets, of which the rear arches are carried on corbels and much splayed. The south-east window is Early Decorated, of two lights, and slightly ogeed, the cill is formed in the centre into a shallow rude piscina. The east window has two lancets, loftier than the others. There are some ancient encaustic tiles in the chancel. The windows of the nave are of the vilest

* The church was restored in 1872, when the wainscot and pews were removed.—H.

description, except one on the north, which has two trefoil-headed lights beneath a pointed arch. The roofs have tie-beams and king-posts, and are covered with tiles. The font is modern. The chancel is nicely arranged; fitted stall-wise; the sacrarium is laid with tiles, and has an ascent of three steps. The altar has a marble slab.

TONG.
ST. GILES. 1871.

The church has nave with north and south aisles, chancel, south porch, and tower placed at the east end of the south aisle. The material is as usual chiefly flint, but the east end of the chancel has been poorly rebuilt in brick. There are several buttresses of brick, in some parts stone is mixed with the flints. The aisles are very low and narrow, the tiled roof is carried over them, and on the north side dormer windows have been inserted. The nave is wide; the north arcade has plain semicircular arches of Norman character; the first pier is circular on square base having tongue-like figures at the angles, square abaci and indented capitals. The other piers are square with moulded imposts and respond. The south arcade has two rude and plain pointed arches with square pier having impost and respond. The western bay is solid wall, and the arch closed up; the western portion of the aisle being an untidy dark place. One of the south piers bears a square recess. The east window of the north aisle is closed. There are no windows in the low walls of the aisles. The nave has a tie-beam and king-post roof. The tower occupying the eastern part of the south aisle opens by plain pointed arches; one on octagonal foliaged brackets, the other on the west is more rude. The tower is of flints and without string, but has buttresses. The belfry has on its east side a Decorated window of two lights, the others are single lancets. On the south is a trefoil-headed lancet; there is no battlement. The foliage of the corbels of the tower arch are well sculptured, and there are two stone brackets on the east side of the tower. The west end of the nave has an odd Decorated window of three lights, below which is a Perpendicular doorway. The chancel arch is pointed, on octagonal corbels; across it is a good Perpendicular wood-screen, with arched compartments of rather curious four-light tracery, an embattled cornice on the top, and good ogee panelling on the lower part. The chancel has a new roof. It has a single lancet in the south wall; and both on the north and the south are pointed arches in the wall as if once opening to chapels. The east wall is modern and has a three-light window of Early English character. The chancel is neat; the altar space well paved; and the altar cloth good. The font has a circular bowl, on octagonal stem—seems new. The pulpit is Jacobean. The porch is of wood, boarded.

NEWNHAM.

ST. PETER AND ST. PAUL. 1871.

A neat church, lately much renovated and partially rebuilt, consisting of nave with aisles, chancel with north and south aisles or chapels, north porch, and tower with spire at the west of the north aisle. The public path is on the north. The porch is new. Near the north door is a stoup. The tower and most parts are of flints; the former much renovated has a new shingled spire. The south aisle is very low and shed-like; the roofs are as usual of tie-beams and king-posts. The south chancel aisle rises higher than that of the nave and is tiled. The south arcade of the nave has three tall pointed arches on octagonal pillars; the northern has two plain pointed arches, with square pier having impost. The aisles have lean-to roofs in the nave. The tower, occupying the western bay of the north aisle, has much solid wall on its south side and opens to the north aisle by a wide pointed arch having strong ribs. The west end of the nave has a square-headed Perpendicular window of two lights; above which, in the gable, is a circle containing three quatrefoils. The west end of the north aisle has a single lancet; other windows of the aisles are of two lights. The chancel arch is a lofty Early English one, with plain soffit on an impost and angle shafts having capitals of foliage. On each side of the chancel is a plain pointed arch without even impost, opening to the aisle. The chancel goes a little eastward of the aisles. The east windows of chancel and north aisle are new. On the north of the east window of the chancel is a lofty canopied niche of Perpendicular date with pediment and cinquefoil feathering. On the south side is a double piscina beneath a trefoil-head niche; the two basins being raised on a ledge. On the south of the sacrarium is a single lancet; on the north a pointed aumbrye. The north chapel has a Decorated two-light window and contains the organ. The south chapel has a moulded bracket for an image; and Perpendicular windows, square-headed and labeled, of two lights. The font is new.

LYNSTEAD.

June .1881. S.P.S.a

ST. PETER AND ST. PAUL. 1871.

A larger church than the others around, yet not very interesting. It has nave and chancel with aisles, south porch, and tower at the west of the north aisle. The walls are mostly of flints. The roofs, high and tiled, have the usual tie-beams and king-posts, but that of the chancel is new. The nave and aisles are lofty and wide. The south arcade has three pointed arches on tall octagonal pillars. On the north the tower occupies the west bay and opens to nave and aisle by pointed arches; beyond which are two pointed arches on large octagonal pillars; the east arch being incomplete and without respond; the west arch is on a corbel. The west window of the nave is Decorated of four lights; that of the south aisle is of two lights. Other windows of the nave are Perpendicular of three lights, but one on the north is Decorated. On the south they are bad. The chancel arch is tall and pointed, without corbels. There are arches between the nave aisles, and chancel aisles. The arch between the north aisle and north chancel is narrower than the corresponding arch on the south. The north chancel has separate high roof covered with tiles. The chancel is divided from the north chapel by two pointed arches on a square pier, and no corbel; and here a new stone screen has been erected. There are two large pointed arches to the south chapel on an octagonal pillar, with some wood screen-work. In the north chapel the windows are Perpendicular, in the south they are Decorated of two and three lights. The east window of the chancel is Perpendicular of five lights, poor in character, with transom and no foils. The nave is pewed and has a west gallery with organ. The tower is of two stages, with single-light windows and surmounted by a wooden belfry-story and spire. The font is new. The rood-loft stair projection is seen on the north.

The north chancel belongs to the Knatchbulls and Hugessens, the south chancel to the Ropers. The north chancel has monuments of 1634 and 1646 with figures in the costume of that period. The south chapel has some sumptuous monuments to the Ropers of like date, and an oblong piscina.

There is a post-Reformation brass to John Wesley and Alice his wife.

DODINGTON.

ST. JOHN. 1871.

A very interesting church, though not striking externally; consisting of nave and chancel, each of which has a south aisle, a south porch, and mean modern steeple of wood at the west of the north aisle on a base of flints. The walls are of flints and mostly stuccoed. The roofs are tiled and high pitched, with

LOW SIDE WINDOW IN DODINGTON CHURCH.

tie-beams and king-posts, except the chancel which is ceiled. The nave has an arcade of three plain Early English arches on square piers with imposts and chamfered angles. The third arch is not wholly complete, but about three quarters. The nave has on the north one single-lancet and two Perpendicular windows of two lights unfoliated. The west window is Perpendicular of three lights; on the south of the nave are some plain two-light windows unfoliated. The chancel arch is Early English, on clustered shafts, with capitals of foliage and bands and continued impost mouldings. In the south pier of this arch is a double hagioscope opening to both chancels. The south chancel opens to the aisle by an Early English arch, like those of the arcade. Between the chancel and south chancel is an arcade of two plain pointed arches on a circular column with square capital moulded, with angles cut off, and a square base. The principal chancel has an Early English triplet* at the east, of equal height, and one set above. In the east wall is a trefoil-headed niche with piscina, and there is a flat-arched recess in the wall south of the altar. On the north of the chancel is a low side or lychnoscopic window next the west, of Perpendicular character and labelled; of the other windows that next the east is a single lancet; another has cinque-foiled head.

The lychnoscopic window has a small shallow niche on its east jamb and a sloping stone desk below, as for a book. On its west jamb is a square aumbry with hinge-hooks. In the arcade is a wood screen. The south chancel or chapel is also Early English; on its south side are three single lancets much splayed, and at the east end two tall lancets with fine mouldings and shafts under which is a string-course, continued along the south but broken by a door more recently cut there. In the east wall is a pointed piscina with a small bowl.

* These windows are very small, and deeply splayed; their inner or rear arches are round headed.—E.

In this chancel is a slab with a cross and Lombard inscription, of the thirteenth century, not easily decyphered: ICI GIST. &c. The pulpit is of Jacobean wood-work. The font has an octagonal bowl with concave sides, on similar stem. The seats are mostly open.

ISLE OF GRAIN.*
ST. JAMES. 1871.

This church has only chancel and nave, of good proportions, with high-pitched roofs, a south porch, and wooden belfry over the west end. The roofs have tie-beams and king-posts. The chancel arch is good Early English pointed, with plain soffit on imposts, and in the angles of the western face are set longitudinal bands of chevron ornament. On each side of the chancel arch, facing west, is a pointed arch diapered with flowers, and one with figures of two mitred saints. The west window is Perpendicular, square-headed and labelled, of two lights; and there is a western doorway. The other windows are modernised in the nave. The chancel is interesting, has on each side single lancets, and an eastern triplet which has excellent mouldings and shafts with round moulded capitals. There is indication of an aisle having once existed on the north of the chancel, an arch appearing in the wall. There are two piscinæ, both north and south; the former under a flat arch, the other, beneath a window, has a trefoil head above its arch and under a horizontal line. Westward of this is a magnum sedile under another lancet. There are also two aumbries with flat arches on the north side. The font is set on a modern base; it has a square bowl charged with semicircular arches. The door within the porch has a continuous pointed arch. Over it is a curious figure of a head with wig, tongue out, and pulling its beard with the hands.

* In the diocese of Rochester.—II.

BIDBOROUGH.

ST. LAWRENCE. 1872.

A small church, much in want of internal improvement and re-arrangement.* It has a small nave, with north aisle, chancel, south porch, and low west tower. The roof is tiled and comes down low over the aisle. There is also a small gabled chapel on the south of the nave, which appears to be modern. The south doorway has remains of the original Norman work; the shafts are visible, with abaci and cushion capitals. The door arch has been altered in Perpendicular character, with the usual mouldings. Two plain low Early English arches divide the nave from the aisle, without any mouldings or chamfer; the pier is square with chamfered angles and imposts. The aisle is very narrow and has small single-lancet windows. On the south are some Perpendicular windows. There is no chancel arch. The chancel has at the east and south Perpendicular windows, the east of three lights; at the south-east is one of two lights which has a Decorated character, and on the north is one single lancet. The chancel roof has tie-beams; south of the nave is a door which once perhaps led to the rood-loft, now to the modern vestry. On the south is one trefoil-headed lancet and one set high, as for the rood-loft. The tower arch is pointed, on octagonal shafts. The tower is low, with tiled pointed roof and corner buttresses. It seems to be Perpendicular, and has on the west a square-headed two-light window, but little architectural character in other respects. The tower has a pointed doorway. The church is prettily situated with a high bank on the north. The font has an octagonal bowl on stem. The seats of the nave are very badly arranged, and the chancel much blocked.

* This church has been enlarged by the addition of a north aisle, and the interior reseated, 1876.—H.

SPELDHURST.

ST. MARY. 1872.

This church has been lately rebuilt (by G. G. Scott, junior), save the curious debased west tower. There is a nave with north aisle, chancel with north aisle, north and south porches, all of the Edwardian character; handsome and well finished with high-pitched roof and good windows. The nave consists of four pointed arches on clustered piers, and all the internal arrangements are satisfactory. Organ on the north of the chancel. The tower arch to the nave has deep mouldings, on clustered shafts. The tower is an odd composition, the lower part is late Perpendicular, with large buttresses and projecting square turret at the north-east. The west doorway has fine mouldings and hood on head corbels, and the west window is square-headed, and labelled of two wide cinquefoiled lights. Upon this substructure is erected an upper story in an ugly style, bearing date 1767: the whole is low and heavy in appearance.

BONNINGTON.

ST. RUMWALD. 1873.

A small church with nave and chancel only, but the nave is unusually lofty and has a high tiled roof. There is a north porch (on which side is the public way) and over the west end a wooden belfry. The east end has a good Early English arrangement, of two obtuse lancets below, and a single one in the gable above. On the north of the chancel is one obtuse lancet, on the south one square-headed Perpendicular window of two lights. The chancel arch is pointed, springing at once from the walls. The chancel is very much lower (and narrower) than the nave. The nave has, on the south, Decorated windows of two lights, the stone of the monials much decayed. One contains some fragments of good ancient coloured glass. The west doorway is fair Perpendicular, with recessed mouldings. The porch is late Perpendicular, of mixed brick, stone, and wood, and some buttresses are of brick.

The church is in a very lonely situation, far from houses.

BILSINGTON.

ST. PETER AND ST. PAUL. 1873.

This church is remote from the village, and curiously cut off in its communications by the moat of the adjoining ancient house.

It is small, and resembles Bonnington, though somewhat larger; consists only of a chancel and nave, with a very low western tower, or rather only part of one, which is constructed of stone in its lower portion, the upper part of wood rising into a tiled pointed belfry. It is scarcely above the high-pitched tiled roof of the nave, and has slit-like openings and no buttress. The nave is both wide and lofty, the chancel is much lower. On the south of the nave is a porch of brick. This side is rough cast, with date 1839, and has some very poor windows of modern date. On the north are some pretty good Decorated windows of two lights, containing fragments of very good ancient coloured glass. The roof of the nave is open and lofty, with tie-beams. The chancel arch is pointed, very plain, and without imposts. The chancel is long but low, rough cast externally; its roof has tie-beams. At the south-west is a single window with obtuse head set low, and there is a single lancet both at the north-east and south-east. The east window is a wretched modern one. The font has an octagonal bowl, but seems to be modern. The church is pewed and unimproved. The walls are patched with brick work. The site is rather elevated and commands a fine view over Romney Marsh.

NEWCHURCH.

ST. PETER AND ST. PAUL. 1873.

This large church, remarkable for so thinly peopled a district, consists of a spacious nave and chancel, each with north and south aisles continued to the end, north and south porches, and western tower chiefly of mixed Decorated and Perpendicular work. There is no clerestory; and the roofs are high-pitched and tiled. The south aisle has two mutilated windows, one of three lights transitional from Decorated to Perpendicular. The western window of the south aisle is of a single light with ogee head and trefoiled feathering. The north aisle has reticulated Decorated windows of three lights, but that at the west end of it is a bad one. The north aisle is wider than the southern. The nave has on each side an arcade of four pointed arches on light octagonal pillars with capitals. The roofs of the nave and aisles have tie-beams and king-posts. The tower arch is Perpendicular of three orders, the inner having shafts with octagonal capitals.

The chancel arch is pointed, but of rude character and continuous, without moulding. On the north side of it is seen the upper rood door. The lower doors are also seen on the north and south. The chancel has some features earlier than those of the nave; and on each side are two plain arches opening to the chapels, pointed, and very plain, on imposts. The chancel goes beyond the arches, and has a new east window containing some rather cold painted glass. On the north side of the sacrarium are two lancets, on the south only one wide and splayed. Under the latter is a piscina set low, with ogee trefoiled arch, and projecting bowl with octofoil orifice. The north chapel has a new Decorated east window, the other windows are poor, and there is a small Perpendicular piscina. The south chapel has a fine wood screen of Perpendicular character, and good Decorated windows, also an oblong aumbry, a cinquefoiled ogee piscina, and a fine old wood chest having Decorated carving. The chancel roof is high and boarded. The seats are all open, and the chancel has been much improved. The font is Perpendicular of black marble and octagonal, with shields on the alternate sides, charged with keys, sword, and rose. The stem has eight buttresses attached. The tower is Perpendicular, its buttresses set square, it has one string-course and embattled parapet, and a stair turret, of square form at the north-east, rising above the parapet. On the west side is a labelled doorway with quatre-foiled spandrels and shafts. Over which is a mutilated window, and in the second stage is a single trefoiled light with square label. The upper story of the tower diminishes upwards, and has a square labelled belfry-window of two lights.

The inner door within the south porch has continuous arch mouldings. The north door has a shouldered arch of Perpendicular character.

RUCKINGE.

ST. MARY. 1873.

The church has nave with north and south aisles, chancel with large south chapel, north porch and massive western tower. The latter is the principal feature, and Norman, save the belfry story. On the west side is a very fine Norman doorway, late in the style, with two orders of shafts, having star ornament in the capitals, and imposts with similar ornament. There are three orders of cylindrical mouldings and one chevroned. The belfry story is later, has its openings curiously arranged, and is surmounted by a sloping tiled roof with *quasi* spire of wood. The north porch is of wood with cusped gable, and on this side is the public way.

The south doorway is Norman; the outer order chevroned, the inner cylindrical, with one order of shafts, having abaci, and sculptured capitals, one abacus is billeted, the other foliaged. The tympanum above the doorway has star ornament. The walls of the church are of rude masonry. The roofs have tie-beams, those of the aisles lean-to. The nave has arcades of three pointed arches on octagonal pillars with capitals. The chancel arch similar. Many of the windows consist of two trefoil-headed lights. At the east of the north aisle is a Decorated one of three lights.

The chancel has on the north two lancets. The east window of three lights seems to be Edwardian, but odd. The chancel has one pointed arch in the south chapel, on octagonal shafts. The chapel is wide and lofty; has Decorated windows of rather curious character, of two lights on the south, at the•end of three. The font has an octagonal bowl on a stem.

WEST PECKHAM.

ST. DUNSTAN.   1873.

This church stands much in need of renovation. It consists of nave and chancel with north aisle to both, a western tower and south porch. The nave is divided from the aisle by two large pointed arches upon a pier of octagonal form. In the wall, east of the arcade, is an opening to the rood-loft above and a door below. The roof has tie-beams. The windows of the nave are mostly square-headed of two lights of Edwardian character, but one is more Perpendicular, one on the south is single with obtuse head. At the west of the aisle is a Perpendicular two-light window, labelled. There is no chancel arch. The chancel has a priest's door on the south and one single obtuse-headed window. The north chapel is formed into a family pew, and has much heavy wood-work; one Decorated window, of two lights, one labelled squareheaded and Perpendicular; its east window is poor and debased. Between the chancel and aisle is an octagonal pier, the arches are gone. The east window of the chancel is Perpendicular, of three lights. In the chancel is a brass on a slab. From the brass the figure of the man is gone, the woman has a winged head-dress. "Orate pro aiāb3 Willmi Culpepper militis et Elizabethe uxoris eius qui quidem Willm obiit x° die Julii 1417 et que quedem Elizabeth obiit. . . . . . In the north chapel the Geary pew has Caroline carved wood; there is also a sumptuous marble monument of a man and woman in wigs, 1722, under a rich sculptured canopy. The font has a square bowl on cylindrical stem surrounded by four legs without capitals on square plinth. The tower is rude and coarse in masonry. The lower part is Norman, and has a low round arch to the nave, hidden by a gallery with traces of imposts. It has no buttresses, the belfry windows are single, and the west door plain. On the tower is a squat *quasi* spire, tiled.

The porch is plain Perpendicular, the inner door has label and spandrels.

WOOTTON.

ST. MARTIN. 1873.

A small church, in a beautifully wooded valley amidst the downs, near to the park of the Brydges family. The plan is merely nave and chancel, with western tower and south porch. The walls are of flint, the nave and chancel rather lofty, the roofs tiled. The chancel arch is pointed on plain shafts. There are some single lancet windows and some double lancets in the nave. The chancel has a pointed low side window, closed, at the south-west. There is a plain pointed piscina at the south-east of the nave and stone seats against the nave walls. In the chancel is another piscina of plain character. Some ancient benches remain, with poppy heads, but the church is as yet unrestored and has high pews. The font is modern. The pulpit has the linen pattern on the wood-work. The poor box has the date 1662. The tower arch is narrow and rude. The tower small, of rough flints, much covered with ivy. The openings are plain single lancets, the parapet has brick battlements. The porch is new, of wood-work, heavy and infelicitous.

SELLINGE.

ST. MARY. 1861.

This church consists of a nave and chancel, each with a north aisle or chapel; a north porch and a tower at the west end of the nave. The chancel is largely developed, according to Kentish fashion, being equal in length to the nave, and the chapel on the north of the chancel is wider than the chancel itself.

The arcade that once divided the nave and aisle has unluckily been removed; the chancel arch is a plain pointed one, on imposts; there are between the north side of the nave and that of the chancel, three parts of an arch now tampered with, and in the north wall a rood door. The tower arch is a plain pointed one on imposts, of the prevalent Early English character as often seen in Kent. The tower is altogether very plain, and surmounted by a pointed roof of shingles. On the south side of the tower is a Norman window deeply splayed. On the west side is a square-headed labelled window,—those of the belfry are of doubtful character. On the east are two lancets. The tower rises but little above the high roof of the nave.

The windows on the north of the nave seem to be modern. The interior has been lately improved in some respects, and further improvement is being carried on in the chancel,* but the removal of the arcade is fatal to its being satisfactory or really church-like. The roof has tie-beams with king-posts, and is supported by wooden pillars. All the seats are open. The chancel is remarkably narrower than its adjacent aisle, and is fitted with stalls. It is divided from the aisle by a plain pointed arch without imposts. The east window has a double lancet under a pointed arch. There is a trefoil-headed piscina, the sacrarium is laid with tiles. The windows on the south of the chancel are Perpendicular of two lights, both square-headed and pointed. In the north chapel is one of two lights trefoiled, and without label, possibly Decorated, and one is square-headed

* The work of restoration has been carried out in this church.—H.

of two lights and labelled. The east window is of three trefoiled lights, probably Perpendicular. In the wall of this chapel next the chancel is a Perpendicular sepulchral arch with mouldings, and in it is placed a later tomb of Elizabethan period. There is a brass to John Bernys and Joane his wife, 1440. In the north wall is a square recess. There are some circles containing crosses let into the walls of the chancel. Many of the windows in the nave have been tampered with. The font has an octagonal bowl, on a circular stem, decorated with new illuminations.

SHADOXHURST.

ST. PETER AND ST. PAUL. 1859.

A small church, of no very remarkable features, consists of nave and chancel only, with a wooden steeple at the west end, having a pointed roof. The nave principally Decorated. There are two-light windows in the nave, early in the style, the lights are trefoil-headed and between them is a lozenge, over them a hood only. There are some odd bracket-like projections in the jambs of the nave windows. The chancel arch is pointed, on half octagonal shafts. The chancel has Early English lancet windows on the north and south, the east window, late Decorated, has some fine ancient stained glass. On the south of the altar is a sedile, sunk in the sill of the south-east window, and a piscina with ogee head, cinquefoiled, and a shelf. The roof has tie-beams and king-posts. There is a good deal of ancient armour hung up in the chancel. There is a large expensive marble monument to Admiral Molloy. There is a stone bracket on the south of the chancel arch. The font has an octagonal bowl on a stem. The porch is of brick stuccoed. The church-yard is very spacious in proportion to the church.

WOODCHURCH.

ALL SAINTS.   1859.

A fine church, in good condition,* consisting of nave with north and south aisles, chancel, with north and south chapels, of which the southern extends wider; a west tower and north porch. The material is stone, the north aisle and porch are embattled. The south side has no parapet, but the south aisle of the chancel has a tiled roof. The north porch has a circular staircase and within it is a stoup. The prevailing features are very good Early English, and the interior is decidedly grand and imposing. The nave has on each side a good arcade of four arches, with pillars of black Bethersden marble, alternately circular and octagonal. The fourth arch of the south arcade, before the commencement of the chancel, is wider than the others, corresponding with the beginning of the widening of the south aisle. The arches have hoods, and there is no clerestory. The columns, divested of whitewash, have a remarkable and beautiful effect. The roof is new and open. The tower arch is on octagonal shafts, also of marble. The chancel arch is very wide, upon marble shafts. The nave is fitted with open seats having square bench ends. The north and south walls have been rebuilt in the Perpendicular period, and have windows of that character, some square-headed. At the west end of the north aisle is a single-light slit-like window, and another to the north of it, as at Faversham, which would appear to have belonged to some inclosed place, separated from the church. There is no window at the west end of the south aisle. The north porch has a parvise, and the staircase door opens into the north aisle; there is also a staircase lighted by slits, containing the rood-steps to the north of the chancel arch, and a labelled doorway, opened in the corresponding north pier. According to a fashion not uncommon in Kent, the south aisle of the chancel is not only wider than that of the nave, but

* Restored in 1846.

extends in a widened state along one bay of the nave. It was probably a private chapel. The chancel extends eastward of both aisles, and is a remarkably beautiful piece of Early English work. It has a fine eastern triplet, with excellent mouldings, and banded shafts of black marble. On the north there are three lancets, on the south two, set on a string, also with fine mouldings and shafts. Beneath the southern windows are three sedilia ascending eastward, with similar mouldings, and black marble shafts detached. Eastward of these is a double piscina, with trefoil-headed arches. On the north is an aumbry with depressed shouldered arch. The sacrarium is raised on four steps, and is laid with rich glazed tiles. The chancel opens to the north aisle by a narrow pointed arch with fine Early English mouldings, rising from black marble octagonal shafts. The arch on the south side is wider and less good in mouldings, but it has marble shafts. There is an arched opening in the west pier on the south of the chancel, and two odd irregular apertures to the east of the northern arcade. The chancel has a coved roof, with ribs and bosses, painted blue; and it is fitted with stalls and an harmonium. The south chapel has a narrow pointed arch opening into the narrower south aisle; it has one Decorated window of two lights, but the other is Perpendicular. The tower is Early English, but has a Decorated west window of three lights and a doorway with hood on corbel heads. The tower is surmounted by a large low shingled spire, and has large buttresses to the north-west and south-west. There are six bells. The belfry windows are single lancets on the south and west, and double on the north and east.

In the south chapel is a fine late tomb of Bethersden marble to Sir Edward Waterhouse, Chancellor of the Exchequer in Ireland, obt. 1591, also some to the Harlakyndens; one has lost the brass [Roger Harlakynden, Esq., son of Wm. Harlakynden, Esq. ,* A.D. 1523; another has been lately renewed. There

* See Parsons' "Monuments," pp. 37: 4–11.

is also a brass of a priest, said to be Nichol de Gore, in the form of a cross, the head of which is a quatrefoiled circle. The figure is small, in Eucharistic vestments; early and curious, circ. 1320.* The font is an early one; the bowl of black marble and square form, sculptured with a rude Norman arcade, the stem cylindrical, with four shafts at the angles on a square plinth. This is one of the most beautiful churches in Kent, and derives much interest from the unusual feature of having the main columns of black marble, divested of whitewash.

KENNARDINGTON.

ST. MARY. 1859.

This church is but a mutilated and insignificant building, placed on a commanding eminence overlooking Romney Marsh. Kennardington church was struck by lightning in 1559, after which it was patched up so as to form the building now existing. The foundations of the former nave may be seen. It consisted once of two aisles or bodies, with a tower at the west end of the northern one; but the northern aisle or nave is now destroyed. The tower is low, without buttresses, and has a tiled pointed roof; on its north side is a circular stair turret. The belfry windows are lancets. On the west side is a three-light Perpendicular window (closed) and a doorway. The materials are flint and stone intermixed. At the west end of the remaining aisle is a Perpendicular window of three lights, with a finial at the apex. On the south side is one two-light Perpendicular window and two Decorated ones of two and three lights, of a good Kentish type, but partially closed. The present east window is Perpendicular, of two lights, and not in the centre. The roof has tie-beams. The nave seems to have been destroyed at an early period, as the wall appears to be Perpendicular. The font is of brick.

* "Surrounded with French Lombardic inscription, in two verses, in a cross; stem lost." Engraved in Paley's "Manual of Gothic Architecture" (frontispiece), and in Boutell's "Series."—H.

WAREHORNE.

ST. MATTHEW. 1859.

This church has nave, with north and south aisles; chancel, and western tower of brick, built about sixty years. It is a large, good building. The nave is divided from each aisle by an Early English arcade of three pointed arches, upon slender circular columns of black marble, resembling those at Woodchurch, and having moulded bases and capitals. The eastern

AUMBRY AND PISCINA, WAREHORNE CHURCH.

arch of the arcade is wider than the others. The roof has tie-beams and king-posts. In the south aisle are some Decorated windows of two lights, and a long one at the east end of the north aisle, under which is a niche. Other windows are of debased character. There have been altars at the east end of each aisle, and there are window seats, which must have been sedilia for the priests. In the south aisle is an aumbry of square form and a trefoil-headed piscina with wooden shelf. There is a door in the north wall, and others high up, connected with the rood-loft. The original tower arch remains, being pointed, with good mouldings, rising from circular shafts, with octagonal capitals. The tower contains six bells.

The chancel has an east window of four lights: good Perpendicular. On the north and south are three square-headed windows of two lights, of Decorated character; the north-east and south-east windows both have their sills extended so as to form a seat; but that on the south-east has beneath it a horizontal flowered band; and in the east jamb of the window is an elegant ogee piscina. In the north wall is a small pointed recess. Over the sacrarium the roof is boarded and panelled. There is a brass (1483) thus inscribed:

> "Qui Rector fuit hic Thomas Jekyn jacet istic.
> Anno M. C. quater X ter et Octavo requievit.
> Quem cœli cœtus dignetur sumere letus."

The outer walls are of rough stone and flint mixed. There is a north porch. There is an harmonium.

ORLESTON.
ST. MARY. 1859.

A small and rather mean church, situated on an eminence, having a nave and chancel only, with a very white shingled belfry over the west end. The nave is very short, has some two-light Decorated windows, and at the west a trefoiled lancet, and a doorway with continuous mouldings. The chancel arch is pointed, on octagonal shafts. The chancel seems to have been shortened, but has two windows of lancet form at the east end; it has on each side a trefoiled lancet and a two-light Decorated window. South of the altar is a plain pointed recess. There is an arched recess in the north wall of the nave. The chancel is ceiled; the nave has tie-beams. There is a west gallery. The east wall is rebuilt in brick. The south porch is boarded. The font is modern. In the churchyard is a seat under a thorn.

KINGSNORTH.
ST. MICHAEL.   1859.

This church has a lofty nave and chancel, south porch, and low west tower. The walls are chiefly of rough stone; the roofs tiled. The chancel arch is pointed and ungraceful, rising at once from the wall without shafts. The chancel arch is not in the middle. The tower arch is curious and double, with fair mouldings upon shafts. The roof of the nave has tie-beams and king-posts. The windows of the nave have rather a debased look; square-headed, labelled, and of two lights; there is one similar on the south of the chancel, and one in the same place which appears to be Norman. There are no windows on the north of the chancel, but an indication of there once having been a chapel on that side. The south-east window sill is extended into a seat. On the north of the sacrarium is a gorgeous marble tomb, with brass figures to Humfrey Clarke, Esq., and Mary his wife, with a group of children, 1579.* The east end has been rebuilt in brick, and has a horrid window. The chancel is stalled: the nave has open seats. There is some stained glass and a figure of St. Michael in one of the northern windows.† The font has an octagonal bowl and stem. The tower is low and apparently unfinished; of rough stone intermixed with brick; it has buttresses and two heights of single trefoil lights. The west doorway is plain, and over it is a three-light window verging from Decorated to Perpendicular. The churchyard is spacious and pretty.

ROLVENDEN.
ST. MARY.   1859.

This church is handsome, and of fair dimensions; consisting of nave and chancel, each with north and south aisles, western tower and south porch. The exterior is mainly Perpendicular, but the windows of the north aisle of the nave are Decorated of

---

* Inscriptions are given in Parsons' "Monuments," pp. 396–7.—H.
† See Parsons, p. 397. H.

two lights, those of the south aisle are Perpendicular of three lights and square-headed ; the tower is rather plain, with large buttresses and battlement and corner turret at the north-west. The west window appears to be Decorated of two lights, the upper part has a modern appearance. The south porch has a parvise, and is lighted by single trefoil-headed windows. Within it is a Decorated doorway with good mouldings and shafts with capitals. The tower arch to the nave is pointed, on octagonal shafts. The nave has Early English arcades, each of five tall narrow pointed arches on piers alternately circular and octagonal, but one of the northern octagonal piers has shafts attached. There is no clerestory. The nave is unfortunately galleried and pewed, though in a uniform style, and kept in good order. At the west end is a large organ. The roof has tie-beams and king-posts. The chancel arch has channeled octagonal shafts. There is a rood door up high. Between the aisles of the nave and those of the chancel are arches with continuous mouldings.

The chancel extends a little beyond the aisles and has a Perpendicular east window of five lights, those at the east of the aisles are of three lights. On the north of the east end of the chancel are two lancets with shafts (probably original) filled with stained glass. That of the east window is poor. There are two uniform Perpendicular arches between the chancel and the north aisle, but between it and the south aisle are two dissimilar arches, one large on octagonal clustered shafts, the eastern small, of Perpendicular character, rising from octagonal shafts attached to the piers. Both the chancel aisles have Perpendicular windows, but not all of the same character. There is a piscina in the south aisle. These aisles or chapels have coved boarded roofs with ribs and bosses. The font has an octagonal bowl, with quatrefoil panelling and blazoned shields, upon an octagonal stem. The style is late Decorated; one side has a circle with wavy lines. There are daily services at a quarter past six a.m., and in the evening.

NEWENDEN.
ST. PETER.   1859.

A small mutilated church, consists of nave with north aisle and south chapel, the chancel being destroyed. At the west end of the aisle is a low oblong tower with pointed tiled roof. The belfry windows are mere slits. The arcade to the north aisle is of three pointed arches on octagonal columns. The porch ranges with the aisle, so as to form the western portion of it. The windows are Perpendicular, some square-headed. The roof in the nave is an open ribbed one with tie-beams and king-posts. The south chapel opens to the nave by a pointed arch upon octagonal pillars, and is inclosed by a fine Perpendicular wood screen with very good panelling. This chapel has a flat wood ceiling.

The font is by far the most remarkable feature; it is a grand Norman specimen, the bowl square, on a cylindrical stem, surrounded by four Norman shafts, set on a plinth and high steps. The four sides of the bowl have varied sculpture. On the north are dragons and grotesque animals, on the south a course of lozenges with fruit, &c. On the west, circles containing stars, &c.

SANDHURST.
ST. NICOLAS.   1859.

This church stands in a very elevated spot, and is a conspicuous object. It consists of nave with north and south aisles, chancel with north chapel, south porch, and western tower, to the north and south of which are small shed-like buildings westward of the aisles. The nave was divided from the aisles by four pointed arches originally, but the two eastern ones on each side are now thrown into one ugly mis-shapen arch.* The piers are octagonal. The clerestory, singularly

---

* The original pillars and arches have been restored; pews removed, and open seats substituted; windows restored, and the south chapel thrown into the church. 1876. H.

enough, appears to be Early English, and has single lancets, but no other part of the church has other than Perpendicular features. The south aisle windows may have been Decorated. The interior is damp and ill-kept, with pews painted blue, and a west gallery containing a barrel organ. The exterior has a forlorn appearance, mutilated and occasionally patched both with brick and with plaster. The north aisle is wider than the other. The clerestory is slated, the chancel has a high tiled roof and there are no parapets. The windows of the south aisle are Perpendicular, with rather flat arches and labelled, those of the north aisle are much mutilated. The tower arch is pointed on octagonal columns and it opens by smaller pointed arches to the north-west and south-west chapels, which also open to the aisles by pointed arches. That on the north has brickwork in the walls, and is damp and dirty, but has on the west side a window in form of a spherical triangle. The north chapel belonged to the family De Betterinden. The southern chapel is wholly modernised, and used for vestry and school.

The chancel arch is pointed, on octagonal pillars. The chancel extends beyond the north aisle, from which it is divided by two pointed arches of unequal size, with a central pier having octagonal attached shafts, whence the arches spring. The windows of the chancel are all mutilated; beneath them is a string-course carried over an aumbry. The north chapel has square-headed Perpendicular windows in good preservation, and at the east end a pointed one of three lights, of which the top is cut by the ceiling. In these windows are some good pieces of old stained glass in which may be seen figures of angels and one of an armed knight.

The font has an octagonal bowl with some fair Decorated tracery on it upon a stem of like form. The tower is a good Perpendicular one, very strongly built and embattled, having a square turret at the north-west. It has strong buttresses, but no string-courses. The west window is much mutilated; below it is a doorway with continuous mouldings. The belfry windows are single, ogee-headed and trefoiled; a smaller window is in the stage below.

The north porch is of brick and late Perpendicular.

BIDDENDEN.

ALL SAINTS. 1859.

A good church with mixed work, consisting of nave with north and south aisles, chancel also with aisles or chapels, and western tower. The tower is Perpendicular, tall and handsome, of the best Kentish sort, having battlement and lofty octagonal stair turret at the north-east; the buttresses are very large. The belfry windows are of two plain lights with square label, but set double on the south. On the west side is a four light window, and a good doorway with label on corbels of crowned and mitred heads. The spandrels have shields and quatrefoils, and the arch mouldings have shafts. The tower arch opening to the nave is open, and the inner moulding rests upon octagonal shafts with capitals, the other mouldings are continuous. The south aisle is wider and loftier than the north aisle. The arcades of the nave are Early English; each of four pointed arches rising from slender circular columns with moulded capitals. The fourth arch next the chancel is not strictly an entire arch, but three parts of a very wide one. The chancel arch is pointed, upon octagonal shafts.

Over the chancel arch has been opened a modern window. The north aisle has two windows of advanced Decorated character, of three lights and rather uncommon tracery: the other windows are Perpendicular in the nave, one square-headed of three lights. The south aisle of the nave has a good open arched roof with ribs and tie-beams, and angel figures for corbels. The nave has lately been fitted with open benches of pitch pine, and is in good condition. The chancel arch is a wide pointed one, upon octagonal pillars. On its south side is a hagioscope from the nave. The roof of the nave has tie-beams and king-posts. The chancel extends beyond the aisles and has on the north and south Decorated windows of two lights containing stained glass by Lavers; on the south are three low equal sedilia, also Decorated, having good mouldings and clustered shafts. Eastward of them, included in the same plan, is a piscina with shelf. Opposite, on the north side, is an aumbry. The chancel is divided from each aisle by two pointed arches, springing from octagonal pillars, which, as well as the capitals on the south side, are concave, as at Rolvenden.

The south chapel, though it has a high gable, has the original roof concealed by a flat plaster ceiling, with ornamental panelling and bosses which are coloured. There is no arch dividing it from the aisle of the nave; but there is a good wood screen of Perpendicular work with vine cornice, and part of a loft now concealed by the flat ceiling. This south chapel has an east window, subarcuated, of four lights and transitional from Decorated to Perpendicular work: also a piscina and some post-Reformation brasses to the Randolphs. There is a Perpendicular tomb of marble, having lozenges sunk in the sides, containing foliation and shields, with a brass plate in memory of one of the Wildgose family, 1541. There are also in the north chapel several monuments, and one to Sir Thomas Mayne, 1566, who had fourteen children, and a canopied tomb of enriched and somewhat debased work, with brass figures of Sir William Boddenden, his wife and children, obt. 1579.

There is an organ in the south chapel. The font has an octagonal bowl of marble with obtuse arches sunk in the sides, upon a cylindrical stem surrounded by eight larger shafts with capitals, and on an octagonal plinth. The pulpit is Jacobean.

The aisles are embattled. The porch plain Perpendicular, and there is a vestry at the south-east.

HIGH HALDEN.

ST. MARY.

July. 1
1859.

The plan is nave with south aisle, north transept, chancel with south aisle, south porch, and a wooden steeple at the west end, of rather unusual construction: the upper part is a small shingled tower, with spire of the same material, set upon a tiled roof which covers a wooden porch. The whole is a curious example of the wooden steeple, and not quite of the ordinary type; the addition of the porch is unusual, the interior has strong timbers, and there are five bells. Between the steeple and the nave is a pointed arch on octagonal shafts, above which two pointed small arches open into the nave. The nave is wide and lofty, of Perpendicular character, has an arcade of three arches with the outer mouldings continued down the pier, and shafts to the inner member. The windows on the north of the nave are Decorated, and so is that at the west end of the aisle. The nave has a roof of king-posts and tie-beams. The chancel arch is pointed and lofty, on shafts with capitals of Decorated character, mounted upon square Norman corbels. In the wall over this arch are four small windows, two plain lancets, two trefoiled, a very uncommon feature. The north transept opens by a plain pointed arch on octagonal shafts.

The chancel has one lancet on the north, the other windows are Decorated, one on the south having some good stained glass, chiefly armorial. The east window has shafts to the interior arch, but the tracery has been mutilated. There is a continuous pointed arch opening to the south chapel, which has Perpendicular windows of three lights and a squint into the chancel. There is a double piscina in the chancel, and on the north a priest's door. The font has a plain square bowl on a cylindrical stem, with four legs, without caps or bases, set on a square plinth. There is one fine carved bench-end with poppy head. Near the south door is a stoup. The south porch is a good one, of timber, with feathering in the gable, and open sides. The roofs of chancel and nave are tiled, and the south aisle has no parapet.

BETHERSDEN.

ST. MARGARET. 1859.

This church follows very much a local type, and consists of nave with north and south aisles, chancel with north and south aisles or chapels, south porch and western tower. The prevailing features are Perpendicular. The aisles are embattled; the nave has a high tiled roof, and no clerestory. The material is chiefly Kentish rag; but several parts are covered with rough cast. The cornice below the battlement is of sharp and good work. In the north aisle are some Decorated windows, square-headed and of two lights, but others of the same aisle are Perpendicular. At the west of the south aisle is a two light square-headed Decorated window. Most other windows throughout the church are Perpendicular, those in the south chapel of the chancel have very flat arches. The east window of the chancel is a new one of Decorated tracery. In some of the windows are fragments of good ancient stained glass. The nave has on each side an arcade of three large pointed arches, of which the eastern is much the widest; the piers are light octagonal pillars with capitals. In the south aisle is a pointed recess in the wall.

The chancel arch is pointed, upon corbels, one of which has a large head, the other an angel. The chancel is divided from each aisle by one pointed arch upon octagonal half-shafts: that on the south of lighter character than the one opposite. There are good moulded arches separating the aisles of the nave from those of the chancel, springing from corbels. The chancel extends a little beyond the aisles.

The church has recently been put into very good condition; the nave fitted with low but rather too plain open benches: the chancel has a new reredos, and the sacrarium is laid with fine glazed tiles. There is a small finger organ at the west of the north aisle.

There are two brasses, one to Thomas Lovelace, 1591, one to

William Lovelace, gentleman, 1459; the former is Protestant, the latter has the "cuius aie ppicietur Deus."*

The font has an octagonal bowl on a cylindrical stem, with steps of marble. The tower-arch to the nave is lofty and open, of Perpendicular character. The roof is of the usual character, with tie-beams and king-posts.

The south porch is tiled, and has side windows, single and trefoiled. The outer doorway has a label, on corbels representing figures, and panelled spandrels. There is a projection on the south side in the angle of the south aisle and south chapel, corresponding with the rood-loft's place, ending in a chamfer and a large corbel head.

The tower is good Perpendicular of Kentish rag, with battlement and octagonal stair turret at the south-east, rising above the parapet. There are two string-courses, and buttresses at the angles. The belfry window is square-headed of two lights, and below it is a single window; on the west side we see a large three light Perpendicular window and a labelled doorway, the label standing on half-length human figures as corbels, the spandrels panelled with shields.

CHARTHAM.
ST. MARY. 1861.

A very interesting church with much good work, especially Decorated. The plan is cruciform, without aisles, and with tower at the west end, but the space is considerable and the interior striking, though still pewed and having a west gallery.†
The walls are of flints, with tiled roofs, but some of the buttresses are of brick. The roofs are high and tiled. There is a south porch which is also of brick for the most part. The north porch has some wood framework on a stone base. The

* See Parsons' "Monuments," p. 418.— H.
† This gallery and the high pews were removed when the church was restored in 1875.— H.

tower seems to be Perpendicular and is plain, with battlement and square embattled stair turret at the north-east; it has corner buttresses chequered in flint and stone. The belfry windows are of two lights without foliation. On the west is a continuous doorway and a plain three-light window without tracery or foliation. The tower-arch to the nave is Perpendicular and continuous.

The nave is early Decorated; as are the transepts. The chancel is more advanced. The roof is coved in the nave, which has windows consisting of two trefoil-headed lancets under a splayed arch, but on the north is one single lancet with hood. It would seem that a central tower had been intended, for there is a crossing at the point of intersection of the transepts and an incipient western arch which springs from shafts in the angles of a *quasi* pilaster having abacus and capital. In the piers north and south of this arch are hagioscopes with cinquefoiled arches. The roof over the crossing has four crossing ribs with bosses which spring from Early English shafts having abaci and cushion capitals, which, together with the remains of the western arch indicate the existence of an earlier tower in the centre. The transepts are shallow and quite uniform. At each end is an early Decorated window set high in the wall, of five lights trefoiled within a larger arch. The transepts have modern plaster ceilings concealing the original roof.*

The chancel is very lofty, light and beautiful, apparently *temp*. Edward III. The east window of four lights, subarcuated, has marble shafts with moulded capitals to the outer arch. North and south of the chancel, are four pretty two-light windows, similar to the eastern, set close, but having buttresses between them on the exterior. Within, a string raised over the doors runs below the windows. These windows have the star tracery so common in Kent; and internally, their hoods are connected by a small trefoil head, in the intermediate spaces; they are all very elegant, and contain much of the original

* The original roof has now been opened.—H.

stained glass. There are no sedilia, which is remarkable in a chancel of such magnitude and beauty. The roof of the chancel has panelling, with ribs and foliated bosses. The chancel is rich in sepulchral remains, principally brasses.

(1). A fine brass on a grey slab, representing the cross-legged figure of a knight, armed in mail, the surcoat bearing the heraldic charge of the Septvans, seven wheat-screens or fans; the arms, also on the shield. In rather unfinished state, and the Lombardic inscription imperfect. Sir Robert de Septvans, A.D. 1306. This is remarkable, as one of the earliest specimens of brasses.*

(2). A priest, Robert London, rector, very small, October 1, 1416. In cope.†

(3). A priest, in surplice and almuce. Robert Sheffelde, rector, 1508.‡

(4). A priest, Robert Arthur, rector, a large figure, in cope, [March 28] 1454. §

(5). A small figure of a lady, "Off your charyte pray for the soul of Jane Dowther of Lewys Clefforht, obt. 1530.

(6). In the north wall, is a segmental arch, having good mouldings, under which is a marble tomb, the sides panelled with trefoiled arches.

The font is modern and poor, erected 1720. There is a small organ.

HORTON. 1861.

A small desecrated chapel, now used as a granary; consists of chancel and nave, divided by a pointed arch. There is a single light trefoiled window on the north, all other windows are closed, and south of the altar is a trefoil-headed piscina. The roof has

* Engraved in "Manual of Monumental Brasses." Introd., p. 146, and in Boutell, p. 35.
† Engraved in Manual, Introd., p. 76. Inscription given in Parsons, p. 95.—H.
‡ See Parsons, ibid.—H.
§ Ibid.—H.

tie-beams and king-posts. The walls are of flint, and the west gable rises into a bellcot, for two bells in open arches. The roofs are tiled; all probably of late date.

UPPER HARDRES.
ST. PETER AND ST. PAUL. 1859.

This church has a nave with south aisle, chancel with south chapel, and tower situated between the two south aisles. The walls, are of mixed flint and stone; the south aisle has a lower roof than the nave, but all the roofs are tiled. The tower is very plain, and has no battlement. There is a Perpendicular labelled square-headed window on the south of the nave, but one lancet, and one Decorated window of two lights, and a single lancet at the west, of small size. The nave has two pointed arches dividing it from the aisle, on a circular column with octagonal capital. The chancel extends beyond the aisle, and is large and good, having four single lancets on the north, and one on the south; at the east end are two lancets containing some fine ancient stained glass. The west window of the nave is Perpendicular of three lights, and full of ancient stained glass: below it is a plain doorway. There is a south porch of brick, and within it a Perpendicular doorway of late date, with a hood on corbel heads. There are several brasses to the Hardres family, 1485, 1575, 1579, 1583, and a fine one of a Priest, on a bracket, John Strete, rector, 1405, in hood, and kneeling.

STOURMOUTH.
ALL SAINTS. 1859.

This church, in an inaccessible situation bordering on marshes, consists of nave with aisles and chancel. The walls are chiefly of rough flints, the nave roof is tiled, and extends over the aisles which are low. Over the west end is a wooden belfry with small spire.

Stourmouth.

The north arcade is plain Early English, with simple unmoulded pointed arches, on square piers with imposts and shafts set in the angles. The south arcade is later and less plain, the arches moulded, the piers circular and octagonal. The chancel arch is pointed on imposts. The windows are mostly Perpendicular, that at the east end, is Decorated of three lights. Many of the southern windows have some good pieces of ancient stained glass. Part of the rood-screen remains. There are some encaustic tiles, and a font which has a square bowl upon four shafts with caps and bases. The west end is strengthened by brick buttresses. The east end has been renewed.

SHELDWICH.
ST. JAMES.
1859.

This church has a nave and chancel, the latter having a north chapel, and the former a south chapel. Western tower. On the south of the nave, is a Norman window closed, and some square-headed Perpendicular windows. On the north, are Decorated windows of two and three lights. The nave is very wide. The tower-arch is Perpendicular, on corbels, and there is a gallery and organ in the tower. The roof of the nave has tie-beams and king-posts. The chancel-arch is pointed and wide, springing at once from the wall. The chancel has a debased east window; it is divided from the north chapel, by one pointed arch, having octagonal eastern respond, but dying into the west wall. This chapel has Decorated windows, and an ogee trefoiled piscina with bowl. In this chapel, is a fine early brass, with figures of a knight and a lady, A.D. 1383.* The chancel has Decorated windows of two lights on the south.

The nave opens to the south chapel, by two pointed arches, with octagonal pier, having shafts attached. This chapel has Decorated windows, and has been recently restored. One is

* Richard Atte Lese, 1394, and wife Dionisia. See Manual, p. 108. Inscription given in Parsons, p. 205. Engraved in Boutell's Series. II,

a circle containing a trefoil, another is of segmental form. There is also some new stained glass, and a good brass, of a knight and lady, A.D. 1426, inscribed "Orate p. aiabs Johes Coly Armigeri et Isabelle ux sue qu. qdem Johannes obiit IX. Oct. MCCCCXXVI., q. a. p. D."*

The chancel is paved with marble. The font is modern. The tower is Perpendicular, of flint and stone, is embattled, with octagonal turret at the south-east, has corner buttresses, two string-courses, and belfry windows plain without foliation. The west window is of three lights, and the west doorway has continuous arch mouldings.

BADLESMERE.
ST. LEONARD. 1859.

A poor small church, without aisles, without distinct chancel, and having a mean modern bellcot. The east window is a good double lancet; there are some Decorated windows, and others modernised. The roof has tie-beams and king-posts. The font has a plain octagonal bowl on a stem. There are some good carved bench-ends with poppy-heads, having an inscription and a representation of the Archbishop's pall.

LEVELAND.
ST. LAURENCE. 1859.

A small church, having nave with north aisle and chancel, and a wooden bellcot over the west end. There are two lancet windows south of the nave, one rather too wide. The chancel has, like Badlesmere, a double-lancet east window; on the north two lancets, and on the south, a lancet and a Decorated two-light window. The aisle has two lancets, one trefoil-headed. The arcade to the aisle, has two straight formed pointed arches

* Compare Parsons, p. 206.—H.

with square pier, having shafts at the angles and impost. There is no chancel-arch. In the chancel is a piscina with hood-moulding and circular bowl; there is also one in the north aisle having a shelf.

The south-west window of the chancel, being Decorated of two lights, has internally a flat rear arch over it. The roof has king-posts and tie-beams. The font is ugly and the church is pewed. There is a mural monument with two kneeling figures, a lady in a ruff, and her son behind her, of the seventeenth century.*

MOLASH.

ST. PETER.   1859.

The church has a chancel and nave only, without aisles, a western tower and south porch. The site is rural and retired. The tower is of rough flints and left unfinished, the upper part is of poor modern brick-work. It has strong buttresses, and only small plain apertures of no architectural character, and rises but little above the roof of the nave. The west doorway has an obtuse arch. On the north of the tower is a shed-like building having a Perpendicular window with a label and double feathering. The tower opens to the nave by a small arch more like a door. The walls are all of rough flints. The porch is of wood and late Perpendicular, having ornamental spandrels to the doorway. The chancel is long in proportion, but there is no chancel-arch: it has lancets on the north and south, and one Perpendicular window of three lights on the south; the east window has three trefoil-headed lights under a pointed arch. There is a piscina, with flattened trefoil arch, on the south of the chancel, and above it a grotesque head. The roof has tie-beams and king-posts. There is a priests' door on the south.

The nave has on the south, one Decorated window of two

---

* Mrs. Katharin Rooper, and her son, Francis Herdson, by her first husband, Thomas Herdson. Inscription given in Parsons, p. 291. H.

lights, and two Perpendicular windows of three. On the north is a transitional window of two trefoiled lights with a quatrefoiled circle above them and no hood; also one of three lights of advanced Decorated character, with rather curious tracery, and a single light, having in the head a quatrefoiled circle. In several windows are pieces of good ancient stained glass. The font has a square bowl of Norman character, bearing a plain Norman arcade. The stem is later and has four angel figures. There is a Longobardic inscription on a slab in the chancel.

In the churchyard is a fine yew tree.

CHALLOCK.

ST. COSMUS AND ST. DAMIAN. 1859.

The church has a nave with north and south aisles, chancel, south porch, and west tower. The arcades are Early English, each of four pointed arches on circular columns, with moulded capitals and bases. There is no chancel-arch, and the fourth arch of the north arcade ranges with the chancel; that part of the aisle being separated from it by a parclose screen of Perpendicular character. On the north side is a rood door. At the west end of each aisle is a single lancet, in the south aisle are Perpendicular windows mostly square-headed. In the north aisle are Decorated windows of two and (at the east end) of three lights. The chancel has been restored and has a boarded roof; it has on the south a Decorated window: the other windows are Perpendicular. The font is a square mass of Early English character, having an arcade all round it.

The tower is Perpendicular, of local type, embattled, and having a stair-turret at the south-east, square below and octagonal at the top, rising above the parapet. There are two stages of square-headed, two light, labelled windows, and a plain west doorway. The material is flint and stone. The situation strikingly beautiful, sylvan and tranquil, is adjacent to the fine trees of Eastwell Park.

EASTWELL.

ST. MARY. 1859.

The church has two equal aisles, with a tower at the west end of the north, which aisle, in its eastern portion, forms the chancel; there is a south porch. The church was restored some years ago, but rather too soon to be entirely satisfactory. The arcade consists of four arches, of which three are in the nave and one in the chancel, pointed, on octagonal columns. The windows are all Perpendicular, chiefly of two lights, except the two east end windows, of which the northern is Decorated of three lights, with pretty tracery, the southern, also of three lights, is of a debased kind. The roofs covered and boarded within, are tiled externally. The chancel-arch and the tower-arch, both spring from octagonal shafts. The fourth arch of the arcade within the chancel, is very wide, and there is some wood screen-work. On the north of the chancel is a sepulchral arch, under which is an ancient tomb. In the south chapel is a very large altar tomb with recumbent figures in marble, to some of the Finch family.* The floors are laid with encaustic tiles, and the seats are open, with poppy-heads. There is also a reredos; the font new.

There is one ancient poppy-head with a figure of St. Peter, and with a rebus, *Hat* and *ton*, for the name of Hatton. There is a white marble monument to Emily, Countess of Winchelsea, obt. 1848.

The tower appears to be Decorated, and has a battlement; its west window is of two lights, one belfry window is Decorated, the others are later and labelled. The exterior is much mantled in ivy.

---

* To Sir Moyle Finch and Elizabeth his wife, who died circ. 1614, and Sir Heneage Finch, their son, ob. 1631, and Frances, his wife, ob. 1627. See Parsons pp. 21-23.—H.

BRASTED.

ST. MARTIN.   1859.

The church has a nave with south aisle, north and south transepts, chancel and west tower.*

In the north wall of the nave is a Norman window, deeply splayed. The arcade of the nave is Early English, and has four pointed arches on circular pillars, with capitals and bases. The tower arch is very small and springs at once from the wall. The north transept opens by a large pointed arch in which is a wood screen. This transept has Decorated windows, one of three lights, two at east and west, of two lights and square-headed. There is on the west side of the south transept a wide pointed arch on octagonal shaft, seen in the wall, and seeming to mark a change of plan. This wide arch, now partially without the wall of the south aisle, shows that the aisle has been at some period, altered, and made much narrower than it originally was. In the south transept is a wood screen, a Perpendicular square-headed window, and a rood door up high with the original steps. The south transept is wholly Perpendicular. There is a tolerable rood-screen with trefoil openings in the lower part. The pulpit is Jacobean. The seats are mostly open and the chancel fitted stallwise. The porch is very mean. The roofs are tiled. There is a barrel-organ. There is no chancel-arch. The chancel has an Early English lancet on the north side, the east window is large, Perpendicular, of five lights, but the arch has, internally, the original Early English shafts with bands and capitals. The east window must have originally been a triple lancet, of which the shafts remain. In the north wall is an aumbry, the south-east window is Perpendicular, but it has been mauled, its cill is extended for a sedile. Near it is a very plain piscina. The chancel is laid with encaustic tiles, and has poor stalls and modern drapery at the east end. In the chancel is a black marble sepulchral slab to Dorothy Chaune, also a slab with

---

* This church, with the exception of the tower, has been entirely rebuilt.—H.

the trace of a beautiful brass cross, with this legend: "Hic jacet magister Edwardus. . . . Rector huius ecclie cuius anim. ppiciet. Deus M. D. C." There is also an inscription in Lombardic character:—"Hic jacet Edmundus de Mepham doctor sacre theologie quondam Rector hujus ecclesie cuius anime propicietur Deus. Amen." The font is a plain octagonal one. In the south aisle are two square-headed Perpendicular windows of two lights, and one of three lights on the north.

The tower in its upper part is Perpendicular, but is earlier below, and of considerable size, without a parapet, it has a tiled pointed roof.* The belfry windows are square-headed and labelled. There are strong buttresses on the north of the tower. On the west side is a singular shallow porch, in a manner, formed out of a buttress. The porch has strong ribs and the doorway has continuous arch mouldings of Decorated character. There are five bells. The walls are of rough flints, much stuccoed and not very sightly.

BOUGHTON-UNDER-BLEAN.

ST. PETER AND ST. PAUL. 1862.

A large church, having nave with north and south aisles; chancel with north and south chapels; western tower, and north and south porches. The walls are chiefly of rough flints intermixed with stone; the roofs high pitched and tiled. The north aisle has a parapet, but not the other portions, and the north porch is square topped, without gable. The north chapel of the chancel has its roof higher than the rest.†

Within, the arcades of the nave are dissimilar. On the north

---

* The lower part of the tower is probably Early Decorated, and has a massive, half military character with its few and small openings, and much extent of bare wall. The three strong buttresses on the north, and three on the west, give it an odd appearance, as if it had sunk at an early period, and required more support. The porch buttress on the west is almost unique. The western buttresses are of irregular form and dimensions, and the tower is extremely large.

† The church has been carefully restored, the roofs relaid, &c. H.

are four pointed arches on pillars, alternately circular and
octagonal, with moulded capitals. On each side, the fourth arch
is imperfect being not more than half an arch. On the south are
two small pointed arches on an octagonal pillar. The south aisle
has been partly extended into a transept, and the arch facing that
portion is very wide and somewhat stilted, on octagonal imposts,
marking an alteration of plan. This transeptal chapel opens to
the aisle by a very plain pointed arch on imposts; its window at
the end is Perpendicular of five lights, but there is one lancet.
The roofs have tie-beams and king-posts. There is a boarded
ceiling over the chancel-arch, which is large and pointed,
with a hood on corbel heads. There is a rood-screen,
partially preserved, with good Perpendicular tracery. The rood
doors remain on both sides. The chancel opens to each aisle or
chapel by two small pointed arches on octagonal columns with
capitals. Those on the south have odd corbels. The east
window is a good Early English triplet with shafts. North
and south of the chancel are single trefoiled windows, also Early
English. The south chapel has a Perpendicular east window of
three lights, of which only the central one remains open. On the
south is a window of two-lights with ogee heads trefoiled; the cill is
prolonged in the centre in a singular fashion, the portion brought
down having a billet moulding, rather puzzling. Near it is a
sepulchral arch with feathering. There are brasses in this chapel
of the time of Elizabeth; also one, 1508, for John Best and his wife,
and one for John Colkins, 1405,* in the nave. The north chapel
has an odd oblong recess under the east window; in this chantry
are some Early English lancets. In it also is a fine high
alabaster tomb with a remarkable brass to Sir Thomas Hawkins,
obt. 1587, aged 101, having some curious lines inscribed in black
letter.† There are screens north and south of the chancel.
The north chantry is dedicated to St. James, the south chantry
to St. John. The font is modern. The tower-arch is open, on

* The inscription is given in Parsons, p. 92.—H.
† See Parsons, pp. 86-87.—H.

octagonal shafts. The entrance to the tower staircase is unusually placed in the south aisle. The tower is Perpendicular, embattled, with octagonal turret at the south-east. The south porch is embattled, and is now used as a vestry. The public way is on the north side, and the north porch is exclusively used. The east gable of the chancel has been raised.

The north chantry is wider and higher than the north aisle, and has externally a sort of tower-like character. The church is very pleasantly situated, a mile from the village, in a retired spot, near hop-grounds, with only the parsonage and schools near it.

SELLING.
ST. MARY. 1862.

A nice church, comprising nave, with north and south aisles: a chancel, with north and south chapels; a north transept, and a central tower; also western and southern porches. The south aisle of the nave is embattled, and has a very high pitched tiled roof. The south chapel of the chancel has also a tiled roof, but less high. The walls, as usual, are mostly of flints. The tower is plain and rather small, and, as seen on the south, ungracefully rises above the tiled roof; it is covered with stucco, and embattled, with a labelled, square-headed belfry window of two lights. There is a south transept, seen internally only, as it is externally absorbed in the large south chantry.

The west doorway within the porch is Early English, with fine mouldings and banded shafts having capitals of foliage. The west porch has been renewed. Over it is a Decorated window of three lights, merely trefoiled. The nave is narrow but lofty, and has on each side an arcade of four tall pointed arches with octagonal piers having caps. The roofs, as usual, have tie-beams. The tower rises upon four pointed arches, of which the east and west are Early English, on square abaci, with chamfered angles and foliage. The north and south arches are Perpendicular on stilted shafts. There is a bold corbel table over the arch between the aisles and transepts. The rood door and steps are seen on the north, and the arch from the north aisle to the north transept is very narrow and Early English. The chancel is chiefly Early English, and has on each side an elegant arcade of narrow arches, on extremely light circular columns having capitals of beautiful foliage and square abaci. These are carried over the windows on the north, and on the south are partly open to the aisle. The aisles of the nave are very narrow. The chancel has one lancet window on the south, and on the north a two-light window without foils. The east window appears to be Decorated, and is of five lights, merely trefoiled, and contains some fine ancient stained glass with figures above and armorial shields below. It has been carefully restored. There are no sedilia, but there is a modern reredos. The south transept may be defined within, it contains the organ, and has a lancet on the west side. The south chantry chapel has, on the south, two lancet windows and one Perpendicular of two lights; at its east end are two lancets. The interior is in a very neat and improved condition, yet the pews, though uniform, have doors. The pulpit is very fair. In the nave is a small brass.

HERNHILL.
ST. MICHAEL. 1862.

The church, prettily situated near a village green, where are several fine walnut trees, consists of a nave, with north and south aisles, chancel with continued north aisle; west tower and north porch. There is no south porch, and the public path to the church is here on the north, as at Boughton Blean. The walls are of the usual masonry of these parts, chiefly rough flints. The roofs are tiled, the north porch embattled. The whole church appears to be of Perpendicular character. The tower is of a kind very common in Kent, resembling those at Boughton-under-Blean, Chilham, Rodmersham, &c.; it has an embattled parapet, with a stair-turret at the south-east, square below and octagonal above; there is good stone masonry intermixed with flints; it has one string-course; the western doorway has continuous arch mouldings. The doorways, of the porch and on the south, have similar arch mouldings. West window of two lights, and belfry windows are square-headed, labelled, of two lights. There are five bells. The windows of the aisles are very uniform Perpendicular, of two lights, except that east of the south aisle, which has three lights. The roof has tie-beams and king-posts. The nave has fair arcades, of Perpendicular character, each of three arches, on light clustered piers of four shafts, having octagonal caps. As at Boughton, the door to the belfry is within the south aisle. The tower-arch is pointed, but is encroached on by a gallery, and the nave has unimproved pews. The chancel-arch is on circular shafts. Part of the rood-screen remains, as does the rood door on the south. The chancel has square-headed windows of two lights, north and south; at the east end is one of three lights, with flattish arch, with new obituary stained glass of poor character to Jane Drake, 1853; there is also a low stone reredos. The north aisle is continued along part of the chancel, it has a three-light east window, and opens to the chancel by a doorway, of which the inner member has a foliated impost. There is more stone masonry in the chancel than in the nave. The font has a plain octagonal bowl, on an octagonal stem. The interior is clogged with whitewash.*

LYMPNE.

ST. STEPHEN.   1862.

A curious church, adjacent to the interesting castellated mansion of the Archdeacons, which is a good domestic specimen of the fifteenth century. The church is of much earlier date, having both Norman and Early English work, but chiefly the latter. It consists of nave with north aisles, chancel, and massive tower situated between the chancel and nave; also a

---

* The complete restoration of this church is now in hand, 1876.—H.

porch on the north, on which side is the public approach to the church, which, on the south, is very near to the declivity of the hill overlooking the marsh. The walls are of coarse masonry, with flints and stone intermixed. There is a tiled roof of high pitch to the aisle; the chancel has a moulded parapet. There are no buttresses on the north, save one flat one near the west end; and the aisle has lancet windows of different sizes. On the south of the nave, the windows, originally Perpendicular, have been mutilated. The west wall of the nave has been rebuilt, too soon and not well. It is very near to the wall of the castle. The nave has, on the north, two rude pointed Early English arches opening to the aisle, without mouldings, on a square pier having an impost, and the angles chamfered. The roof of the nave is flat pitched and Perpendicular. The aisle is carried along the tower; but the portion corresponding with the latter is divided off for a vestry. The roof of the aisle is a well preserved one, with tie-beams and king-posts; it has at its east end two lancets, and in the wall is a sepulchral arch under a window, the inner member slightly ogeed and foliated. There are some stone brackets internally against the tower walls above the west arch. The north porch is plain; over the door is the date 1708. The tower is plain and rude, and has an unfinished appearance, being without parapet. On each side of it are two rude semi-Norman belfry windows, and there are flat buttresses. The tower opens to the nave internally by a rude pointed arch like those of the arcade, opened in a large mass of plain wall; above this arch are seen two rude windows opening into the nave. The tower has a large pointed arch on the north, opening to the aisle, much resembling the western arch and those in the nave. The eastern arch opening to the chancel is semi-circular, rude, and without mouldings; but the impost is sculptured with starry ornament. On each side of this arch is a smaller pointed one of hagioscopic character, as frequently seen both in Kent and Sussex, and elsewhere: Pinvin, and Wyre-Piddle, Worcester; Little Shelford, Cambridge; Coombes, Sussex. The chancel is very long, and externally has strong buttresses. It is not pewed, but has some modern wainscoting, and a poor modern roof of flat pitch. The east window has three lancets, but the central one is closed up by an ugly modern tablet on which is the Decalogue. There are single lancets north and south, and those at the north-west and south-west, now closed, have a lychnoscopic look. The fittings are mean, and need improvement. The font is modern. There is a slab with a flory cross. There are five bells. The churchyard is very extensive, but all on the north side.

TILMANSTONE.
ST. ANDREW. 1863.

A small church, having chancel and nave only, with western tower and south porch. The material is of flints, chiefly rough. The tower has a plain parapet and no buttresses, the belfry windows are single and obtuse-headed; on the west is a lancet; the roof is tiled. On the north of the nave are two single lancets, and at the north-east a narrow slit-like lychnoscopic window, having internally a pointed arch. On the south of the nave is a double lancet near the west, and an odd window with a flagged sill.

The chancel arch is pointed, on octagonal pillars. The chancel has on the north one narrow Norman window, on the south a Perpendicular one of two lights and square-headed, at the east end a square-headed Perpendicular one of three lights. In the churchyard is a very large ancient yew tree.

April . 1884.

DOVER CASTLE CHURCH.
ST. MARY. 1863.

This ancient church, long in a state of hopeless ruin, has been lately restored and is used as a garrison chapel. Mr. G. G. Scott has done the restoration very judiciously. The plan is cruciform without aisles, with a rude central tower. The walls are lofty, of rough flints with intermixed bricks, and were till lately without roofs. The masonry has been made good, but so as to keep up the original rough character. The nave is fitted with open benches, the chancel has a plain groined roof, which has a good effect. The arches under the tower are semi-circular, and very plain. The windows of the nave are set high in the wall and of early character, with semi-circular arches; those on the south have internally shafts and mouldings. The west end has two plain Norman windows in the gable. The chancel and transepts are Early English. The former has an eastern triplet, and on the north and south two double lancets. There are some Perpendicular windows west of the south transept, some original Early English windows, and some newly inserted. On the north is a new Early English doorway with shafts. The tower has on the north, near the parapet, two obtuse windows, and circular openings rather irregularly disposed: there are also some circles in the north transept.

The font has a square bowl on an octagonal stem with four legs.

ELMSTONE. *Aug: 1885.*

ST. ——. 1863.

This church has chancel and nave with north aisle to the south porch, and a tower set on the north of the west front. The walls are chiefly of rough flints, and the roofs tiled. The aisle is short, and only eastward of the tower, which is engaged, and opens to the nave and aisle by two pointed arches on octagonal pillars. One of these arches is in the arcade, but shorter than the other two. The first pier is wide; the two eastern arches are higher, and upon a slender octagonal pillar. There is no chancel arch. The nave roof has tie-beams; the aisle is ceiled. Some of the old benches remain, but with pews mounted upon them. The porch is occupied as a vestry. The west window is a poor modern one. There is one Norman window in the nave and on the north two square-headed ones of Decorated character. At the east of the aisle is a curious square-headed window of three lights, late Decorated in character. On the south of the nave near the east is a lychnoscopic single window with trefoil head. In the chancel is a modernised square-headed window on the north, also lychnoscopic. North of the chancel is a single Norman window, and a shouldered flat-topped door. The east window is of three lights, without foliation, of doubtful character, and contains poor modern stained glass. There is a square recess in the east wall of the aisle. The font has a circular bowl of marble with four projecting figures, on a cylindrical stem surrounded by four legs on a plinth. There are stone corbels in the nave, both north and south, corresponding to the tower. The tower itself is small, it has a trefoiled lancet on the west, a single lancet belfry window, and corner buttresses. There is an harmonium.

PRESTON, (By Wingham.)
ST. MILDRED. 1863.

This church presents quite a model of successful restoration, in the true spirit of what should be applied to a village church, without unnecessary rebuilding or the application of unsuitable ornamentation, in contravention of the original character and prevailing style of the county. The church consists of nave, with north and south aisles, chancel with north chapel, western tower, and north porch; the most frequented approach being on that side. The materials, as usual, are chiefly flint, the porch of wood and brick. Within it is a good Early English doorway with toothed mouldings. The tower is of flint, without buttresses, and of Early English character, with plain lancet openings, and surmounted by a pointed tiled roof. It opens to the nave by a pointed arch with plain soffit, upon imposts. The arcade on the south of the nave is of three tall pointed arches that die into the piers, which are plain and square, without capitals. On the north there are three pointed arches lower than those opposite, on square piers, with imposts. There is an arch of similar character between the north aisle and the north chapel of the chancel. Some well-contrived dormer windows have recently been inserted in the roof of the nave to act as a clerestory. There are no windows in the south aisle; but in the north aisle are square-headed windows, of three lights with Decorated tracery. At the west end of each aisle is a single lancet. The chancel arch is Early English pointed, upon *quasi* pilasters having moulded imposts with chamfered angles. Within it is a nice new wood screen. The chancel opens to its north chapel by a pointed arch on circular shafts. The chancel has at the east end a triple lancet, filled with very good stained glass by Lavers. On the south of the chancel is a piscina, of which the arch head is filled with masonry. There is in the same wall a double lancet, and a single one, the former having marble shafts; there is also a lychnoscope. The north chapel has good Decorated windows of two lights, and at the east end is one of three lights without foils. On the north side is a lychnoscope, and a priests' door with flattened trefoil head. There is also a piscina in the south aisle. The nave is fitted with neat open benches; the chancel is stalled, and occupied by a surpliced choir. The north chapel contains a good organ. On the east gable of the nave is a good cross, and the north door has some very pretty new iron-work.

The church is remote from the village.

ADISHAM.

HOLY INNOCENTS. 1863.

A fine church, cruciform in plan, with a central tower, a north porch, and a western chapel adjoining the north transept, but no aisles. The cruciform plan is very well developed, and the chancel is grand and spacious. The main original features are Early English. The walls are of rough flints, partially stuccoed and patched with bricks; the roof high pitched and tiled, save in the chancel, where the covering is of ugly modern slate.*

The windows of the nave are Decorated, of two lights, having externally ogee heads with finials. The west window is a very bad modern one: below it is a doorway with hood and continuous jamb mouldings. The porch is of wood and plaster; within it is a doorway with hood on foliaged corbels.

The nave is internally much disfigured by very ugly high pews of deal. In the south wall is a pointed arched recess. The tower, which is plain and embattled, and has single lancet belfry windows, rises on four Early English pointed arches, of which the western is the loftiest, and has, as well as the southern, a plain soffit on imposts which have zigzag mouldings, somewhat mutilated. The northern and eastern arches are lower, but not quite similar, the eastern having a plainer soffit, but both have continuous mouldings without imposts. The south transept has a Decorated window of three lights on the west side, without tracery but merely trefoliated lights, and contains some ancient stained glass. The south window is similar, but of four lights. On the east side was evidently a chantry altar with a projecting Decorated window gabled externally. Within this windowed recess is a trefoiled arched piscina with shelf.

The north transept, as well as the nave, has a roof of tie-beams and king-posts. On its east side is a triple lancet, closely set, and on the north side a three-light Decorated window, with a lancet closely adjoining it, rather an unusual feature. This transept has deal pews and fittings and an harmonium, it is used by the choir. The chapel on the west of this transept is partitioned off and occupied by rubbish and dirt; it has a lancet window to the north, now closed, and part of a wood screen. It is divided from the transept by a plain Early English pointed arch with plain soffit, on imposts, now closed up.

* Ad........ s very judic.... y restored, and fitted with op.. n.. eat. – H.

The chancel has a more decidedly uniform Early English character than the rest of the church; it is spacious and unincumbered, except by some stalls and desks with poppy heads in a very ruinous state. Part of the base of the rood-screen remains in the eastern tower arch.

The chancel has on each side five single lancet windows, and a triplet at the east end. On the north side is a doorway, and near to it a benatura; on the same side is a shallow aumbry. On the south is a double piscina with trefoil arch having fine mouldings, a hood, and marble shafts with moulded caps and bases, all of the best execution. There is a slab with flory cross in the chancel, and several fairly preserved encaustic tiles are to be found about the church. The font is early, and has a square bowl charged with plain round arches, upon a square pedestal.

EYTHORNE.

ST. PETER AND ST. PAUL. 1863.

This church has nave with north aisle, chancel with north aisle, and tower on the north of the nave, forming a porch in its lower story.

The walls as usual in the locality are of rough flints, partially covered with rough-cast; the roofs are of good pitch and covered with tiles. The tower is low, buttressed at the corners, and embattled, of flints patched with brick; it has no string of division, the belfry windows are single lancets, other windows are cinquefoiled lancets. The outer doorway has continuous mouldings. The lower part, forming the porch, is groined, with ribs simply crossing, upon corbels, having an opening in the centre for the admission of bells. The inner doorway is Early English, of two orders with imposts, the lateral windows are single lancets.

The interior is fearfully disfigured with pews and galleries.*

* This church has been thoroughly restored and refitted throughout.—H.

The nave is divided from its aisle by two very plain pointed Early English arches without mouldings; the pier is an oblong wall with imposts, and the western arch is larger than the other. The roofs of every part of the church have tie-beams and king-posts. The west window is Perpendicular, of three lights. On the south side, the windows are wide lancets. The aisle has two lancets on the north; and a wide one at the west end. One of the northern lancets is shortened, and one has an oblong opening below it, of lychnoscopic character. There are dormers in this aisle roof, and a door up steps opening into the tower above the porch door.

The chancel arch is pointed, with hood and chamfered orders, without imposts. The chancel has a fine Perpendicular east window, of four lights, on each side of which is an ogee canopied niche, with foliage. On the south side of the chancel is a good square-headed Perpendicular window, containing some heraldic glass; on the same side are two rather wide sedilia of Early English character, on shafts with abaci and capitals of foliage, the western having rich mouldings, but not the other. On the north of the chancel are two pointed arches, much smaller than those of the nave, opening into the aisle or chapel. The eastern is particularly small, and looks as if it had been connected with a tomb. The western has jamb mouldings continued to the ground without capitals. The east window of this chapel is Perpendicular of three lights, with tracery, having at first sight a Decorated appearance. A small pointed arch, slightly chamfered, on imposts, divides this aisle from the aisle of the nave. The north chapel is full of hatchments and modern monuments.

The font is attached to a pier; it is a circular bowl of lead with the date, 1628, having rude figures upon it. The stem looks of Norman character. There is a small organ in the west gallery, and a closed doorway under the west window. There is no south door, and the vestry south of the chancel is modern.

BOUGHTON MONCHELSEA.

ST. PETER. 1863.

This church has nave with north aisle, chancel and central low tower, without transepts, and a south porch. The north aisle passes the tower, which however is clear on the south side. The nave, especially on the north side, has been much modernised in consequence of a destructive fire about thirty years ago.* The north wall seems altogether new, as is the slated roof. There are however on this side some Perpendicular windows of three lights, and one at the east end of this aisle. The east window of the aisle has, internally, circular shafts with octagonal caps and bases. The arcade seems to have been tampered with; the piers are clustered. The arch next to the tower is upon an octagonal corbel. The west window is Perpendicular of three lights, and beneath it is a good doorway of the same period, with label, panelled spandrels, and small shafts in the jambs. The window on the west of the aisle is square-headed, of two lights and late Perpendicular. There are indications of earlier work, and the form of the church, with central tower, seems to mark an early origin ; but there is little decidedly early work, except in the chancel, which has some lancet windows on the north; the east window is modern. On the south of the chancel are two trefoil-headed lancets, and one square-headed Perpendicular window of two lights. The tower is very low and massive, and seems in its upper part to be Perpendicular, with battlement and two-light square belfry windows. On the south side of the tower is a two-light window in the lower part, and at the south-west of the tower, a large octagonal turret containing the stairs to the rood-loft, and lighted by small openings. On the south of the nave are windows of two and three lights. The tower has north-west and east arches opening internally. That on the north has its inner member on shafts with octagonal caps : the east and west

* This church has been greatly enlarged, and thoroughly repaired and restored, 1876.—H.

arches are also on octagonal imposts corbeled, and apparently altered in modern times. The font is modern.

The site is beautiful; on the declivity of a fine range of hills, shaded with fine trees, and commanding a lovely view over the Weald. On the north is a very handsome ancient mansion of the fifteenth century.

RIDLEY.*

ST. PETER. 1863.

A small church, of rather mean appearance, consisting of a nave and chancel, with north and south porches, and a wooden belfry over the west end. The chancel has been rebuilt in flints, the rest is stuccoed, with old walls probably of flint. The porch is a new one of brick. There is the trace of a small aisle, or chapel, on the north of the chancel, once opening to it by a plain pointed Early English arch on imposts. In the north wall of the chancel is an oblong aumbry. The chancel has an east window of three lights, and others of two, of Decorated character. On the north side of the nave is a small narrow Norman window, set high in the wall. At the west end, and on the south of the nave are Decorated windows of two lights, which seem to have been renewed, and there is a little mediocre new stained glass. The chancel arch is pointed, upon octagonal corbels. The seats are open.

ASH (juxta Wrotham).†

ST. PETER AND ST. PAUL. 1863.

A respectable church, having nave and chancel, each with north and south aisles, a south porch and western tower. The walls are of flints with stone dressings, the roofs are tiled.

The porch and south aisle of the nave have parapets. The nave has on each side an arcade of three pointed arches on

† Diocese of Rochester.—H

octagonal pillars. The windows of the south aisle and of the north aisle also are Perpendicular; some of them are masked. The roof has tie-beams. The south chapel of the chancel has been rebuilt, and a solid wall divides it from the south aisle of the nave. The chancel arch is pointed on octagonal columns. The east window of the chancel is Decorated, of three lights. The north aisle or chapel is chiefly Perpendicular; but its east window is Decorated, of three lights and good, with portions of old stained glass. It opens to the chancel by one pointed arch on corbeled imposts, and in the chancel northward of this aisle is a closed lancet. The south chapel has been in great measure rebuilt, in Perpendicular character. The chancel has on the south two pointed arches in the wall, not opening to this chapel; one filled with window tracery of Perpendicular character; the eastern loftier, but plain and hooded. This marks that the chapel has been an addition. The north aisle is continued without interruption along the chancel. There is an organ, and a small new octagonal font. Some of the buttresses are of brick. The porch outer doorway has continuous arch mouldings, and near it is a stoup, labelled, of Perpendicular character.

The tower is Perpendicular, embattled, buttressed at the angles, with belfry window square-headed, labelled, and of two lights, and string course under them. The west window is of two lights, and there is a doorway below; over the west window is a slit opening, and there is an octagonal stair turret at the south-east, which encroaches on the west window of the south aisle. The nave roof is much higher than that of the chancel, but has no clerestory.

HARTLEY.*

ALL SAINTS. 1863.

A small church, in a dreary situation, consisting of nave and chancel; south porch, and a wooden belfry with small

---

* Diocese of Rochester.—H.

spire over the west end. The walls have been lately reconstructed in great measure, and a new vestry added on the north. The materials are flint and rubble; but some brick buttresses have been added. The west window is Perpendicular, of two lights. In the nave on the north, appears the little narrow single Norman window, set high as at Ridley. On the south is another Norman window; and one with two cinquefoiled lights. One window is of two lights without foil, and another on the south, next the chancel, is oblong and set low. The chancel arch is pointed, very small and plain. In the chancel on the north is a lychnoscopic single lancet trefoiled. The east window is a new one, of three unfoliated lights. The interior has open seats, and seems to be well arranged. The doorway within the south porch has a semi-circular head internally; the door has some remarkably good old iron-work.

BOXLEY.

ALL SAINTS. 1839 and 1866.

The church has nave with north and south aisles, chancel, west tower, and a curious narthex, or galilee, chapel appended to the west of the tower, and now forming the principal entrance. The church is of mixed flint and stone, and has tiled roofs. The tower is Perpendicular, with battlement and octagonal turret at the north-east. The belfry windows are labelled, and of two lights, there is a single one in the stage below. The buttresses are of excellent stone. The western chapel, or narthex, is Perpendicular, as the tower; its west window of three lights; there is a good western door, but no side windows. On the north is an odd arch set obliquely in the corner, and a closed door. The roof is plain, and covered with tiles. The west doorway of the tower opening to this chapel has good Perpendicular mouldings, and a hood upon corbels representing a crowned and mitred head. The nave has Early English arcades, three pointed arches on each side, on large circular columns with capitals. The roof has tie-beams. The windows of the aisles are mostly Perpendicular, of two lights, but there are some of flowing Decorated; the two western ones of good Kentish Decorated; and at the east of the north aisle one has Flamboyant tracery. Some have new stained glass. There is a cinquefoil piscina in the south aisle, and a stoup near the south door. There is a squint to the south of the chancel arch, and the rood turret is in the north aisle. The nave has neat open benches of pitch pine. The chancel arch is pointed, upon octagonal shafts. The chancel has on each side two Flamboyant windows, which seem to have been renovated, containing pretty good memorial coloured glass. The east window, also new, has some good coloured glass, and there is very pretty colouring of the east wall. There is an organ in the chancel, the north side of which is stalled, the southern pewed.* The tie-beams of the chancel cut the arch and window too much. There is a south porch with continuous interior doorway; the north doorway is closed, but has good arch mouldings and hood. There is a doorway and not a high arch from the tower to the nave. The chancel externally is stuccoed.

The font has an octagonal bowl, on a buttressed stem.

BRENZETT.

ST. EANSWITH. 1868.

This church has a nave and chancel, each with north aisle, and boarded belfry over the west end, terminated by a small spire. The nave has an arcade of three very rude pointed arches with oblong wall piers having mere imposts, but against the most western pier, which is very large, is attached an octagonal shaft, whence springs the arch, which arch is cut by a wooden partition dividing off the west end. At the south-west of the nave appears another pointed arch in the wall, on octagonal

---

* This church has been undergoing recent repairs, with new roofs, and internal rearrangement, 1876. H.

shafts, now walled up, but once opening to a small shed-like building curiously placed there, and of uncertain purpose. It seems, however, to be original; it is tiled, and has a closed trefoliated lancet at its west end; it ranges with the belfry.*

At the west end of the north aisle is a single lancet closed, and in the north aisle is a plain doorway. The wall of the north aisle is remarkably low, and devoid of windows, but there is a dormer in the roof. The north chapel has a separate and loftier roof. At the west end is a plain pointed doorway and bad window. The nave has two Decorated windows on the south which are of two and three lights. The aisle is very low, and the tile roof comes near the ground. The chancel arch has two chamfered orders, and is pointed, upon imposts. The chancel is small and confined; its east window an obtuse single light. The south window Decorated, of two lights. From the chancel to the north aisle or chapel opens a plain rude pointed arch without mouldings. The north chapel has on the north a single lancet. The eastern part is inclosed by a wood partition, and contains an ogee cinquefoiled piscina. This chapel is divided from the aisle of the nave by a half arch. In the north chapel is a fine marble tomb to John Fagge, Esq., of Rye, his wife, and son, 1639 and 1646, the two men are in armour.† The font has a plain square bowl attached to the pier. The south porch is plain, the door has plain pointed arches. There is a small closed priests' door.

The interior is clogged with whitewash, the west gallery painted blue, after the manner of the Marsh.

July 1879. R.A.S.

SNARGATE.

ST. DUNSTAN. 1866.

A large church, rather out of keeping with the very scanty population of the parish on the dreary flat of Romney Marsh.

---

* This church has been almost rebuilt. —H.
† The inscriptions are given in Parsons, p. 384. —H.

The church has nave with aisles, chancel with north and south chapels, western tower, and south porch. The whole is of fair stone masonry, and has tiled roofs. The external features seem to be wholly Perpendicular. The tower, wholly so, has battlement and turret at the north-east corner, and buttresses at the angles, belfry windows of two lights, and string-course beneath. On the west side is a three-light window, and a labelled doorway which has panelled spandrels. The window at the west of the north aisle is of two unfoliated lights. The other windows of the aisle of the nave are square-headed and labelled, of two lights. The north doorway has a flat arch. Within the south porch is a good doorway with arch mouldings. The south aisle does not reach quite to the tower. The nave is long, and has on each side an Early English arcade, with pointed arches having circular pillars with moulded capitals and square bases. The responds vary; the arches on the north die into the wall. On the south the western respond is circular, with Early English foliage and corbeled; the eastern has a square abacus and head. The tower arch is a fine one, with good mouldings and shafts. The roof has tie-beams and king-posts. There is a stoup near the north door. There is no chancel arch, but the lower part of the rood screen may be traced, and in the pavement may be seen some ancient encaustic tiles. The north aisle has tie-beams in the roof; the south aisle has a flat roof.

The chancel has a Perpendicular east window, of three lights, curiously placed quite out of the centre. It is divided from each chapel or aisle by two pointed arches on octagonal pillars; that on the south is very light. Both these chapels seem to have once been private chantries, until lately they were completely separated from the church by boarding, and in a disgraceful state of dilapidation and dirt. Through the laudable exertions of the present curate (who is endeavouring to place the whole church in a state of good repair and ecclesiastical propriety) the south chapel has been opened to the church and put into an improved condition, but is still without pavement.* It has a lean-to roof, and its exterior is stuccoed. At the east end is a doorway opening now to the outside, but which must probably once have opened into a vestry. The east window is square-headed, and of three lights. The other two gables of the chancel and north chapel are pointed : over the east window of the chancel, in the apex of the gable, is a square containing a quatrefoil. There is a rood door on the south, and a Perpendicular tomb in the chancel on the north. The north chapel is still dilapidated, with holes in the roof, and boarded off. It was once, and not so very long ago, occupied for the purposes of smuggling! It has a two-light east window, a square piscina, and traces of an altar; the rood-staircase remains in the western pier of this north side. There are wood screens in both chapels. The font has a square bowl on stem and base of like form. The pews are painted white and the interior has a glaring whitewashed character. If nicely arranged and put into good repair, the interior would be really handsome and striking.

DENTON.

ST. MARY. 1866.

A small church, prettily placed on a secluded site, amidst fine woods, near the rectory and manor house, but far from other dwellings. It has nave and chancel only, with western tower; the walls are of flints, partially stuccoed. The roofs are tiled. The chancel is long in proportion, it has a Decorated east window of three lights ; on the south is a Decorated two-light window and one single lancet. On the north, is one long single lancet and one lychnoscopic window of two lights (Decorated) of which the lower part is closed. The nave has two lancets on the south and one on the north ; on the north side is a pointed doorway. The

* The church has recently been restored and put in good order throughout.—H

tower is embattled, without string or buttresses, with a single obtuse-headed belfry window.

Several windows contain new coloured glass.

SWINGFIELD.
ST. PETER. 1866.

This church has a nave and chancel without aisles, south porch, and western tower. The walls are of flints, in the chancel chequered, in the nave rough. The porch is of wood, and within it is an Early English doorway of two orders, having fair mouldings on imposts. On the north is a doorway closed. There is one Decorated window, of two lights, on the south of the nave, also one square-headed Perpendicular, and one modernised. On the north are two small Norman windows much splayed. The roof of the nave has the Kentish tie-beams and king-posts. The nave has been lately fitted neatly with open benches. The chancel is damp and out of condition.* There is no chancel arch. The east window is Perpendicular, of three lights. On the north are two single lancets, on the south one Decorated window, and one square-headed Perpendicular, both of two lights. The chancel has a coved roof and tie-beams. The tower arch is plain and rude. The tower is square, it has two string courses, a plain unfinished parapet, and at the south-east a very large circular turret, rising high and lighted by slits. The belfry window on the east is square-headed, the other three look of Decorated character. There is a fair labelled Perpendicular doorway, and over it a single labelled window. The font is a new one, with octagonal bowl. There are some brackets on the north wall of the nave.

ACRISE.
ST. MARTIN. 1868.

This small church, situated close to the Hall, is with difficulty found, being closely surrounded by trees. It consists merely of

* The whole church has been thoroughly restored.—H.

chancel and nave, with south porch, and over the west end a tiled belfry with slated spire. The walls are of flints, quite rough; the south porch of brick. There is one single lancet on the south of the chancel, and one on the north. The east window looks as if it had been modernised. On the south the windows are all bad. The west end has a double buttress in the centre. The roof is high pitched and tiled. There is some cold new coloured glass. The cemetery is unusually quiet, shaded by many trees, and much ivy grows on the walls of the church.

PADLESWORTH.
ST. OSWALD. 1868.

A small church in a dreary, elevated site, consisting only of nave and chancel, with walls of flints, and a modern bellcot over the west end. There is much of Early Norman work, of which are the north and south doorways, the chancel arch, and one small original window in the nave. The north doorway has a square head, and a plain, semicircular, arched tympanum. The south doorway has a semicircular arch with plain soffit and imposts, and shaft on each side, of which the western is large and chevroned; the eastern is small, and set in a nook.

The chancel arch is of like form, with a plain soffit, and shafts, in nooks which have square abaci on the capitals. To the south of this arch is an arched recess in the wall facing west, where was once an altar, and there is a hagioscope. On the north of the nave is one small Norman window, and two on the south, between which is a Decorated one of two lights. One window on the north of the nave has two obtuse plain lights. The roof of the nave has tie-beams and brackets. The chancel has a small single lancet on the north and south, and on the south an oblong lychnoscopic opening. The east window is a single lancet, containing coloured glass. On the north of the altar is an oblong recess, perhaps an ambry. The nave is fitted with new open seats with heavy poppy ends. The font is cup-shaped on a low base. There is a modern buttress of brick added on the west side.

WALTHAM.
ST. BARTHOLOMEW. 1868.

The church stands on an eminence, at a distance from anything like a village, and the country about it is steep and not easy to traverse. It consists of a wide and spacious nave, with a short chancel, and a small tower placed between them. It is now in good condition, has new open seats, and a new roof. Some windows of the nave have the appearance of being Norman, but it is doubtful, as they are rather large. The windows seem to be mostly modern, with brick casing externally. There is a bad modern west window; one on the north is Decorated, of two lights; one on the south has two obtuse-headed lights. The walls are of flint, but there is an admixture of brick. The tower is very narrow from east to west, and externally presents a modern appearance of flint and brick; internally it rests on pointed arches opening to the nave and chancel. The western is very plain, upon imposts; the eastern is later, and upon octagonal shafts. On the south of the western arch, in the wall facing the nave is a plain pointed arch upon imposts. The chancel windows are modern and bad. On the south of the altar are three Perpendicular sedilia in one plan, with ogee cinque-foiled arches and trefoil panelling in the spandrels; the shafts between these have octagonal capitals, and above is a panelled and embattled cornice. On the north is a cinquefoiled niche, which looks like a piscina; if so, it is singularly placed. The west doorway has a pointed arch, the hood on head corbels. A similar doorway on the north is closed. There are three bells. The font has a plain octagonal bowl on a stem.

STELLING.

ST. MARY. 1868.

This church has a wide nave with south aisle, chancel, south porch, and western tower. The walls, as usual in the vicinity, are of flints, partly rough, partly fairly polished. The nave and aisle have separate high roofs, covered with tiles. At the west end of the aisle is a single lancet; two on the south have a single light, trefoiled, with ogee head, and at the east of the same aisle is a large, fine Decorated window of three lights, of which the upper part has been closed. The nave has on the north one single window, as on the south, and one short, two-light window with Decorated tracery; on the north is a closed doorway. The south doorway is a pointed one, with hood and good moulding, within a porch much patched. Between the nave and aisle the arcade, perhaps of two or three arches, has been thrown into one large wide arch, upon octagonal shafts. The west end of the aisle is carried past the tower. The tower arch to the nave is a plain pointed one on imposts; between the tower and end of the aisle is solid wall. The roofs of nave and aisle have tie-beams; as also that of the chancel. The chancel arch is pointed, and looks as if it was modern and of wood. The chancel is long, has on the north a single lancet, on the south two lancets, at the east end a good three-light Decorated window of reticulated tracery. There is a piscina on the south of the chancel, with trefoil head to the niche, and a shelf. The font has an octagonal bowl.

The nave is remarkably wide, but short. There has been no attempt at restoration or improvement; the pews are ugly, and there is a gallery in the aisle. The tower is very plain and low, reaching but little above the tiled roof of the nave; it is without parapet; on the west is a plain doorway and a single light, cinquefoiled window of Perpendicular character; in the stage above is a slit opening. The tower has been strengthened by buttresses of brick. The situation is bleak and lonely.

ELMSTEAD.

ST. JAMES. 1868.

The church is prettily situated, near a kind of spacious green, and a large ancient picturesque farmhouse, no regular village being close by. The church has a nave and chancel, each with north and south aisles carried to the east end, and a small tower at the west end surmounted by a wooden belfry, and a short spire, which is slated. The tower, which seems to be Early English, has a single lancet and added brick buttresses; on each side of it is a small wing north and south, with sloping roof, and opening to the tower internally by pointed arches. The belfry is boarded and supports the short spire. The walls are of flint. The nave is short and the south aisle does not extend quite to the west end. The arcades of the nave are Late Perpendicular, with Tudor-shaped arches and octagonal pillars. The chancel arch is pointed, and may be Early English, upon corbels with good mouldings, partly flowered. There are pointed arches between the aisles of the nave and those of the chancel, the northern having corbels resembling those of the chancel arch. The nave and aisles have tie-beam roofs with king-posts. The tower arch is pointed, on octagonal pillars, much hidden by a western gallery. The windows on the south side, both of nave and chancel, are mostly Perpendicular, but one near the west is of two unfoliated lights. In the north aisle they are also Perpendicular, of three lights, simply foliated. Near the east window of the south aisle are two stone brackets. The east end of the chancel presents three equal gables, two of which have Decorated windows, but the southern is Perpendicular, of three lights. There are some fragments of coloured glass in the east window of the south aisle. On the east respond on the south of the chancel is the figure of an angel bearing a scroll inscribed : " Pray for the sowlles of Cristofer Gay,* Agnes, and

---

* " He died 1507 " (see Hasted). Parsons, p. 57.—H.

Johana, his wyfes, their children and all xtian sowlys, on whose sowlys Jhu have mercy" (it is of the fifteenth century).

The font has an octagonal bowl, each face moulded with shallow arches, on a cylindrical stem with eight legs. The south porch is of flints, and has an open wood roof. In the south chancel are monuments to the Honeywoods,* and some post-Reformation brasses.

STOUTING.

ST. MARY. 1868.

This church has been almost wholly rebuilt, and now consists of a nave with north aisle, chancel, and a curious but unsightly steeple at the west end, which probably will be destroyed, as the base of a new tower is in progress at the west end of the aisle. The present steeple consists of a brick basement, with tiled sloping roof, upon which is set a boarded belfry with pointed roof, the upper part overhanging the lower. It seems not to be original, and is perhaps of the seventeenth century. The walls of the church are wholly of flints.

The aisle is an addition to the original plan, and is divided from the nave by three new pointed arches on octagonal pillars with round capitals. The nave has a covered roof; the floor is laid with tiles, and the seats are all open. The whole in very nice condition. The aisle has new double windows with trefoil-headed lights. On the south is one single lancet, and one Perpendicular window of three lights and square-headed, containing some fine old coloured glass,† with figures of saints under canopies and inscription: "Orate p. aiabs Rycardi—Stotyne et Juliane uxoris." The figures of the donor of the window, his wife and family, are represented kneeling. There is on a scroll "Miserere mei." The chancel arch is pointed, on new foliated

* The inscriptions are given by Parsons, pp. 54–59. H.
† "In this church the painted glass seems to have been preserved with some attention." Parsons, p. 134, where the glass is described. H.

corbels. The chancel has one lancet on the north, and two on the south; at the east is a flowing Decorated window, the arch carried on shafts. In the south-east window is a sedile graduated for three seats. There is a new piscina and fine reredos of stone. A vestry is added on the north, divided by a wood-screen. There is also a new font. All about the church is beautifully kept. The porch is of wood.

IVYCHURCH.
ST. GEORGE. 1868.

July 7. 1879.

A large church in the midst of scanty population, in Romney Marsh. It consists of nave and chancel, undivided, with north and south aisles, western tower and south porch, all of stone and principally of Decorated character verging to Perpendicular. The chancel is undivided from the nave without any break, and the aisles reach quite to the east end. The arcades are thus uninterrupted, each consisting of seven pointed arches on light octagonal pillars over which is a clerestory of quatrefoil windows, now closed, contained under a flat arch. The roof is of tie-beams and king-posts. The aisle roofs are flat. The windows of the aisles mostly Early Perpendicular of two lights, of nearly uniform pattern, but some are mutilated. On the north side one is Decorated, and at the west end of the same aisle is one of three lights with something of flamboyant tracery; a cinquefoil in the head. Another in the north aisle of the chancel is Decorated, and has a good hood on corbels internally. In the south chancel aisle two windows are Decorated. The east window of the chancel is a bold one, of five plain unfoliated lights beneath a pointed arch. That of the north aisle is a large Perpendicular one of five lights, that of the south aisle a flat arched one of three lights containing some fair fragments of coloured glass. The chancel occupies three bays out of the seven, and is marked by a portion of wood parclose screens, still remaining, and some of the original stalls with carved Perpendicular fronts. There are three steps of ascent to the sacrarium. The north aisle is almost wholly bare and waste, the raised altar platform remains, and in the east wall is the bracket of an image. The south aisle has also the altar platform and a stone bench against the wall. The font has a plain octagonal bowl on a large stem, raised on two steps. The interior is naked and forlorn, and very glaring, but the few scattered white painted pews, however ugly, do not block up the church, which is sadly too large for its scanty population. The tower arch is open, upon octagonal shafts. The tower is embattled and divided by two string courses, all of sandstone, has large buttresses on the west side, and at the north-east angle a polygonal turret reaching above the parapet, and having slit lights for a staircase. On the west side is a labelled doorway with quatrefoils in the spandrels, and a three-light window, of rather curious tracery, resembling Decorated. The belfry windows are Perpendicular of two lights, some pointed, one square-headed. There are five bells. There is a circular stair turret with slits at the north-west angle of the nave. The roofs are tiled; the buttresses of the body set at intervals. Under the aisle windows is a string, and on the north a plain doorway with continuous arch mouldings. The aisles have parapets. The south porch is large and embattled, having a parvise lighted by slits, and corner buttresses. The doorways are plain.

BROOKLAND.

ST. AUGUSTINE. 1868.

This church has a long nave with aisles, and a chancel undivided from the nave, but one bay of the arcade is carried along it, a north porch, a south porch, and a most curious detached belfry or campanile, wholly of timber, set at some distance away on the north side.

The church is of considerable length, and has high-pitched tiled roofs; the walls for the most part are covered with rough cast, modern brick buttresses have been added, and there has been some mutilation of the original work at the west end of the north aisle. Many of the windows of the nave are ugly Late Perpendicular with square heads. That at the west of the nave is better Perpendicular of three lights. The exterior has altogether rather a patched appearance. The arcades of the

LEADEN FONT, BROOKLAND CHURCH.

nave, which are out of the perpendicular, are each of six bays, the arches being pointed, on light octagonal pillars. The east respond on the north is an octagonal one, on a corbel-head. The north aisle is narrower than the south aisle, the roof of nave and aisles has tie-beams and king-posts. There is no arch of separation, or ascent to the chancel, along which each aisle is carried one bay, but the northern portion is separated for a vestry. The chancel has three single lancets on the north, and one on the south, with excellent arch mouldings within, and shafts on the north, the hoods are connected by strings. The east window is Perpendicular of three lights. Under the south-east window are two Early English sedilia, ascending eastwards, having good mouldings and shafts, and to the east is a piscina of similar design. The east window of the north aisle, or vestry, is Decorated, of three lights, containing some portion of good ancient coloured glass, of which there is some in other windows on the north. The east window of the south aisle is a large Perpendicular one of five lights. The interior is glaring with whitewash, and the pews are painted white, and very high. There is a fine Norman font, wholly of lead, having a cable moulding round the top, and surrounded by semicircular arches in two tiers, each springing from shafts, and each containing figures representing the signs of the zodiac, the names of the corresponding months being inscribed.* The north porch has a tiled roof and wood gable, its outer doorway is Perpendicular, with quatrefoiled spandrels. Adjoining this porch is a square turret for a staircase rising above the roof of the aisle and having trefoiled lights.

The curious belfry is wholly of wood, and holds five bells. It is of octagonal form, with conical shingled roof of three portions overlapping, all supported on very strong timbers set on the ground and crossing each other. It has no special architectural details.

DYMCHURCH.

ST. PETER AND ST. PAUL. 1868.

This church is not of tempting external character, being much modernised, in fact most of the outer walls have been rebuilt.† It has nave with north aisle and chancel, with a small

---

* The font is described and engraved in the "Archaeological Journal" for 1849, and also a full description, with engravings, is given in "Archaeologia Cantiana," vol. iv., p. 87. H.

† The church has recently been restored. H.

western tower. The latter seems to be modern, is without any architectural detail, and has a tiled belfry story. The nave and aisle are thrown into one by the removal of the arcade, but the seats are all open. There are Norman doorways at the west and south, almost exactly similar, having large shafts with indented capitals and abaci. There is a Norman chancel arch having a plain soffit, upon imposts, and an outer moulding with chevron ornament. The shafts are set in the angles, the northern has foliage, the southern sculpture in the capital, and to the south of this arch is a pointed arched recess in the wall, and adjacent to it in the south wall another of the same character.

The chancel is short, has a single lancet at the east end, and also on the north and south. On the south of the sacrarium is an oblong recess; and on the north side of the chancel there is a Norman doorway with cylindrical mouldings and shafts.

APPLEDORE.

ST. PETER AND ST. PAUL. 1868.

This church is on a commanding cliff, looking over Romney Marsh, and immediately above the military canal.

The church has a wide nave and chancel, each with south aisle (and a chapel north of the latter), and a western tower which is low and massive, scarcely rising above the high-pitched tiled roof of the nave. The greater part of the south side of the church is finely mantled in ivy.

The nave has on the south an arcade of four chamfered pointed arches on octagonal pillars with large plain capitals. The tie-beams in the aisle are set upon good spandrels with pierced tracery. There are some long windows on the north of the nave, of two lights, containing some fair fragments of old coloured glass in which canopies may be seen; these are of Early Perpendicular character. On the south of the nave is one Decorated window of two lights, and another similar at the west end of the aisle. There is also a later window of three lights with curious ogee arch, and another of late character, but dissimilar. There is no chancel arch or division of chancel. The roofs have tie-beams and king-posts, but there is a wood-screen across the entrance of the chancel, and dividing the south chancel from the south aisle of the nave. The interior is still pewed, and has a western gallery. There is a rood door up high on the south. The chancel roof is lower than that of the nave. The chancel is divided from the south aisle or chapel by a pointed continuous arch. This was formerly a chantry chapel, and has a pretty good Perpendicular east window of three lights; also a large piscina of the same character, with ogee canopy trefoiled and a stone shelf; also on the south side a fine sepulchral arch under a window, having good double feathering, and in the spandrels circles containing quatrefoils. The chancel has a plain pointed arch upon imposts on the north side, now closed, which once opened to the north chapel. On the same side is a priest's door. The east window is Decorated, of three lights, and has been restored. There are two lancets at the east end of the north chapel, which is set on transept wise. The north chapel is now wholly excluded and used as a school. The chancel is carried eastward of both side chapels. The font is Perpendicular, has octagonal bowl with shields and flowers, on stem of like form. The south porch is plain. The tower may possibly have some Early Norman work in its lower portion, but it is mostly Late Perpendicular, and has a stunted and unfinished look, being almost buried in the tiled roof of the nave. Its western doorway is large and good, the arch upon shafts, with excellent mouldings; the shafts have small octagonal capitals, and there are panelled spandrels; the whole is surmounted by a large label upon angel corbels bearing shields. Above are three heraldic shields. Above the door is a late features arrangement, consisting of three square-headed windows, the central one of two, the lateral ones of one light, all surmounted by one label. The tower has two string courses, and large buttresses at the angles. The belfry windows are late and square-headed, of two lights, labelled, except on the south, where they are replaced by two quatrefoiled circles. There are also similar quatrefoiled circles on the other faces, which displace the belfry window. The tower is covered with ivy, and has a plain bald battlement. The churchyard is very pretty, and shaded with trees.

OLD ROMNEY.
ST. CLEMENT.

July. 1879

1868.

This church has a wide nave, with south aisle not reaching to the west, and north chapel or aisle, chancel with north and south aisles, altogether a very irregular form, and a tower engaged at the west end of the south aisle; there is also a north porch. The masonry is rude; the roofs of high pitch and covered with tiles. The east end presents three equal gables. The nave has two rude pointed arches on the south upon a vast square wall pier with plain imposts, and a third arch, low and pointed, opens to the tower, which has on its east side a rude pointed doorway opening to the aisle. The north transept or chapel opens to the nave by a similar rude pointed arch on imposts. The nave is glaring with whitewash, and thoroughly unimproved in condition; the pews high, and mostly painted white. The west window is Decorated, of two lights. The roofs have the usual tie-beams and king-posts. There is a two-light Decorated window in the north transept, and one single light closed on its west side.

The chancel arch is wholly modernised, and masked in wainscoting, and the whole of the chancel has modern wainscoting. The east window is Decorated, of two lights. There is a plain pointed arch opening from the chancel to each aisle. The north aisle, now used as the vestry, has a lancet single window on the north, and at the east end a Perpendicular window, of three lights. In this chapel is a sepulchral slab with a kind of rude cross with herring-bone figure. The south chapel, which is now occupied by rubbish, has a Decorated east window, of three lights, an open roof, and some remains of wood screen work. It opens to the aisle of the nave by a rude pointed arch, like all the others on imposts. The font has a square bowl, on a central plain stem, and four angle shafts having square bases and capitals with Early English mouldings and varied figures and foliage. The north porch is plain. There is a pointed doorway at the west end of the nave. The tower is low, plain and rude, capped by a short shingled spire, has a single lancet at the west end, and buttress to the south-west.

ALDINGTON.

ST. MARTIN. 1873.

The church, standing conspicuously, but remote from the village, has a nave and chancel, each with south aisle, a south porch, and a lofty western tower. There is a very fine view from the churchyard over Romney Marsh. The tower is of very good Perpendicular work, and though lofty has never been properly finished at the top, which wants both parapet and pinnacles. It has large buttresses at the angles, on the west side is a good doorway, having Tudor arch and spandrels enriched with quatrefoil panelling. The arch mouldings are very good, and above the door is an ornamental tablet, with a series of panels, the centre having a fine ogee arch with niche and pierced spandrels. The tower has base mouldings with quatre-foiled panels containing shields. Near this door is a stoup. Over the door is a three-light window set between two fine canopied niches, the belfry windows are square-headed, of three lights and labelled, the intermediate stage has a single light labelled. At the north-east is an octagonal stair turret rising to the top. The church is earlier than the tower. The north side, which is not much seen, is plain and rough, bearing signs of decay and neglect.* It has two mutilated windows, the masonry is stone but inferior. The south aisle has also bad or mutilated windows, but near its west end it has a small slit window, which may have opened into some separate chamber. The chancel is of good stone masonry, and extends somewhat eastward of the south aisle. It has on the north three windows of two lights and good Perpendicular character. The east window, of five lights, is also good Perpendicular. The south chapel, which is chiefly of brick, has indications of Early English work, and at its east end are two lancets now walled up. On the south-east of the chancel is a two-light Decorated window. The arcades have pointed arches. The porch is of wood.

BECKENHAM.
ST. GEORGE. 1829.

This church is situated within a churchyard so completely shaded with trees as to darken the interior, but the scene is highly picturesque and beautiful. The building itself seems to be wholly Rectilinear, and consists of a nave with an aisle on each side, not co-extensive with the nave, a large chancel, and at the west end a square tower, crowned by a lofty spire of wood covered with lead. The windows have mostly square heads, and there is a plain south porch. Two pointed arches with octagonal piers, open on each side from the nave to the aisle. The roof is lofty, and the beams have pierced brackets. Above the pier, upon each side, is a large head corbel. The south aisle belongs to the Burrell family, and contains a monument to the late Lord Gwydyr. The north aisle contains a monument to the Hon. Mrs. Vansittart, wife of Lord Bexley. The south aisle contains a wood screen of late character. In the chancel is the print of a brass on a flat stone, which represented a figure beneath a crocketed canopy. In the north wall of the chancel is

* The church has been well restored.- H.

also a brass, date 1548, representing figures of a man and woman with several children. In the same wall is the monument of Mrs. Jane Clarke, who died 1757, with a beautiful epitaph by Gray, " Lo, where this silent marble weeps," &c.

The church also contains monuments to the late Lord Auckland and his Lady, and to Mrs. Lambton, first wife to Lord Durham. At the west end is a barrel organ.

BROMLEY.

ST. PETER AND ST. PAUL. 1829.

This church has a nave with aisles, a chancel, and a tower at the west end of the nave. The latter is Rectilinear, and built of flints, embattled, containing eight bells and a clock. The exterior of the church is much modernised. The original church consisted only of a nave and south aisle, the north aisle having been erected in 1792 at the expense of the then Bishop of Rochester. The south door is enriched with some curious wood carving, and has a singular old rude lock. In the interior the arches and piers have been removed, in order to facilitate the erection of galleries, excepting only the two west piers on the south, which are of octagonal form. The south aisle is carried to the west wall of the tower, and the west portion of it has a wood coved roof. There are north, south, and west galleries, the latter containing a fine organ. The chancel is small, but has a chapel on the south. The east window is large, and the arch supported within by shafts apparently Early Curvilinear; the mouldings of the arch are bold and good, but the tracery is gone, and most part walled up. In the north wall of the chancel is an arch of Curvilinear character, with triangular canopy, deep mouldings, feathering and shafts, with rich flowered capitals; within this arch was formerly a tomb, now destroyed.*

* This graceful relic of the Edwardian period is very small, and had originally in its centre a cylindrical aperture of about 6 or 8 inches diameter, within which was a deep rectangular sinking, or hole. It possibly was the shrine of a heart,

There is also a brass to one of the name of Thornhill, of about 1600, well preserved. The font is early, of square form, and of black marble, moulded with plain semicircular arches. The pedestal is modern.

WEST WICKHAM.
ST. JOHN.   1833.

The church is situated on high ground at a distance from the village, and contiguous to the mansion called Wickham Court. It is a plain structure of the age of Henry VII., consisting of a nave and chancel, each with a north aisle, and a plain square tower on the south of the nave, the lower part of which forms a porch. The exterior is rough cast. The windows are all of one character, late Rectilinear, and of two lights, except those at the east and west ends, which are of three lights. The nave is divided from the aisle by two plain pointed arches, having a massive octagonal pier with square capitals, the character of which appears earlier than the remainder of the church. The chancel opens to the nave by a pointed arch, and to its aisle by two pointed arches with mouldings, and an octagonal pier, lighter than that of the nave. Between the nave and chancel is a wood screen, coeval with the church. The ceilings of the church are of wood, flat, with plain panels. The north chancel has several fine portions of ancient stained glass in the windows, representing the Virgin, St. Catharine, and other saints. This chancel is hung with several ancient banners and helmets, and contains monuments to the Hobbes and Leonard family. There is also a trefoil niche and piscina. There are two well preserved brasses of rectors. The font is a plain octagon. The tower has the lower story forming the roof vaulted in stone.

which was enclosed in a case, and deposited within this deeply-sunk aperture. The mouth of the aperture has lately been filled in, with a closely-fitted piece of stone. Of nearly the same period is the small brass inscription to the memory of Isabella, wife of Richard Lacer (lord mayor of London). She died in 1361. There are late monumental brasses in the floor. There is also an inscription to the memory of Elizabeth, wife of Dr. Samuel Johnson, the lexicographer.-- R.

KESTON.

ST. ———.   1832.

This is a very small church, consisting only of a nave and chancel, built of flints, with a small wood turret at the west end. There seems to have been a south aisle originally, as there are two rude semicircular arches with a square pier built into the south wall. The chancel arch is semicircular and plain. In the chancel are some trefoiled lancets; the other windows are mostly modern. The interior is neatly pewed. The doorways are pointed, but plain.

DOWN.

ST. ———.   1832.

This is a small church, all in one space, with no distinction of chancel, and a plain tower at the west end, built of flints, and surmounted by a heavy shingled spire. The windows are chiefly Rectilinear and square headed, but there is one lancet on the south side. The tower opens to the nave by a pointed arch, and in its lower portion forms the vestry. The interior is neatly and even elegantly fitted up, the pews and pulpit are handsome, and there is a barrel organ. The roof is coved and boarded. The chancel contains a feathered niche. The east window has modern stained glass; the altar rails and table are handsome, and the altar cloth is a curious ancient one of damask. The font is a plain octagon. There are two brasses with small figures of the fifteenth century, and one larger one in the chancel of later date to John Vezeglini, Esq., born at Venice, and Elizabeth his wife, of the ancient house of Vanburen & Mace, of Antwerp. He died 1606, she 1607. Their figures are large and well executed, their costume being very good, and they are attended by groups of children. In the churchyard is a very fine yew.

ELTHAM.

ST. JOHN THE BAPTIST.   1830.

The church is a mean fabric, much patched and modernised; with scarce a trace of anything like good work, and from repeated alterations, the plan has become irregular. The nave has a south aisle, cased in brick; and a north chapel of stone, bearing the date 1667, with square-headed labelled windows, and a door of mixed Italian character. The chancel is wholly of brick. At the west end of the nave is a tower of flint, cased in brick, with large buttresses and pointed doorway, and surmounted by a spire of wood, covered with lead. The interior is neat and well pewed; with galleries all round, and a double one at the west end with an organ. The north chapel opens to the nave by three pointed arches with octagonal pillars.

The banqueting hall of the Palace remains in a very tolerable condition, and is a remarkably fine specimen of domestic Rectilinear architecture. It is built partly of brick, but chiefly of stone. The parapet is plain, the windows are set in pairs, each being of two lights; and there are doors with Tudor arch and label. The roof is a most splendid one of timber, the interstices of the framing being filled with pierced panelling. At the extremity of the hall, on each side, is a fine oriel, the windows long, and the ceiling elegantly groined.

The view from the Palace is remarkably rich and extensive.

DARTFORD.

HOLY TRINITY. 1829.

This is a large church, but the exterior has been much patched and modernised. It has a nave and chancel, each with side aisles. The tower is placed between the north aisle of the nave and that of the chancel; the lower part of the tower appears Early, the upper part is plain, and has an abrupt termination. The greater part of the church was originally constructed of flints; but parts have been rebuilt in brick, in an incongruous style. The west door is Curvilinear with good mouldings and shafts with foliated capitals. Above it is a good window of the same character, of five lights. Some other windows are Curvilinear, and some of Rectilinear character.

The clerestory windows of the nave are square-headed. The nave is wide and lofty, but the south aisle is narrow; the nave is separated from each aisle by three pointed arches, with octagonal piers. The nave has crowded pews and galleries, and an organ at the west end. The chancel has a fine wood ceiling, coved and panelled, and enriched with painting and gilt stars. To the north aisle it has three Early English pointed arches, and to the south two pointed arches with an octagonal pier. There is a good deal of wood-screen work about the chancel. In the east wall are traces of painting, and a niche for an image. In the south chancel are some brasses, much mutilated. On the north side of the chancel is a vestry, with some lancet windows, and a Rectilinear one at the east end.

In the chancel are two very fine brasses, one representing a male and a female figure beneath a rich canopy, with the following inscription, in black letter running round. "Hic jacent Ricardus Martyn de Derteford qui obiit vicesimo die mensis Aprilis anno dni millmo quadrengentesimo . . . . mensis ffebruarii anno dni millmo quadrengentisimo secundo, quorum aiabus ppicietur deus." Another in very fine preservation, commemorates the Lady Agnes Molyngton, daughter of John Appleton, Esq., who died 1454.

In the nave is a brass (date 1590) to Wm. Death, Esq., his wife and sixteen children. The font is an octagon, each face sculptured with two rude Early pointed arches; the pedestal is also octagonal.

HORTON KIRBY.

ST. MARY. 1831.

This is a neat cruciform church, built mostly of flints, with a modern tower rising from the centre of the cross. There are no side aisles, and the nave is very wide; the windows of the nave are mostly Rectilinear of three lights, but that at the west end is Curvilinear. The transepts and chancel contain some fine

Early English portions. The tower rises from four very lofty pointed arches, the piers having plain mouldings; the arches are not equal in breadth to the nave, and a bad effect is produced by their not being in the middle, but nearer to the north wall. The south transept has a triple lancet window, and two lancets on the east side, stopped up within larger arches. Beneath the windows runs a string course. Each transept has on the west side two semicircular arches; one of which, on the south side, is cut exactly in half by the wall of the nave, so that one half forms an opening into the nave, beyond the pier of the tower; the other arch is in relief in the transept wall. On the north side, the arch is cut so as to form a much narrower opening into the nave, and in an oblique direction; in the wall within this arch, is a small niche and piscina. There is a slab bearing a cross flory; and some brasses much mutilated or concealed by pews. The chancel is a very good Early English specimen; on each side are lancet windows having shafts internally, banded, and with fine foliated capitals; on the exterior some labels have been added which appear to be Rectilinear. The east window consists of three lancets, the central being the highest; the shafts have particularly rich foliated capitals. The whole interior is covered with glaring whitewash, but is very neatly pewed. The west doorway of the nave has on the exterior very good mouldings and clustered shafts, apparently Curvilinear; within the south porch is a plain stoup.

MEOPHAM.

ST. JOHN THE BAPTIST. 1831.

This is a large church beautifully situated, wholly built of flints, consisting of a nave with aisles and clerestory, a chancel, a tower at the west end, and porches north and south. The whole of the body is Early Curvilinear; but the tower is Early English, of massive proportions, divided into stages by string courses, and having small trefoil openings: it is surmounted by a shingled spire rising from a very heavy square base. Many of the aisle windows are Rectilinear of three lights; but at the east end of the north aisle is an Early Curvilinear one of three lights. In the chancel the side windows are of two lights without dripstones, but the east window is an elegant one of three lights, containing some fine stained glass; beneath the chancel windows runs a string course. The south porch is placed almost in the centre of the nave, and not as usual, nearer the west extremity. There is also a plain north porch. The nave has on each side five pointed arches with light octagonal piers. The clerestory has circular windows, containing quatrefoils set one over each pier. The chancel has on the south a priest's door, the head of which is of the form called a "shouldered arch." The font is a plain octagon with fluted sides. There is an early piscina on the south of the chancel. The exterior is of good flint work. On the north side of the chancel is a hagioscope, in which the original iron grating, or *grille*, may still be seen, although the opening is bricked up.

Meopham Church revisited, 1863.

The church is said to have been built by Archbishop Meopham, *temp.* Edw. III., with which period its architectural character agrees.* The roofs of the nave and chancel are high pitched and tiled. The seats are open; the pulpit is of fair Caroline woodwork.

TROTTESCLIFFE.

ST. PETER AND ST. PAUL.

July 1891. S. G. S.

1831.

This is a small church of mean exterior, consisting of a nave and chancel all in one space, with a plain tower on the south

* I have discovered at Lambeth in Archbishop Reynolds' Register (folio 135, b.) a record of the rededication of Meopham Church, after it had been rebuilt. The ceremony took place upon the 2nd of the Ides of May, 1325. W. A. S. R.

side, the lower part of which forms a porch. Some of the
windows are lancets, those of chancel on the north side very
obtuse; there are also some Curvilinear windows of two lights,
one of which contains good stained glass. The pulpit has some
curious wood carving of late date, apparently in the Dutch style.
The situation is very retired and lonely, immediately under the
range of chalk hill.

Exterior very finely restored - especially West wall

WEST FARLEIGH.
ALL SAINTS.

This small church is most pleasantly situated upon a bank,
overlooking the Medway, commanding a rich and delightful
view. It consists of a nave and chancel, with a small tower
at the west end of Rectilinear date, surmounted by a wooden
turret. The west door of the church within the tower is
Norman, of which character there is one window set very high
in the wall of the nave on the south side; the other windows of
the nave are both of Curvilinear and Rectilinear character. The
arch to the chancel is Norman and very low; in the east wall are
three small plain Norman windows set high, the central one
being the highest.

EAST FARLEIGH.
ST. ———.

This is a larger church than the preceding one, and consists
of a nave and chancel, each with a south aisle, and at the west
end a plain massive tower without buttresses, having a lancet
belfry window and surmounted by a heavy shingled spire. The
walls are mostly built of the Kentish rag stone; there is a large
Rectilinear porch of two stories on the south side; several of the
windows are Rectilinear, some are trefoiled lancets; one north of
the chancel is Curvilinear of two lights, and the east window is
Rectilinear of three lights. The nave is very neatly pewed, and
has four pointed arches dividing it from the aisle, with octagonal
pillars. The arch to the chancel appears to be Rectilinear; its

shafts have octagonal capitals; one plain pointed arch divides the chancel from its south aisle. In the south aisle of the chancel there is an arch in the wall, with good ogee canopy with feathering and finial, but the tomb is destroyed. In the north wall is a rich arch, with double feathering within a square compartment, the spandrels enriched with foliage and panelling. The font is a plain octagon. The situation of this church, overhanging the river Medway, is very pleasing, and commands a charming prospect.

TONBRIDGE.

ST. PETER AND ST. PAUL. 1833.

This church consists of a nave with aisles (the southern aisle having been recently added), a chancel, and a square tower at the west end, which opens into the nave by a low Early English arch, and has some trefoiled lancet windows; the belfry window is square-headed and the parapet embattled. The whole of the nave and tower are stuccoed; the chancel is not, it has a high tiled roof. The windows north of the nave are mostly Rectilinear, but one is Curvilinear of three lights. The south aisle is modern and quite plain; the nave is wide, and opens to the north aisle by five pointed arches of Early English character; the piers are lofty and circular, except one which is octagonal. There are galleries north and south, and one at the west end contains a fine organ. There is in the north aisle a monument to Alexander Weller, 1670, consisting of an open book inscribed with verses. The chancel arch is very wide. On each side of the chancel is a small plain Norman window; there are also some both Curvilinear and Rectilinear. The east window is of the latter character of three lights. In an arch in the wall south of the altar are alabaster figures of a man and woman, representing Sir Anthony Denton and his Lady, 1617.

The ruins of the Castle are highly picturesque and beautiful, but consist almost exclusively of the gateway, which is very perfect and handsome. It is flanked by two large round towers, and has above the arch two tiers of windows, the lower containing three trefoiled lancets (facing the south), the upper two windows of two lights with elegant Curvilinear tracery and dripstones. On the north front there are no corresponding windows. The arch of the gateway itself has bold and deep mouldings and a portcullis. The house, which is inhabited and adjoins the gateway, appears to be constructed of the old materials, and on the west side is a high mound, now planted, on which stood the keep, commanding a fine view; the whole is enclosed within private garden grounds.

WESTERHAM.
ST. MARY.

This church is beautifully situated on a rising bank, and if its steeple was more imposing would be a picturesque object. It appears to be wholly of Rectilinear work, consisting of three equal aisles; and at the west end is a low massive tower stuccoed, surmounted by an equally heavy shingled spire. The west door has a label, and over it is a window of three lights; the belfry window is square-headed, and there is a small door on the south side of the tower. The east end has three equal gables, each of which has a window of different character; that of the centre aisle of five lights is a mixture of Curvilinear and Rectilinear form; the south window of five lights is Curvilinear, and the north of three lights Late Rectilinear. Of the latter character are all the other windows of the church. The south porch is of wood, with a feathered gable of modern work. The interior is very neat and well fitted up. The nave has on each side four arches springing from light piers composed of four shafts with a hollow band in the intermediate spaces. In the chancel the arches (two on each side) are of Tudor form. Those on the north are lower; on the south there is one wide and one narrower. The southern arches have better mouldings than the northern. There is at the west end a good organ, which can be played either with keys or barrels. In the east wall is a piscina, trefoiled at top. The chancel is rather lower than the nave, and there is no clerestory. The font is octagonal, ornamented with quatrefoils, and has a panelled pedestal. Over the south door is the monument of General Wolfe. The windows on the south are later, merely foliated lights without tracery. On a brass :

> Orate pro aia Thome Potter filii Johnes Potter gēnosi q. quidem Thomas obiit vi' die Junii ano dñi MVCXXI. cui aie ppicietur deus.

There are some post-Reformation brasses.

Westerham Church has been fairly restored since 1850. The sacrarium is laid with fine new tiles. There is a new pulpit and some good wood-carving.

PENSHURST.*

ST. JOHN. 1829.

The church consists of a nave and a chancel, each with side aisles, and a large square tower at the west end, the whole Late Rectilinear, except the pillars on the north side of the nave, which are circular with banded capitals and on square bases; they appear to be Early English. The southern arches spring from octagonal pillars, and on each side of the nave are three arches. The tower is built of fine stone, and has an embattled parapet and four octagon turrets at the angles, crowned with large pinnacles. There is a west doorway of Tudor form, and the belfry windows are square-headed, of two lights with labels. The nave and chancel are in one continuous space, and are covered with a heavy tiled roof. The aisles of the nave are very narrow, and have tiled sloping roofs. The windows throughout the church are square-headed with labels, and Late Rectilinear, both

* Some improvements have been effected in Penshurst Church since this account was written.

in aisles and clerestory. At the west end of the north aisle is a plain lancet. The interior of the nave is rather handsome, being very wide and lofty, while the aisles are small. There is no architectural distinction of chancel, but its north and south aisles seem to have been later additions. It opens to that on the north by one Tudor arch on corbels, and one smaller arch, evidently opened in the original wall to the south aisle by two pointed arches upon an octagonal pier. This aisle has been adorned in a modern Gothic fashion, and contains an altar tomb of Late Rectilinear work to Sir William Sydney,* beneath a canopy adorned with the Tudor flower and panelling containing blazoned shields. The church is rich in monumental inscriptions; there is a brass in the form of a cross inlaid in a flat stone, in memory of Thomas Bwlloyen, son of Sir Thomas Bwlloyen. Another with brass effigies of a knight and lady thus inscribed: "Of your charitie pray for the sowle of Pawle Yden, gentleman, son of Thomas Yden esquyre, and Agnes his wyfe; the which Thomas deceased the 6th day of August, in the year of our Lord 1514, of whose sowle Jesu have mercy, Amen." There is in the chancel a piece of the effigy of Sir Stephen de Penchester,† in chain armour, with a shield; only the upper part remains and is set against a pillar. There are also other monumental remains. The font is octagonal, panelled with quatrefoils, containing shields charged with various devices: one, a cross; one, emblems of crucifixion; one, arms of the see of Canterbury; one (ihc x̄p̄c); one, I H R, &c.; the pedestal is panelled and enriched with tracery, but the whole is barbarously painted blue and red.

There is an organ which can be played either with fingers or by barrels. The churchyard is sequestered and shaded. In it is an ancient tomb, also one of modern date to Frances and

* Chamberlain, and after Steward to Edward VI.; died 1553, and the "fyft of that name."

† "Syr Stephen de Penchester" was warden of the Cinque ports, obt. temp. Edw. I.

Susannah Allnutt, with a poetical inscription, and dressed with evergreens and flowering shrubs.

> If tender pity ever touch'd your breast,
> Mourn for these much lov'd sisters, now at rest,
> And with their sorrowing parents drop a tear
> O'er every virtue which could life endear.
> There is no balm to heal parental grief,
> For worldly pleasures fail to yield relief.
> Sweet filial love can never be forgot,
> And Rachel weeps her children who are not.
> But deepest grief by Xtian hope is shared,
> And Faith's the rock on which that hope is rear'd.
> Hope points triumphally to joys more sweet,
> Where Faith has promised kindred souls shall meet.
> Maternal love records their early doom;
> O, could her prayers recall them from the tomb!

The Hall of Penshurst, originally a very grand ancient mansion, but now much altered and spoiled. The hall has a fine open roof and Curvilinear window of two lights, as well as a singular one of four lights in a depressed arch above the screen; and again above it, in the gable, two smaller windows of like character. The screen is of Gothic wood-work, and the brackets supporting the beams of the roof rest on large bold corbels representing figures.

LAMBERHURST.

ST. MARY.

The church is situated eastward of the village, closely adjoining the house of Mr. Morland, by whose grounds it is nearly surrounded. It is a picturesque building of grey stone, of the two later styles, and consists of a nave and chancel, each with a south aisle, and a tower with a shingled spire stands engaged at the west end of the south aisle. The windows on the north and south are all Curvilinear of two lights, that at the west end is Rectilinear of five lights, and the east window of the chancel is of the same character. The chancel has an arcade of three arches lower than those of the nave, and a fourth next the east is very much smaller and lower, with ruder capitals and bases set lower;

rather puzzling, whether part of an earlier construction or connected with a tomb.

In the third arch is a low stone screen, with circles containing pierced quatrefoils for ornamentation, and apparently forming a magnum sedile, or three seats thrown into one, having a stone elbow on the west end. Eastward is a rude pointed piscina, and an oblong aperture over it, perhaps for the same purpose as a stone shelf.

There is also an earlier kind of piscina or stoup, in form of a Norman capital, but loose and not *in situ*.

The walls lean outwards.

The roofs of both nave and chancel are good specimens of Kentish wood roof with tie-beams and king-posts.

The south porch is Rectilinear, and has a fine labelled doorway with spandrels panelled with quatrefoils. The tower is Rectilinear, and embattled with an octagonal turret on the south; on the west side a three-light window and square-headed belfry windows. Many of the buttresses of the church have triangular heads. The nave is divided from the south aisle by four pointed arches with octagonal pillars, and the chancel from its aisle by three smaller arches, with pillars of the same form, within one of which arches is part of a stone screen with some pierced quatrefoiled panelling on one side. There is a pointed arch between the aisle of the nave and that of the chancel, and south of the altar is a small square aperture in the wall. The font is a plain octagon. There are several modern monuments, but none of early date, or very remarkable character.

In the churchyard is a very fine yew tree.

HORSMONDEN.

ST. MARGARET.

This church, distant a mile and a half from Lamberhurst, and the same from Goudhurst, is beautifully situated at a distance from the village, upon rising ground in the midst of lovely rich and woody scenery. It consists of a nave with aisles, a chancel

with south chapel, and at the west end a very handsome
Rectilinear tower of excellent masonry, and built of picturesque
grey stone. It has a battlement and an octagon turret on the
south side, crowned by a plain pinnacle rising above the parapet.
The belfry windows are square-headed with labels; on the west
side is a very handsome doorway, the arch deeply moulded with
a label and shafts, and the spandrels filled with shields charged
with armorial bearings. Above is a good window, of three
lights. The body of the church has no battlement, the clerestory
has a tiled roof, which on the north side is carried down to the
side aisle so as to obscure the windows. The north porch is of
wood, having the gable with rich feathering. The chancel has
had the exterior scraped and modernised, but there remains a
cross on the gable. The windows are principally Late Rectilinear, some of two lights with flat arch and label, and some
square-headed. In the south chancel, which is evidently Late,
they are of three lights. There is one Curvilinear window of
two lights at the west end of the north aisle, also one on the
north of the chancel. The east window is likewise of three
lights, with good Curvilinear tracery. The south clerestory
windows of the nave are modern. The nave is divided from
each aisle by three pointed arches, the pillars alternately circular
and octagonal, the extreme arch towards the west, on the south
side, springing from a curious triangular bracket. The chancel
opens to the south chapel by two arches of contracted form with
an octagonal pier, within which is placed a wood screen of good
character, on which may be discerned the following inscription:
"Orate pro bono aie Alicie Campion." There is a little
stained glass, and over the east window of the south chancel is
a curious very small square opening glazed. South of the altar
is a cinquefoil niche, and in the chancel is a rich brass to an
ecclesiastic; above his figure is a rich crocketed canopy, and a
scroll on his breast is inscribed. The font is an octagon, with
roses and shields on the alternate faces. There are some
modern monuments to the family of Marriott.

GOUDHURST.
ST. MARY.

This is a large handsome church, of plain work externally, consisting of a nave and chancel with side aisles, and a low massive tower at the west end of the nave. The exterior is to all appearance of Late Rectilinear character; the tower is low, and altogether of debased work of the seventeenth century. It has a battlement, square-headed belfry windows, and a large window, of three lights, which exactly resembles those of St. Catherine Cree, Leadenhall Street, *temp.* Charles I., inserted on the west side; the north aisle is narrow and embattled; it has a boarded flat roof covered with lead; the south has a tiled roof and no battlement. On the north side, between the nave and chancel, is an octagonal turret for the rood stairs. At the west end of the south aisle is an adjunct of two stories, which seems to have been a vestry with priest's chamber over it, with embattled parapet and single windows with feathering and labels. Near the south door is a plain stoup. Most of the southern windows, and many of those of the north aisle, have been sadly mutilated; but the south chancel has at the east end a fine Rectilinear one of five lights, and on the south a square-headed one of three. There is a curious kind of oriel window in the south aisle, in good condition, and with tracery of Edwardian character, which has externally an embattled parapet. The interior is light and spacious, though it wants a clerestory; it is remarkably well pewed and neatly kept. The nave has five pointed arches on each side, with various piers: on the south there are two octagonal, one circular, and one of Rectilinear character with a shaft attached to each side. On the north two are circular and two octagonal. The south aisle is much wider than the others, and has a separate high-pitched roof, with good gables to the east and west, and a coved ceiling with ribs and bosses and tie-beams. The chancel is divided from each aisle by two pointed arches, with octagonal pillars. The church is very rich in tombs and monumental remains, many of which are particularly beautiful. Within the oriel on the south side of the nave is inserted a tomb beneath the sill of the window, with the wooden effigies of a knight and lady in very perfect condition, of the sixteenth century; the lady has a chain collar and head-dress; the man a collar and arabesque ornament on his legs; at the feet is a dog. On the sides of the window is some sculpture representing the Deity in clouds, and the story of Cain and Abel, and in another compartment are two figures kneeling at a desk with children behind, also kneeling. Within this oriel it is rather remarkable that a tree should be growing actually inside the church. The south chancel contains numerous monuments, to the families of Colepeper, Courthope, and Campion, among which may be noticed a rich brass representing a knight in armour beneath a rich ogee canopy with a lion at his feet; there is also an altar tomb of Rectilinear character, panelled with shields, &c., set under a canopy formed by a flat arch enriched with trefoils and roses, and richly panelled spandrels. Above it runs a rich band of panelling, and the whole is of unusual character, but has a good effect. There is likewise another mutilated brass to one of the Colepepers, to which family is also a large monument, commemorating Thomas Colepeper of Bedgebury, " eldest son of ould Sir Alexander C. also Sir Alex^r his sonne and Mary his wife, daughter of William Ld Dacre. (1599)." Their figures are sculptured, and also those of their children. There is a handsome marble monument to William Campion of Combwell, Esq., who married Frances third daughter of Sir John Glyn, Knt., and died 1702, aged sixty-three—with a fine bust. South of the altar is another large monument to Wm. Campion, Esq., of Combwell. The font is an octagon, the basin painted and modernised, the pedestal panelled with figures of animals, &c.

A gallery at the west end contains a neat finger organ, and the tower has a fine peal of eight bells.

(SUPPLEMENTARY ACCOUNT.)
1873.

Goudhurst church has been nicely restored, fitted up with neat open benches (save the south aisle, where are still high pews) and the chancel with stalls for surpliced choir, the organ being moved to the south aisle of the chancel.

The south aisle is still unrestored, but the altar tomb, panelled with shields bearing wooden effigies of a knight and lady of the Colepeper family, has been well restored and coloured. In the jamb of the window is some curious sculpture representing the Trinity and the Virgin Mary.

Near the tower arch within the nave are indications of original Early English mouldings. The tower arch is tall, pointed on octagonal shafts. The arcades of the nave have each five pointed arches, the pillar varying, both circular and octagonal, on high bases. One on the south is different and later, of fifteenth century. The nave has a new boarded roof. The chancel arch is pointed, the chancel has a new coved roof. The east window is of five lights and Perpendicular; it appears to replace an earlier window, of which there are some indications. But much of the wall is new. On the north of the sacrarium is a good two-light Perpendicular window with good new coloured glass. On the south is a pointed recess and plain oblong piscina. The reredos is tiled. In the north chapel is the base of the original screen, with good wood-carving. The south chapel has a good five-light east window, the south windows square-headed.

Brasses:—1. Knight in plate armour under ogee canopy. 2. Knight and lady (lady's figure gone). Colepeper.

YALDING.

ST. PETER AND ST. PAUL.

This is a good spacious church, consisting of a nave with side aisles, north and south transepts, and chancel, with a massive square tower at the west end, standing within the nave, and opening to the nave and aisles by pointed arches. This tower is earlier than the other parts of the church, and has obtuse lancet windows of rude workmanship; at the south-east corner is a circular turret: the top of the tower is plain, without battlement or cornice. It contains six bells. There are large porches north and south. West of the aisles are Curvilinear windows of two lights. The windows north of the nave are Rectilinear, but there is a Curvilinear one in the north transept: on the south most of them have been mutilated. The nave has no clerestory, but opens to each aisle by four pointed arches with octagonal pillars; a fourth arch on each side opens to the transept. The roof of the nave is coved and boarded, part being divided into panels, with good bosses at the intersection of the ribs. In the south transept are some niches in the east wall, stopped up. In the south wall is a tomb under a fine Rectilinear arch, with double feathering and panelled spandrels; the effigy is gone; near it is a niche with triangular head.

The chancel has, on the south, two lancet Early English windows with dripstones connected by strings. The east window is Rectilinear, and there is one of a like character on the north side.

The font is a plain octagon, on a pedestal of like form.

NETTLESTEAD.

ST. MARY.

This small church displays some specimens of very handsome Rectilinear work. It consists only of a nave, a chancel, and a small tower at the west end with a tiled roof, greatly inferior in character to the rest of the church. It is built of good stone; and the nave is very lofty; it has on each side three large windows, each of three lights, containing some very good painted glass, one on the north side being entirely filled with representations of saints beneath rich canopies, and armorial bearings;

the colouring is very fine; beneath one of the south windows is a porch with doorway of Tudor form; the buttresses have triangular heads. The interior is neat and well pewed. The chancel is lower than the nave, it has side windows of two lights, and one at the east end of three lights, with much painted glass.* The arch between the nave and chancel springs from shafts with octagonal capitals. The altar-piece is very neat, in the Corinthian style. The font is a plain octagon, upon a square pedestal. The church stands on rising ground above the Medway, and commands a charming prospect.

WATERINGBURY.
ST. JOHN.

This church consists of a nave, with large chapel on the north, a chancel, and a tower at the west end, surmounted by a shingled spire. The tower is Early English, having three stages of plain lancets, and opening to the nave by a plain pointed arch upon imposts. On the west side of the nave by the tower is a plain lancet window. The other windows of the nave are Rectilinear of three lights. There is also a south porch of Rectilinear character, the doorway having a label. The chapel on the north side of the nave has been rebuilt, and has a window which is a very fair imitation of Rectilinear work; it opens to the nave by a large wide pointed arch. The chancel is lower than the nave and has an east window, Rectilinear, of two lights; on the south side are windows with square heads. On the north side is a vestry of the same style. South of the altar is a Rectilinear

* Two of the scenes, now inserted within the east window, were formerly portions of the painted glass which formed " St. Thomas's window " (the westernmost upon the north side of the nave). Mr. Charles Winston considered that they were painted between 1425 and 1439. He identified one scene as depicting the triumphal entry of Archbishop Becket into Christ Church, Canterbury, after his reconciliation with the King, when all the monks of Christ Church met and welcomed him at the old cemetery gate of the monastery, in Burgate, which stood a few yards eastward of the existing gateway. The other scene shews sick people at Becket's shrine. (*Vide* "Archæologia Cantiana," vol. VI., 129-134.)—R.

niche, and on the north a very large and gorgeous monument to several of the Style family, of the age of James I.

The font is octagonal, with plain panelling, upon a shaft of the same form. The churchyard is finely shaded with trees, and contains a remarkably fine yew.

BARMING.
ST. MARGARET.

This church is in a lovely situation, very retired, and entirely surrounded by wood and hop gardens. It consists only of a nave and chancel, with a square tower at the west end surmounted by a tall shingled spire of rather elegant proportions. The tower is of good stone, and of plain Rectilinear character, with a battlement and an octagonal turret on the south side. The south porch is plain; in the nave are some Curvilinear windows of two lights, and on the south side is one small single light, feathered and set very low down. The chancel opens to the nave by a pointed arch springing from octagonal shafts. The east end of the chancel is very early and plain, and contains three small plain Norman windows, one set near the apex of the gable, the other two in a line lower down, but high up in the wall. The font is a small plain octagon.

DITTON.
ST. PETER.

This is also a small church, consisting only of a nave and chancel, with a plain square tower at the west end, having neither buttress nor battlement, but apparently of Rectilinear character. In the nave are two windows of two lights, the tracery of which appears to be Curvilinear, but the arch is of a contracted form. One of them contains some stained glass. The chancel arch is pointed and quite plain. In the chancel are some single-light windows with square heads, feathered, and others of very bad modern character. There is an organ, played with the fingers.

WEST MALLING.

ST. MARY.

The remains of the abbey form the principal object of attraction in this place, and their chief feature is a very fine Norman tower, of considerable dimensions and great beauty. This tower is square in its lower part and octagonal above; it has corner turrets of corresponding form, which are crowned by large pinnacles. The tower has several tiers of ornament, the lowest containing a range of rude semicircular arches without mouldings or shafts. The upper part is clearly of later date; it has ranges of semicircular arches, with rich chevron ornaments in the mouldings, and clustered shafts with fine capitals; those in the highest stage are banded round the middle. There are some windows of later date inserted in the tower. Besides this, there is another large square tower, very strongly built, of rude, plain Norman work. The gateway is principally Rectilinear, and has doorways with Tudor arches, having shields in the spandrels, and finely moulded, but there is one very early Norman arch in the gateway, upon imposts, resembling the Roman character, and very low. The Abbey House, now occupied as a farm, is of good Rectilinear work, about Henry VI., the gables have wood feathering, and the windows are square-headed.

The parish church is a large building, the nave of which is modern, and built of Kentish ragstone in 1778, in a neat style, but not harmonizing with the rest of the building. The tower at the west end is a very early Norman specimen, said to have been erected by Gundulph, Bishop of Rochester. It is massive, and has very thick walls; the buttresses are flat. Some of the windows have pointed heads, but all are rude and plain. It is surmounted by a lofty shingled spire. The chancel is Early English, and has on the north three lancet windows, with plain mouldings externally, but within they have richer mouldings and shafts. On the south is one trefoiled lancet. The east window has three lancets, included within a moulded arch, with shafts having bell capitals; beneath the windows runs a string course. South of the chancel is a range of three arches in the wall, with good mouldings, one forming a doorway, and on the south of the altar is a vestry, and a large, gaudy, marble monument to Sir Robert Brett. Knt., 1620. There is an organ at the west end of the nave.

OFFHAM.

July. 1891. R.A.

ST. MICHAEL.

This church is situated in a churchyard entirely shaded by large trees, and at a distance from any houses. It consists of a nave and chancel, with a tower placed on the north side, about the centre. The exterior is plain, the roof tiled; there are some Early English portions, and some of later date. The tower opens to the church by a very rude pointed arch, and is of very plain character, without buttresses; the upper part is later, with a single-light belfry window having a label, and the parapet is plain. On the east side of the tower is a small Curvilinear window of two lights. The windows of the nave are mostly square-headed, with Curvilinear tracery; that at the west end is Rectilinear, and above it is a small circle quatrefoiled, but now walled up. The south porch is Rectilinear. The interior is mean and neglected. On the south of the nave is a trefoiled Rectilinear niche with piscina. The chancel opens to the nave by a pointed arch. The chancel has several lancet windows, and on the south is a low side window, with square head and Curvilinear tracery. The east window is Curvilinear, of three lights, and contains some good stained glass. On the south of the altar is a trefoil niche and piscina. The exterior is very ragged and out of repair. In the tower are three bells.

BYRLING.

ALL SAINTS.

This church stands upon a lofty bank, and is a tolerably large building, consisting of a nave with aisles, a chancel, and a tower at the west end. The tower and chancel are Rectilinear, but the nave contains some earlier work. In the south aisle are two trefoiled lancets, and at the east end of the same is a double lancet, with trefoiled heads. There is also a similar window on the north, and one Curvilinear of two lights. The roofs are all tiled, and there is no clerestory. The nave is wide, and divided from each aisle by four pointed arches with octagonal piers. The chancel is lower, and has a flat boarded ceiling, panelled; on its south side are four square-headed windows, each of two lights, with label, and quite uniform. On the north are three very curious plain windows of small size, with square heads, and set obliquely in the wall, looking towards the east. The east window is of six lights, within a contracted arch. On the north side of the chancel is a tomb arch in the wall, and a doorway stopped up. South of the altar is a plain stone stall, and a niche with piscina; there are also some ancient wood stalls and pew ends. In the south aisle of the nave is the brass of an ecclesiastic, with this inscription, "Of your charite pray for the soule of Water Meylys sum tyme Tewter unto my lord of Bergavenny, the whych decesyd the xv. day of Marche, 1522." The font is a plain octagon. The tower has a battlement and an octagonal turret on the south-east corner; the belfry windows are square-headed of two lights. The west doorway has a Tudor arch, and quatrefoils in the spandrels; above it is a two-light window. There are six bells.

SNODLAND.

ALL SAINTS.

The church stands close upon the River Medway; it is a neat structure, in very good repair, and of tolerable size, con-

Snodland.

sisting of a nave with side aisles, chancel, and a massive tower on the south side of the nave, the lower part of which forms a porch. The latter is Rectilinear and embattled, has the windows all with square heads, and opens to the church by a moulded, pointed arch. The nave and aisles are included under one tiled roof, without a clerestory. Most of the windows of the nave are Curvilinear, of two lights, but there is one on the south side of Norman character, set high in the wall, and in a transverse direction. The pews are modern and uniform, and there is a barrel organ, presented by the Rev. Mr. Phelps, the present rector. The nave is divided from each aisle by four pointed arches with circular pillars; their capitals and bases are moulded. The east end of the north aisle is inclosed by a wood and there is some ancient stained glass in the heads of the windows of this aisle. The chancel opens to the nave by a pointed arch with octagonal shafts. The chancel has some windows Curvilinear, others of lancet form, of which one has a trefoiled head. The east window is Rectilinear, of four lights. The altar table is handsomely carved, *temp.* James I. South of the chancel is a large feathered arch, within which is a stone seat, and also a trefoil niche with moulding. There are a few brasses, with figures of ecclesiastics, and one with a cross flory.

The font is a plain octagon.

WROTHAM.
ST. GEORGE.

This is a large and respectable structure, principally of the two later styles, consisting of a broad nave with aisles, a chancel, and a tower at the west end. The roofs are tiled, and there is no battlement or clerestory. The tower is of plain Rectilinear work and has a turret attached to the north side; it is chiefly remarkable from having a curious arched passage through the lower part, having strong stone groining. There is a large south porch, also of Rectilinear work, having two stories, the lower has a good groined ceiling, the ribs having shields for bosses; there is a niche over the door, and an octagonal turret attached to the west side. The room over the porch is used for parish meetings. The nave is of considerable width, and is separated from each aisle by four pointed arches* with circular pillars having moulded capitals. Some of the windows of the nave are Curvilinear with square heads, others are of Rectilinear character. The arch to the chancel springs from circular shafts, and has within it a wood screen, on the north side of which is a staircase turret.

The chancel has on the north side a very elegant Curvilinear window, of three lights; and on the south one of Rectilinear character. The east window and several others have been shamefully mutilated.† The chancel is paved with marble, and there is a vestry on the north side. There are some brasses of the fifteenth century to the family of Peckham, and a more recent monument to Mrs. Helen Betason, who bequeathed large sums to Bromley College, and other institutions.

The font is Early English, of octagonal form, each face moulded with two plain pointed arches; the shaft is of cylindrical form, and is attached to one of the pillars of the nave.

IGHTHAM.
ST. PETER.   1831.

This beautiful village presents one of the most picturesque scenes in the county, and contains some ancient houses with gables enriched with most elegant wood feathering. The church is a plain structure, consisting of a nave with narrow aisles, a chancel and a tower at the west end of plain work, much patched and modernised: the north aisle is also rebuilt in brick. The south porch has a wood roof; the windows of the aisles are mostly of Rectilinear character, but not good. The

---

* Of Early English character.—R.
† This church has since been admirably restored throughout. —R.

nave is separated from each aisle by two wide pointed arches, springing from octagonal pillars. The chancel has the east window Curvilinear, and on the north a square-headed one of

WINDOW, IGHTHAM CHURCH.

two lights, with tracery, also of Curvilinear period,* beneath which, in the wall, is a monumental arch, richly feathered,

* This window was inserted by the executors of Sir Thomas Cawne, whose will, made about 1373-4, set apart the sum of £20 " for one window to be made in the north part of the church of Eyghtham." ("Archæologia Cantiana," IV., 223.) E.

surmounted by a label, and the spandrels panelled; beneath the arch is the effigy of Sir Thomas Cayne, in complete armour, with belt, sword, and dagger, and on his breast the armorial bearings, a lion couchant à la double queue. On the south side of the chancel is a small window with trefoil head set obliquely, as those at Byrling, and containing painted glass representing a figure with the inscription on a scroll, "*Dñe miserere mei.*"

The roof at the nave is coved, and has beneath it a cornice with small battlements in wood. The pulpit and the west gallery are of the age of James I., the latter bears the inscription, "The work of Sir William Selby of the Mote, Knyte, to the glory of God and use of this church," 1619. The font is a plain octagon. The pew belonging to the Selby family is inclosed by a wood screen.

In the chancel are some very rich monuments to the Selbys of the Mote in this parish. One of the age of Elizabeth or James I., to the memory of Sir William Selby, is in two stages, each containing a recumbent effigy. Another, most highly curious, is to the memory of Dame Dorothy Selby who died 1619. It is at the east end, on the north side of the altar, and is a mural monument containing the half-length figure of an elderly female within an oval recess, probably an excellent portrait; at the back of the figure within the recess are two tablets, supposed to represent some of her needlework, the upper of which represents Adam and Eve in three different situations, first, receiving the apple, then falling down prostrate when detected, lastly, driven out of Paradise. The lower tablet, which is of slate, is a curious allegorical picture relating to the Popish Plot, above which is inscribed in one line, "Trinuni Britannicæ bis ultori in memoriam classis invincibilem subversæ proditionis nefanda delicta Dei;" below this on the left side is a tent inscribed " In perpetuam Papistarum infamiam;" and there are represented the Pope, Cardinals, Monks, and a Spanish Don assembled at a council board. Above all is a figure with distended cheeks blowing a blast after the ships which occupy the centre, above the wind is inscribed, "*Diflo.*" Over the ships is represented Jehovah and an angel blowing a blast bearing the inscription "*Dissipo.*" The right hand side represents the Parliament house and Guy Faux with a dark lanthorn attempting to set it on fire; over him inscribed, "*Fax Faux quantillum abfuit.*" An eye in the clouds darts a ray inscribed, "*Video, rideo,*" over the Parliament house is "*Opus tenebrarum.*" The whole of this is very difficult to distinguish from below, and is much concealed by the bust. The monumental inscription runs thus:—

D. D. D.

TO THE PRETIOUS NAME AND HONOR

OF

DAME DOROTHY SELBY

THE RELICT

OF

SIR WILLIAM SELBY

THE ONLY DAUGHTER AND HEIRE

OF

CHARLES BONHAM, ESQRE.

She was a Dorcas
Whose curious needle turn'd the abused stage
Of this bad worlde into the golden age,
Whose pen of steele and sileken inck enrolled
The acts of Jonah in records of gold.
Whose arts disclos'd that plot which had it taken,
Rome had tryumph'd, and Britain's walls had shaken.
She was
In heart a Lydia, in tongue a Hanna,
In zeale a Ruthe, in wedlock a Susanna.
Prudently simple, prudently wary,
To the world a Martha, and to heav'n a Mary.
Who put on } in the yere of her   age 69.
immortality }   Redemption 1641.

EAST PECKHAM.

ST. MICHAEL.

This church, from its very elevated situation forms a most conspicuous object from the neighbourhood of Tonbridge, and for some way along the Hastings road. It stands quite at a distance from any houses, and the view from the churchyard is very grand and extensive. The building itself is large, and chiefly of Rectilinear work. It has a nave and chancel, with a co-extensive north aisle, and at the west end a lofty, but very plain, tower, without battlement. The nave is divided from the aisle by three pointed arches with circular pillars; the chancel has two wide arches with an octagonal pier. The windows are all Rectilinear, of different sizes and tracery, but mostly of three lights, those on the north are mostly with square heads; there is one set very high up, as if to give light to the rood loft. The south porch has a Tudor door-arch with label, and panelled spandrels. There are scraps of stained glass in some of the windows. The east end of the north chancel is inclosed by a wood screen of late date.

SEVENOAKS.
ST. NICHOLAS.

July 1885.

This is a large and handsome church, built of Kentish rag, and all of Rectilinear work, excepting perhaps part of the north aisle, which has windows of two lights, apparently Curvilinear. The exterior is very well preserved, and the general outline good. The nave and chancel have each side aisles, the nave has a clerestory, the aisles and the south porch are embattled; the latter is large and handsome, of two stages, with an octagonal staircase turret. The tower at the west end is lofty * and good, resembling many others in the neighbourhood. It is three stories in height; the west door is set in a square compartment with panelled spandrels, above it is a good window of five lights; the belfry windows are square-headed; there is a battlement and octagonal corner-turret. It contains a clock and eight bells. The windows are mostly of three lights, except those on the north before mentioned; and those of the clerestory are of four

* The tower is said to be 99 feet high.—R.

lights, but not large. The interior is handsome and in good order, the length very considerable; the nave has five lofty pointed arches on each side with octagonal piers, the chancel has two, with light lozenge piers of clustered shafts. The roof of the nave is groined in wood; that of the chancel is coved, boarded, and panelled. On the north of the chancel is a vestry embattled. The font is octagonal panelled with quatrefoils.* At the west end is a very large organ. There are few monuments deserving of notice, but Lambarde, the Historian of Kent, is buried here, and the Lambarde chapel is at the west end of the north aisle. The view from the churchyard is very delightful.

SEALE.

ST. PETER.

This church has a nave, chancel, and south aisle,† and at the west end a Rectilinear tower which is quite a counterpart of that at Sevenoaks, containing five bells. The south doorway has the spandrels panelled. There are some Rectilinear windows, and some square-headed ones that appear Curvilinear, some containing scraps of stained glass. The nave is divided from the aisle by three pointed arches, with one circular and one octagonal pillar. The chancel opens to its aisle by one wide contracted arch with octagonal shafts; in the pier between the nave and chancel is a square aperture for a door to the rood loft. The pews are very neat and uniform, and there is a double gallery at the west end. In the south wall of the chancel is a small niche with a piscina of octagonal form, likewise a square recess in the wall. Within the altar rails is a very fine brass of a knight, in

---

* Containing carvings, each panel bearing a different subject : (i.) a shield bearing the instruments of our Lord's Passion ; (ii.) arms of the See of Canterbury ; (iii.) and (iv.) Tudor roses ; (v.) a lion's head within a circular cable ; (vi.) a shield bearing a chevron between three trees ; (vii.) a grotesque head ; (viii.) defaced. The pulpit now in the church is dated 1635 ; it originally belonged to Wrotham Church.—R.

† A north aisle has since been added.—R.

perfect preservation; he is represented with a lion at his feet, the arms are three piles, the inscription which runs round is perfect, and as follows: "Hic jacet dns Willms de Bryene, miles quondam dns de Kemsyng et de Sele, qui obiit. xxiii° die mensis Septembr anno dni Mccclxxxxv cuius ale ppiciet° Deus, Amen." At the four angles are medallions bearing the emblems of the four Evangelists, the Angel, the Bull, the Lion, and the Eagle. This is one of the earliest brasses that is to be found. The font is a plain octagon. The pulpit is carved, *temp.* James I.

CHEVENING.

ST. BOTOLPH. 1835 and 1859.

This church consists of a nave and chancel, each with a south aisle, and a good tower of Rectilinear character at the west end. The latter has a door on the west side with label and panelled spandrels, above which is a four-light window; there is also a corner turret. The south aisle does not extend to the west of the nave, but quite to the end of the chancel, its eastern part being appropriated as a burial chapel of the Stanhopes; and divided from the rest by a pointed arch. There are three Early English arches in the nave, and two in the chancel, with circular columns. In the north wall are seen three similar arches and pillars, showing that a north aisle once existed. The roofs are tiled. The nave is divided from the south aisle by three wide pointed arches with circular pillars having moulded capitals. The windows are some Curvilinear with square heads, but mostly Rectilinear. The chancel is divided from its south chapel by two pointed arches with a circular pier. There is no chancel arch, and the chancel has a coved waggon roof with ribs and bosses. The chancel windows are Perpendicular. The tower is Perpendicular, embattled, with octagonal turret at the north-east. The tower arch is lofty and continuous. There is a modern font, and a barrel organ.

In the south chapel of the chancel is a piscina with shelf and three sepulchral arches, and there is a square locker in the east wall. It contains also some handsome monuments to the Stanhopes, of the sixteenth century, and one most beautiful modern one by Chantry to Lady Frederica Stanhope, considered one of the best specimens of modern statuary. There is a vestry north of the chancel. A south porch has a wooden gable.

The church was restored in 1858, and fitted with open seats, and a new south porch was built. The newly inserted windows are Decorated, of two lights, but one ancient small Norman one remains south of the nave.

FARNBOROUGH.
ST. GILES.

This is a small church, of little beauty or interest; consisting only of a nave and chancel, with a very low tower at the west end. It is built of flint and chalk, and the roof is tiled. On the north side of the nave is a kind of projection, opening to the nave by a wide pointed arch. The windows of the nave are mostly Rectilinear, some modernised. The chancel is Early English, and has three plain lancet windows on each side; at the east end is inserted a square-headed Late window, in the place of one of Early English date, of which remain the foliated capitals of shafts now gone. North of the chancel is a good marble monument, date 1673, to Thomas Brome, Esq. The font is a good one, apparently of Curvilinear period; its form octagonal, and three faces are enriched with varied tracery of excellent character. At the west end of the nave is a double gallery, and a small barrel organ. The church is said to have been rebuilt in 1639.

OTFORD.

ST. BARTHOLOMEW.

This church has a nave, chancel, and south aisle, with a massive early tower at the west end, surmounted by a heavy shingled spire. The walls of the tower are very thick and without buttresses; it has a few small rude windows, some with pointed, others with semicircular heads. It opens to the nave by a plain pointed arch, and has on the west side a semicircular arched doorway, in front of which is a wooden porch of the sixteenth century. The north side of the nave has Curvilinear windows of two lights; the south aisle is evidently a later addition, and is separated from the nave by a row of wooden pillars. The windows on that side appear to be of Late debased character. The chancel has an east window of five lights, of very good Curvilinear tracery; on the north side is a small vestry of Rectilinear character, which contains a fine tomb of the same character, under a canopy with panelled soffit and a cornice of Tudor flower. There is also in the chancel a fine marble monument to Charles Polhill, Esq., who died 1755.

Near the church are considerable remains of the castle or palace of the Archbishops of Canterbury, exhibiting a fine specimen of brickwork, *temp.* Henry VI. There is a handsome octangular tower of three stories, having double square-headed windows, besides many other interesting portions.

EYNESFORD.
ST. MARTIN.

The church is a very interesting building, constructed of flints, and consisting of a nave with north aisle, a south transept and a chancel with semicircular east end, forming an excellent specimen of Early English work. At the west end is a tower of Norman work, surmounted by a tall shingled spire. The tower is plain, and has very thick walls; on the west side is a Norman doorway, within a porch of Rectilinear style; this doorway is of excellent character; the outer arch is enriched with double chevron ornament, and has shafts, the capitals of which have the abaci enriched with lozenge ornament and the rope under them; the head of the arch is fitted with stone-work, divided into a number of small panelled compartments each containing a kind of lozenge ornament; the door itself has a pointed arch, small and low, evidently a later insertion; the shafts are very richly ornamented with the chevron and twisted ornaments. The arch from the tower to the nave is pointed. The windows of the nave are all Rectilinear of late date; the north aisle, which does not extend to the west end, is divided from the nave by two pointed arches with an octagonal pillar. The roof beams of the north aisle rest upon carved brackets. The south transept is Early English, and has three plain lancets upon each side; at the south end there is a circle in the gable now walled up. The transept is walled off from the church. The chancel is by far the finest portion, and is of rich and beautiful Early English work. It opens to the nave by a pointed arch springing from octagonal shafts, having upon them pedestals for statues. The east end of the chancel is semicircular and has three fine lancet windows, the exterior arches of which have plain mouldings; but the interior arches are very richly moulded, and have shafts with bell capitals and bands. On the north side are two smaller Early English windows, opening to the interior by moulded arches with shafts; over them are moulded pointed arches in the wall, which seem intended to have formed a groined stone ceiling; these windows present, externally, an appearance of later work, having labels over them. The roof of the chancel is of timber, and there was above the windows a wooden embattled cornice. The space enclosed within the altar rails is unusually large; there is a niche with mouldings and shafts containing a piscina; the paint has been taken off this niche, but the rest of the church is glaring with whitewash. In the chancel are two stone coffins. The font is an octagon, each face charged alternately with shields and roses, the shields bearing different devices. At the west end of the nave is a double gallery.

FARNINGHAM.

ST. PETER AND ST. PAUL.

This church consists of a wide nave and chancel, with a square tower at the west end. There are no side aisles. The tower is Rectilinear, and also the windows of the nave; the tower is embattled, with an octagonal corner turret, and opens to the church by an arch of Tudor form. The chancel being unusually narrow leaves room for windows on each side of the arch in the nave. It has three lancet windows on each side, and opens to the nave by a plain pointed arch, on each side of which is an octagonal turret lighted by a lancet window on the east side. There is also a wood screen in the chancel arch; in the south wall there is a feathered arch for a tomb, and some niches walled up. The font is the most remarkable object about the church, and is a beautiful specimen of Curvilinear or Rectilinear work. The form is octagonal, and each face is richly sculptured with figures, in fine condition, possibly representing the Seven Sacraments. This font is engraved in the Custumale Roffense. Round the base of the shaft is a panelled band with quatrefoils. The whitewash has been carefully taken off. The interior of the church is neatly arranged, and the churchyard offers a pleasing scene, shaded by high trees. The church is wholly built of flints.

DARENTH.

ST. MARGARET.

This church consists of a nave with south aisle and a chancel, with a square tower at the west end of the south aisle, crowned by a shingled pyramid, the base of which overhangs the tower. The tower appears to be Early English, having small lancet windows; the nave and aisle appear to be Rectilinear, but the chancel is much earlier and highly curious, being in two divisions, the western of which opens to the nave by a pointed arch, and is of Early English character; the eastern portion is Norman of a very early character. The nave is divided from its aisle by three pointed arches with octagonal pillars: the last arch at its eastern extremity, springs from a bell capital with a head corbel. The western part of the chancel had once an aisle on the south, there being built into the south wall two pointed arches, with a massive circular pier having a square capital, upon which there are traces of some ancient painting. In this portion are some lancet windows and one Late Rectilinear one. In the interior on each side against the wall is a stone seat, eighteen inches in height, running beneath the windows, and upon it stands the circular pillar on the south side.

The eastern portion of Norman work, is approached by an ascent of several steps; it has a stone vaulted ceiling somewhat low, forming a semicircular arch, of very plain character, without ribs. At the east end are two heights of windows; in the upper are two of lancet shape walled up, situated between the vaulted ceiling and the real roof; between these lancets is a circle. Above these, in the upper part of the gable, is a cross worked in flints. The lower stage contains at the east end three very narrow windows, the central one being the highest, with semicircular heads, giving light to the chancel. They are deeply recessed in the wall, and externally are surrounded by a course of stones set alternately in large and small squares. A similar course runs up each corner of the east end; this appears to be a test of very early work. On the north side of this chancel is a Norman window; on the south is inserted one of Rectilinear date, but in the south wall is seen a string of chevron ornament.

The font is a very splendid Norman one, of cylindrical form, sculptured all round with a range of semicircular arches rising from shafts with square capitals; within the arches are figures of centaurs, griffins, &c., but in one is the figure of a king, and in another is represented the rite of baptism.

SOUTHFLEET.
ST. NICHOLAS.

This church is a good structure consisting of a nave with aisles, a chancel, and a square tower at the west end; all being of Curvilinear work with no admixture of other styles. The walls are principally of flints, and the tower chequered, the latter is three stages in height, crowned by a battlement with a turret attached; the lower stage has a plain door and a two-light Curvilinear window, the two others have single trefoiled windows. The nave and aisles are wide, but the aisles do not quite extend to the west end, and each opens to the nave by three pointed arches with octagonal pillars. The windows are invariably Curvilinear, excepting those at the east ends of the aisles, which are Rectilinear. Of the Curvilinear windows in the aisles the greater part are of two lights, and some square-headed: one or two have three lights, and some contain portions of ancient stained glass.

The chancel has on each side three very good Curvilinear windows of two lights, below which runs a string-course carried as a dripstone over the doors. The east window is of five lights, of plainer tracery but very good, and contains some ancient stained glass. On the south side are three ascending stone stalls with ogee canopies having crockets and finials, supported on shafts of Purbeck marble; there is also a trefoiled niche with a drain and shelf. In the pavement are several ancient tiles, and there are many remnants of ancient stalls and carved pew ends.

There are several monumental remains and brasses; in the south aisle is a marble tomb to Sir John Sedley (1561) richly painted and gilt, and near it, in the wall, an ogee arch with rich crockets, finials, and feathering, upon each side of which is the figure of an angel. On a flat stone is a brass figure of unusually small size, kneeling, with this inscription: " Pray for the sowle of Thomas Cowell on whoose soule Jhū have mercy. Amē for charite."

Southfleet.

An altar-tomb is charged with the figures in brass of a man and woman with this inscription: "Hic jacet Johñes Sedley comes auditor Dñi Regis de Scaccio suo et Elizabeth uxor eius qui quidm̄ Johñes obiit — die — anno dñi M°CCCCC et dīa Elizabeth obiit X° die Januarii anno dñi M° —."

Another brass of a female with this inscription: "Hic jacet Johña quondā uxor Johīs Urban Armigeri filia Johīs Reikmer Milit' de com̄ cornūb qui obiit X° die Junii a° dñi M°CCCCXIV quae aīa ppiciet de°. Amen." Below are inscribed the common monkish Latin verses beginning, " Sis testis Xp̄e," &c., &c. At the east end of the north aisle is a large slab with an ornamented cross. There are two small brasses to ecclesiastics in the chancel. The font* is very good, of octagonal form, each face charged with sculpture, representing respectively: 1. The Pope; 2. The chalice; 3. The Resurrection of Our Saviour; 4. His Baptism; 5. The Lamb; 6. St. Michael the archangel; 7. A shield inscribed Jhu.

SWANSCOMBE.

ST. PETER AND ST. PAUL.

This church is principally Early English, with several insertions of later date. It consists of a nave with aisles, a chancel, and at the west end a tower crowned by a lofty shingled spire. The tower is without buttresses, of flints with courses of stones at the corners; the belfry windows are lancets variously arranged, on the west side triple.† The lower part of the west side has a two-light Curvilinear window. The spire is square at the base, and covers the whole area of the tower. The body

---

* Engraved in the *Registrum Roffense*. The fonts at Shorne and Southfleet are almost exactly alike.—R.

† On the south side of the tower is a doubly-splayed, round-headed window, which is supposed to be of Saxon work of Edward the Confessor's reign. In the quoins of the tower are some masses of Roman masonry, each mass having been inserted as if it were one solid block of stone.—R.

has no battlement, the nave is leaded, the chancel has a high tiled roof. The windows of the side aisles are all Rectilinear, except a Curvilinear one east of the south aisle. The nave is divided from each aisle by three Early English arches with circular pillars having octagonal capitals, some of which are enriched with foliage. Over the south arches is a clerestory with trefoil windows. The arch to the tower is plain and pointed, within it is a wood screen, apparently of Early Curvilinear work, with trefoil arches and shafts with bell capitals and bands. The south porch is plain. The chancel has two Early English lancets on the north and a Curvilinear window of two lights on the south. South of the altar is a trefoil niche and drain. Within the altar rails is an elegant wood lectern of plain Rectilinear character, enriched on one side with a circle containing a pierced quatrefoil, and on another side is a small ogee canopied opening. Such lecterns are rarely found in churches. The font is cased in wood.* There are six bells.

LONGFIELD.
ST. MARY.

This small church is built of flints and consists of a small nave with north aisle, and a chancel, with a wooden turret over the west end. The nave and aisle are divided by two pointed arches with an octagonal pier. There is one small Norman window at the west end of the aisle (probably reinserted in the later wall), the others are chiefly Rectilinear and squareheaded in the nave. In the chancel the east window is Curvilinear, of three lights, and some others are of the same character. There is a wood screen between the nave and chancel, and some small seats with carved ends. South of the

---

* The wood casing has since been removed, and the font's outer surface, now much mutilated, seems to have been carved with the emblems of the four Evangelists. There are some good monuments—to Dame Eleanor Weldon, Anthony Weldon, and their son, Sir Ralph Weldon, who died in 1602.—R.

altar is a stone seat in the wall, and an aumbry and piscina. The font is a plain octagon. The whole church is very small but prettily situated.

NORTHFLEET.

ST. BOTOLPH.

This is perhaps the largest and most interesting church in the diocese,* and is principally of Curvilinear work. The walls are chiefly of flints, with stone buttresses, and the exterior plain. It consists of a spacious nave with side aisles, in two distinct divisions, a partition being placed between them and the western portion not used for service.† The chancel and eastern portion of the nave are appropriated to the service, and pewed; thus the church is of considerable length. At the west extremity is a plain tower, built in 1628, within the ruins of the original one, of which parts of the walls remain. It contains six bells. The side aisles are embattled; the nave and chancel have tiled roofs. On the south side is a Rectilinear porch of chequered work, and there is some ivy growing up that side. The windows of the nave are principally Curvilinear of two lights, but one is of three lights at the east end of the south aisle; all have good tracery; some on the north side of the eastern division of the nave are Rectilinear. The western portion of the nave is left open without pews; it has on each side three pointed arches, those on the north having octagonal piers, on the south alternately circular and octagonal, the former having square bases. The roof of this portion is a fine plain timber one, the supports of the beams being pierced. Between the western and eastern division of the nave is a pointed arch, and there are similar ones in the side aisles. Across the whole runs a screen and a singing

---

* Northfleet is in the diocese of Rochester.—R.

† Since Sir Stephen Glynne's visit, this church has been completely restored, and every part of it is now made available for use at the frequent daily services.—R.

gallery facing the east division, which is now fitted up for the service. This part has on each side two pointed arches, with octagonal piers having plain capitals, above which are small single clerestory windows with trefoiled heads, walled up. Over part of the north aisle is a painted panelled ceiling; at the east end of the south aisle are three stone seats, under arches finely moulded and trefoiled. Between the body and chancel is a very curious wood screen, which appears to be of Early English work, of which few specimens in wood are to be found. It has in the centre an arched doorway, and on each side of it seven arched compartments, each of which contains within it a trefoiled arch, between which and the arch head is a pierced trefoil. All the arches spring from shafts with bell capitals and bands. The door in the chancel screen has some fine ancient iron work. The doorway appears of later date, but has a trefoiled head; the spandrels are filled with vine leaves and other foliage, and the whole is flanked by buttresses with crocketed canopies; above runs a cornice containing heads. The chancel is large and stately, but somewhat neglected. Its east window is a very fine one of five lights, with rather Early Curvilinear tracery, and shafts supporting the mouldings of the arch. On the south side are four windows, all Curvilinear of two lights; on the north are three Curvilinear and one Rectilinear window with string running under all. There are some stone seats extremely mutilated, the canopies being destroyed, and an ogee canopied niche containing a piscina and shelf. The ceiling is coved and boarded, with a small embattled cornice running under it. In the chancel is a brass figure of an ecclesiastic beneath a canopy with a mutilated inscription to Peter de Lacy, rector of this church, and prebendary of Swordes in the cathedral of Dublin, obt. 1375. There are two slabs near the west end, each charged with a cross flory; there is also a good monumental bust of Mrs. Fortresse, who died 1740, and a rich marble monument of   Critch, Esq., and his wife; the figures remarkably well executed.

The font is a plain octagon.

CHALK.

ST. MARY. 1862.

This church stands remote from houses near the turnpike road from Gravesend to Rochester. It consists of a nave with north aisle, the south aisle being destroyed; a chancel with north aisle, and a square tower with an embattled parapet at the west end. The body is chiefly of flints, but the tower is principally of stone, and has an octagonal turret rising above the parapet, and square-headed belfry windows. On its west side is a Rectilinear porch; there is a stoup, and over the doorway a niche, supported by a grotesque figure of a man holding an ale-jug in his hands. In the south wall of the nave are three pointed arches in the wall; there are square-headed windows inserted, and one of Curvilinear character, so that the aisle was evidently destroyed at an early period. The nave is divided from its north aisle by three very plain Early English arches without mouldings; the piers square, having shafts set in the hollows at the angles. The chancel has similar arches on the north side. The interior is dark, but neatly pewed; the windows on the north side of the nave are walled up. The chancel has a small Early English doorway on the south side, and two square-headed windows of Rectilinear character; at the east end are three Early English lancets. The north aisle of the chancel has at the east end a Curvilinear window of two lights, and is very low and small. On the south side of the altar is a stone sedile with trefoil head, having very elegant mouldings, and near it, on corbel heads, a piscina of like form, with head corbels.*

SHORNE.

ST. PETER AND ST. PAUL.

This church is tolerably spacious, and consists of a nave and chancel, each with side aisles, and a plain embattled tower at

* On the north wall of this north chancel is some wide, low, arcading.—R.

the west end of Rectilinear character, having an octagonal turret attached, the belfry windows are square-headed, and on the west side is a pretty good door and a window, the former in a square compartment, with panelled spandrels. The rest of the church contains much earlier work, and is built of flint and stone. The south aisle both of nave and chancel* is very wide; the nave has on the south side three tall pointed arches with octagonal pillars; on the north are three arches, all dissimilar, having large piers forming very wide intervals. The first arch from the west end is very high and pointed, but partly walled up; † the second is also pointed, but less high, and of Early English character, springing from circular shafts.‡ The third arch is semicircular, very plain and rude. The chancel is divided from its south aisle by three tall pointed arches, with pillars alternately of circular and octagonal form; from the north aisle it is divided by three arches, the two eastern of which are very fine lofty ones of Early English character, with a circular pillar having the capital moulded; the third arch is also Early English, but lower and plainer. Both the side aisles of the chancel are partitioned off from the chancel and used as schools,§ the arches being filled with plaster-work; on the north side remains some wood screenwork. The windows that have escaped mutilation are chiefly Curvilinear of two and three lights; but there is one lancet at the west end of the north aisle, and that at the east end of the chancel is Rectilinear of five lights, with a transom. The roof of the nave has tie-beams upon pierced brackets. The font is a very fine one of Rectilinear character, of octagonal form, each face presenting a different piece of sculpture, among which are figures of (i) St. Peter; (ii) Our Lord rising from the Tomb; (iii) Our Lord receiving Baptism; (iv) the Holy Lamb; (v) a

* The south chancel has since been rebuilt upon a narrower plan.—R.
† This arch has since been thoroughly opened.—R.
‡ Over this arch a round-headed window arch, *doubly splayed*, is now visible. It must have been a clerestory window in the latest Saxon or early Norman period.—R.
§ Long discontinued. No school is held in the church. The arches have been completely opened.—R.

shield inscribed with Jhu.; (vi) an Angel with a balance; and (vii) the Sacramental cup. The shaft has also fine panelling. There is the effigy of a crusader (Henry de Cobham, le oncle) rather mutilated, and in the chancel is a brass with a representation of a chalice and I H S, without figures, but bearing an inscription to Sir Thomas Elys, late vycar, 1569.* The church is neatly pewed and has a barrel organ.

ROCHESTER.

THE CATHEDRAL CHURCH.

It is needless to give a detailed account of this venerable structure, which is so well-known and illustrated by prints, that a brief description of its general outline and character will be sufficient. The plan consists of a nave with side aisles and transepts, and a choir which is somewhat longer than the nave, contrary to custom, and reaches to the extreme east end. A line of chapels is carried along the western portion of the choir, forming aisles, the southern being much wider than the northern, beyond which is a regular second cross aisle or transept, not extending beyond the breadth of the aisle on the south side. Each end of the transept has on the east side a small chapel. The choir extends about fifty feet in length beyond these transeptal chapels without aisles. The tower rises from the intersection of the western or great transept with the nave and choir. Adjoining the north end of the great transept, on the east side, is a massive square building, now in ruins, called Gundulph's Tower. The south end of this transept has a large chapel, called St. Mary's, joining it on the west side, which is of Late Rectilinear character.

The nave is of Norman work, except the two eastern arches on each side, and the windows, which are almost all insertions of Curvilinear or Rectilinear date. The west front is a very noble specimen of Norman work, but inserted in it is a very large Recti-

---

* Other brasses commemorate John Smith, 1437; John and Marian Smith, 1457; William Pepyr, vicar, 1468; Edmund Page, 1550; Elynor Allen, 1583.—R.

linear window of eight lights. Its doorway is very rich in ornamental mouldings and shafts, the door itself square-headed, and the head of the arch filled with sculpture. The front of the centre aisle is flanked by square turrets, finished by octagonal ones, and that on the south by a plain pinnacle. The whole façade has several ranges of arches, some semicircular, some intersecting, with shafts and various enrichments; but these are stopped by the insertion of the window. The west ends of the aisles have Norman windows with rich chevron-work and shafts, as well as ornamental tiers of arches. The rest of the exterior of the nave is plain. The interior of the nave has five Norman arches and two pointed ones on each side. The Norman arches have chevron ornaments in their mouldings; the piers are, some octagonal, some with shafts attached. Over each arch is a triforium, a large semicircular arch with chevron moulding, containing two smaller ones divided by a shaft; the space in the head has the scale work ornament.

The clerestory windows are Late Rectilinear. The nave and aisles have plain timber roofs. The two east arches of the nave and the whole of the eastern portions of the church are Early English. The choir and transepts have plain but good stone groining. The arches under the tower spring from fine clustered banded shafts. The north transept is richer than the south, but both have two tiers of lancet windows, differently arranged and plain externally, but presenting to the interior beautiful arcades with delicate mouldings and shafts. The choir, of which William de Hoo, when sacrist, is the reputed builder (he was afterwards, in 1239, made prior), is raised considerably above the nave, and approached by a flight of steps, there being beneath it a spacious crypt, approached by a good doorway, with toothed ornament in the mouldings, on the north of the choir. There are four compartments on each side of the choir, each containing in the lower part two lancet arches with billet work in the mouldings, which spring from clustered shafts of marble; but these arches are walled up. Above is the clerestory with single lancet windows, each presenting to the interior a triple arch with toothed mouldings and marble shafts, which kind of work is continued along the whole of the Early English portion, the character of which is very good, though not rich, and externally, singularly plain. The interior has much of the toothed and billet ornaments, and marble shafts. One window in the south-east transept has a semicircular head and chevron ornament on the exterior. In the chapel adjoining this transept is a very fine Curvilinear window, and also a beautiful door of later date, opening to the chapter house (*now rebuilt*) with a crocketed ogee head, and a hollow moulding filled with images of saints and bishops beneath canopies, and also two small bands of foliage. The east part of the choir has some Early English lancet windows, in which has been inserted tracery of Curvilinear and Rectilinear character, and the east wall has in the lower part three lancets, above which is a large Rectilinear window. There are three Rectilinear stalls on the south side of the altar. The choir was fitted up in 1743; * the stalls, pews, &c., are neat, but plain and out of character. There are several fine tombs— that of Bishop Merton, who died 1277, is in the north-east transept, it is a beautiful specimen of the transition from Early English to Curvilinear. The canopy is double, each portion having a triangular finishing, with crockets, flanked by pinnacles. The north-east transept is called St. William's chapel, and the narrow aisle which joins it on the west is approached by an ascent of several steps and contains the tomb of Bishop Hamo de Hethe, beneath a canopy of Curvilinear work, consisting of a contracted arch with rich feathering, sur-

* Very much of the original woodwork of the 13th century, and other portions which were added in the 16th century, remained *in situ* when Sir Stephen Glynne visited this cathedral, and have been conscientiously respected and preserved *in situ* by Sir Gilbert G. Scott in his restoration of the choir, 1874-5. He likewise preserved and reproduced the 11th century wall-painting which formerly, as now, filled the space between the tops of the stalls, and the string-course beneath the windows. The singular paving patterns, in the eastern transepts, formed of small plain red tiles of various shapes, have also been preserved and reproduced.

mounted by a crocketed triangular canopy, the intermediate spaces much enriched. In the aisle of the north-east transept has recently been discovered a fine tomb with the effigy of a bishop, richly painted and gilt, and the colours well preserved, having been long concealed. In the eastern part of the choir are on the north the tombs of Bishops Glanville, 1214, and St. Martin, 1274; the former has a range of Early English niches, and is much mutilated; the latter has an Early Curvilinear canopy, and the effigy is perfect. On the south are the tombs of Bishops Gundulph and Inglethorpe, 1291; the former is only a plain stone, the latter has the effigy perfect, in Petworth marble, a crosier in his hand, head on a pillar, beneath a trefoil canopy. In the south aisle of the choir, called St. Edmund's Chapel, is the mutilated tomb of Bishop Bradfield, 1284.

At the south-east corner of the cathedral are some Norman remains of the ancient chapter house and cloisters, unusually placed, so far to the east. The eastern portions have lately been much repaired and restored within and without; but the exterior is generally plain and not attractive in appearance, and it is doubtful whether it is improved by the transformation of the original steeple (a low tower with a short and inelegant, though venerable spire) into a lofty but very ordinary tower with battlement and pinnacles, quite repugnant to the general style of the edifice, and yet entirely wanting in grandeur and beauty.

ST. NICHOLAS CHURCH.   1831, 1839, 1853.

This structure stands on the north side of the cathedral, and is a plain building without pretensions to beauty, consisting of a nave and side aisles and a chancel, with a low tower on the west side of the northern aisle. The windows are of a character which resembles Decorated tracery, but they were probably inserted in the seventeenth century, when the church was much repaired and partly rebuilt. The divisions of the aisles are formed by two rows of pointed arches, five on each side, with circular columns, having square capitals, and evidently debased. The interior is neatly pewed, and contains a good organ. The chancel is wholly modernised within, and the east window closed.

The west window is of five lights, and below it is a Perpendicular labelled doorway with spandrels. At the west end of the south aisle is a three-light Perpendicular window. The tower, which is engaged in the west front, is also Perpendicular, low, and small. The walls are chiefly of flints.

ST. MARGARET'S CHURCH.

This church consists of a nave, a chancel with south aisle, and a square tower at the west end, with a battlement and corner turret. There are many modern alterations, both within and without, but some original windows remain of the two later styles. There is also an ancient font.

(SUPPLEMENTARY NOTICE.)

1811.

St. Margaret's Church has been wholly rebuilt, except the Tower, in an Italian unecclesiastical style, which ill accords with the ancient tower. The latter is Perpendicular, plain in character, but resembling other specimens in the neighbourhood. An organ has been erected.

The Castle of Rochester presents a very noble specimen of Norman work. The principal part comprises a very large square tower with flat buttresses, and a turret at each angle, three of which are square, and one circular. There are several tiers of small windows with semicircular heads; the walls are very thick, and the whole is three stories in height. The interior is divided into two equal parts by a wall which opens on each floor by arches, and in the centre is a curious well, which is accessible from each floor. The second floor seems to have contained the state apartments, and has some semicircular arches and pillars of excellent workmanship.

Around is a considerable extent of the outer walls remaining, and the entrances show great ingenuity in the several contrivances for securing them.

FOOT'S CRAY. *Aug: 1869. E.A.S.*

ALL SAINTS.

This is a small rustic church, beautifully situated in a churchyard shaded by fine trees. It consists of a nave and chancel, with a chapel on the north side of the nave. Over the west end is a small turret and spire of wood. There is a west porch of wood, with feathering in its gable, and within it a Rectilinear doorway, with label and shields in the spandrels. The windows of the nave and its chapel are all square-headed of the Rectilinear period. The nave opens to the chapel by two arches of pointed form, but very dissimilar proportions. The chancel has some plain lancet windows, and a square-headed one at the east end. On the north side of the altar is an arched recess in the wall. On the south side of the church, at the eastern extremity of the nave, is a square turret lighted by small windows containing a stone staircase which now leads to the pulpit. It opens to the interior by a Rectilinear doorway with foliage in the spandrels. In the north chapel is an arch in the wall, beneath which are the effigies of a knight and lady, the latter has a head-dress of singular character. In the chancel is a brass with this inscription in black letters: "Hic jacet Thomas Myton quodm Rector isti' ecclie qui obiit XXX° die mēs Januarii M°CCCCLXXXIX cui^s aīe ppiciet deus. Amen."

The font is a large square one of Norman character, made of granite, each side is moulded with a range of plain semicircular arches, the pedestal is cylindrical with square base. At the west end is a double gallery, and there is one on the north.✗ The interior is quite dark from the shade of the numerous trees which surround the church.

✗ *Removed, & the church lengthened at the west end* –

St. Paul's Cray.

ST. PAUL'S CRAY.
ST. PAULINUS.

This church consists of a nave with south aisle, and a chancel, with a square tower at the west end surmounted by a shingled spire. The walls are all of flints, and the general character is Early English. The west doorway of the tower has very elegant mouldings, with the toothed ornament, and shafts having foliated capitals. The tower has some lancet windows, and one Curvilinear of two lights, also in the upper part on the west side are two circular apertures. Near the west door is a stoup. The nave had formerly a north aisle now destroyed, but two pointed arches are seen in the wall. On the south side of the nave is a range of three elegant acute arches, with slender circular pillars, one of which has the capital enriched with varied sculpture of foliage, angels' heads, &c. In the south aisle are some lancet windows, and one square-headed Rectilinear one. On the north are inserted late windows with flat arches. The chancel had a north aisle, now partly destroyed, the rest of it is used as a vestry, and has lancet windows. To this aisle opened two Early English arches, one rising from foliated imposts, the other from a pier with shafts in the angles. The east window is Rectilinear but walled up. The altar rails are partly composed of old wood screen-work. The chancel has no arch to the nave, but is all in one space with it. There is a little door up on high, which led to the rood-loft. The font is a plain one in the form of a barrel.

ST. MARY CRAY.

This church is entirely constructed of flints, and consists of a western tower surmounted by a shingled spire, a nave and a chancel, each with side aisles. There is a large south porch, chiefly of wood, two stories high.* The tower is plain, with some

* From the upper story, which was probably a priest's room, opens into the church a hagioscope, or squint, through which the occupant of the upper room

lancet windows, and there are circular belfry windows with a quatrefoil within the circle. In the north aisle of the nave are some early Decorated windows of two lights; that at the west end of this aisle is particularly good. In the south aisle the windows are late Perpendicular. The nave is divided from each aisle by three Early English arches on circular pillars, and the chancel arch is similar. On the south of the chancel arch is the door to the rood-loft. The chancel has a narrow pointed arch to the south aisle, and a larger one to the north aisle. Beyond the east end of the south aisle is a vestry. One south window of the chancel is late Perpendicular, one on the north is Early English. There is a wood-screen in the south aisle. In the north aisle of the chancel, which is dirty and neglected, is a feathered niche with piscina, and a wood screen which has rather a Decorated character.

There are some brasses to Isabel Colsale; Richard Avery, 1558, and three wives; two to Richard Manning, 1605; a fifth to Philadelphia Greenwood, 1747, and a sixth to Benjamin Greenwood, 1773.

CHISELHURST.
ST. NICHOLAS.

This church is situated within a lovely churchyard shaded by fine trees. It consists of a nave with north aisle, a chancel with north chapel, and a tower of flints at the west end of the aisle, which is of Perpendicular character, having a tolerable doorway with moulded arch and three-light window. It is surmounted by a wooden spire. The walls are all of flints, and the whole is Perpendicular, save part of the chancel; most of the windows are square-headed, or have very obtuse arches. The body is divided from the aisle by five pointed arches, on light piers of four clustered shafts, the tower occupying the space of one arch.

in the porch could see the altar. This "squint" is still visible above the entrance door.—R.

At the east end of the aisle is a good wood screen. The east end of the chancel has a window of advanced Early English, with three trefoil lights within a general arch; above it, on the point of the roof, is a pierced quatrefoil, not glazed. There is one lancet stopped up on the north of the chancel.

ALLINGTON.

ST. LAWRENCE.

This is a very small church, consisting only of a nave and chancel; the nave lofty. There is a north porch surmounted by a wooden belfry. The features are early. A south doorway has a rude semicircular arch, now walled up, and the north doorway is Early English but plain. The nave has lancet windows, one trefoiled, and the chancel has two on each side. The chancel arch is semicircular and quite plain. South of the altar is an odd piscina of trefoil form. The font is octagonal and simple. The walls are of flint and plaster.

CRAYFORD.

ST. PAULINUS.

This church is almost entirely Perpendicular, except part of the chancel, in which there are some windows of which the tracery appears to be Decorated. The whole is built of flints, and the work is coarse and ordinary; the chief singularity is, that though the nave and chancel are about equal in width, the former consists of two broad aisles with a range of arches in the centre, while the chancel has three divisions, a centre and a north and south aisle—accordingly a most irregular appearance is produced within, the arches of the nave running in a line with the middle of the chancel arch—they are four in number, and a half arch abutting against that leading to the chancel, which looks as if the chancel was a remnant of a more ancient building, and that in building the nave they had not accurately

Y 2

calculated the dimensions of the arches, and had only room for half the easternmost; the piers are formed of four clustered shafts. The chancel has but one arch to each of the side chapels, which seem to have been private chantries. Most of the windows are square-headed; the tower at the west end of the southern aisle is very plain and without a battlement, and there is a plain south porch. The interior contains several large heavy monuments of the seventeenth century; the font a plain octagon.

BRENCHLEY.
ALL SAINTS.

This is a large church, consisting of a nave with side aisles, north and south transepts and chancel, and at the west an embattled tower, which is of Perpendicular character, and has the staircase turret so common in this part of Kent, but it is of very ordinary workmanship and ill-finished. The nave is wide, and is divided from each aisle by four pointed arches upon circular pillars which are probably Early English. Above is a clerestory of square-headed Perpendicular windows. Most of the windows have been spoiled or entirely modernised; but there is one of very large size in the north transept which has shafts within, although the tracery is entirely destroyed. In the same transept are two plain lancets. The roof is coved, and that part of it which is over the eastern portion of the nave, where was the rood-loft, is enriched with panels and foliated bosses. The chancel is wholly modern; the font is a plain octagon.

EDENBRIDGE.
ST. PETER AND ST. PAUL.

This church consists of a nave and chancel, each with a north aisle, and a massive tower at the west end surmounted by a large shingled spire; the tower is plain Perpendicular, and has a labelled doorway with panelled spandrels. The walls are of stone and flints mixed, and there are portions about the church of all the three later styles. The nave is divided from the aisle by four handsome pointed arches with octagonal pillars, the extreme arch towards the west springing from a half circular column. The chancel has three pointed arches with lighter octagonal columns, and the door to the rood-loft is seen on the north of the chancel arch. There are several square-headed Perpendicular windows in the nave, and one lancet on the south. The windows are :—one lancet, one of transition character, with a cinquefoil between the heads of two lancets, one of three lights, early Decorated, east of the south aisle, and others Decorated of two lights. The east window of the chancel is Perpendicular, of five lights. On the south side of the chancel is a small piscina with a shaft. The chancel is very wide, and there is a little stained glass. There is an altar-tomb of Rectilinear character.

CHIDDINGSTONE.

ST. MARY.

This church has three equal aisles, without any distinction of chancel, and a fine lofty western tower of good Kentish stone, of Perpendicular character, with a handsome battlement, and octagonal turrets at the angles, crowned by crocketed pinnacles. There is also the Kentish stair turret rising high; the tower is three stages in height; the west door has fine mouldings, a label, and panelled spandrels. The west window is of three lights, and the belfry window is large. The body has a high tiled roof; the north chancel has a moulded parapet, and is of finer workmanship than the nave, the windows, having good arch mouldings, are late Perpendicular in style. There are Decorated windows, of two lights, at the west of the aisles, the others in the nave are Perpendicular, and square-headed or with flat arches. The east window of the chancel is rather dubious; that of the south chancel has Decorated tracery, but is square-headed. The gables of the chancel and its south aisle are surmounted by crosses. The interior is neat, but the only interesting features are, some monuments to the Streatfeilds, which, however, are not ancient. There are on each side six pointed arches with octagonal pillars, and the ascent of one step is the only indication of the chancel. There is a little wood screen-work. The font is octagonal, late, and poor.

HEVER.
ST. PETER.

The church has a nave and chancel, each with a north aisle, and a western tower surmounted by a tall shingled spire of lighter proportions than Edenbridge. The tower is Perpendicular, and built of stone, without buttresses; its windows have no dripstones. Most of the windows have very flat Perpendicular arches, but one is Decorated with a square head. In the chancel is one Decorated window, of two lights, that at the east end is Perpendicular, of three lights. The nave is divided from the aisle by three pointed arches with circular pillars. The chancel has two flat Tudor arches with an octagonal pillar. In the north chancel is an altar-tomb with panelling of late Perpendicular character. There is also a fine brass.

Hever Castle is a curious specimen of a mansion of the fifteenth century, built round a quadrangle, it has a fine gateway tower with a portcullis; there are some fine gables in the external elevation with some fine bay windows, beneath which are bands of panelling. An apartment over the gateway has been modern Gothicised in bad and frippery taste.

AYLESFORD.
ST. PETER.
1836.

This church is tolerably spacious, but as usual in Kent, with rather a plain and coarse exterior, it is built of stone and flints intermixed. It has a nave and chancel, each with north aisle, and a western tower, the lower part of which seems to be early, is without buttresses, and has some rude small openings of Norman character, the upper part is Perpendicular, embattled, and has a square-headed belfry window. The south porch is two stages in height, and within it is a door with good mouldings and shafts which have a Decorated character. Several windows are Decorated; at the west of the north aisle is a good one, of three lights, others are of two lights, and some on the north side are square-headed. There are also some Perpendicular windows, especially south of the chancel; on the north side is a single low side window with trefoiled arch. The interior is rather gloomy; the nave is separated from its aisle by five pointed arches, with clustered piers of lozenge form, having four shafts with octagonal capitals, which appear Perpendicular; the last arch next the chancel is curtailed by about one-tenth. In the chancel are two lower pointed arches with an octagonal pier, and on the south side of the chancel arch is an embattled octagonal turret for stairs to the rood-loft, opening to the interior by a small labelled door. In the chancel are several large and gorgeous monuments to the Milner family, and some banners. The font is a plain octagon. The view from the churchyard is very pleasing over the Medway with its woody banks.

MILTON (next Gravesend).
ST. PETER AND ST. PAUL.

This church is but small, and sadly disproportioned to the large and increasing population of the parish. It consists of a west tower, nave and chancel, and a south porch. The tower

and porch are Perpendicular, and the whole is built of flint and
stone, sometimes ranged in horizontal courses. The tower is
plain, with a battlement, a square-headed belfry window, a west
window of two lights, and a plain west door; it opens to the nave
by a pointed arch. The porch has small windows, and over its
entrance is an ogee niche with panelled spandrels. There is also
within the porch a small niche with benatura. The entrance to
the porch is by a large moulded arch upon shafts. The body
has a moulded parapet, but the whole is covered by a hideous
modern projecting roof. The windows on the north are all
of two lights and mostly Decorated, but one is Perpendicular.
On the south some are Decorated, some Perpendicular, but all
are of two lights.

There is no architectural distinction between the nave and
chancel. The east window is Perpendicular of three lights.
The interior is much modernised, with a flat ceiling, walls
painted blue, a large west gallery, and smaller side galleries
north and south, which, though not deep, are very unsightly in
this narrow church. In the west gallery is a tolerable organ.
The pews encroach very much on the altar. On the south side
of the chancel are three elegant Decorated sedilia deep in the
wall, with trefoil feathering, clustered shafts with moulded
capitals, and good groining with bosses. A fourth niche of
similar character contains a piscina. There are square stone
brackets with corbel heads, &c., which must have supported
the beams of the original roof. The font is modern.

STONE.

ST. MARY.

This very elegant and interesting church, though externally
plain and rough, like most Kentish churches, presents internally
some of the finest specimens that can be found of work verging
from Early English to Decorated, and in some respects not
unlike Lincoln Cathedral in its eastern portions. The church

has a massive west tower, nave with side aisles, and chancel
with chapel and vestry on the north. The tower is engaged

EAST WINDOW OF SOUTH AISLE, STONE CHURCH.

ONE PANEL OF MOULDED STRING-COURSE ON THE
NAVE WALLS OF STONE CHURCH.

with the west end of the aisles, and is constructed of mixed
flints and stone, the battlement being of stone, the belfry windows

are square-headed, and on the west side is a Decorated window of three lights. On the west side is a large square turret projecting at the angle, full of small openings and terminating in a kind of gable. The west door has a pointed arch on shafts. The walls of the church are mostly flint, some smoothed, some rough, and a good deal of the chancel is of stone to which brick buttresses have been added on the south. There is no clerestory.

CAPITAL OF WINDOW MONIAL, IN THE CHANCEL OF STONE CHURCH.

The roof is tiled over both nave and aisles, and the chancel is of equal height with the nave. On the north side of the chancel are some curious flying buttresses; also an embattled parapet and a large Perpendicular window. The vestry is low and beneath the window sill. The east window is Perpendicular, of four very wide lights, those on the north and south of the chancel are of like character, of three lights. On the south of the chancel are brick buttresses.

The plainness of the exterior causes surprise at the unusual elegance within, in which both nave and chancel participate. The windows of the aisles of the nave are three on each side, of two lights, and at the west end of four lights, all of elegant

Stone by Dartford.

tracery, with circles and quatrefoils of the incipient Decorated character, about the end of the reign of Henry III.* Externally they are plain, but internally there is an unusual degree of

BOSSES ON CUSPS OF THE CHANCEL ARCADING, IN STONE CHURCH.

enrichment; two windows on each side have the tracery repeated in open stone work on the inner side, as in the

* Mr. Street, the architect who restored this church, believes that it was erected during the episcopate of Lawrence de St. Martin, Bishop of Rochester (1251-74), and that its architect was the architect of Westminster Abbey. ("Archæologia Cantiana." III., 108.) R.

clerestory of the choir of Lincoln, the mouldings are of peculiar beauty with head corbels, and detached shafts having elegant foliated capitals. The centre window on each side has not the interior tracery, but has very good mouldings and toothed ornament on the capitals of the shafts. The east window of the north aisle is closed by the vestry, that of the south aisle is of two lights, also closed, but with fine corbels and marble shafts. The west windows are of four lights, and very elegant, having three circles in the heads, very fine toothed mouldings, and shafts with foliated capitals, of the best execution. The tower being within the nave opens on the north, south, and east by three lofty moulded pointed arches springing from piers of clustered shafts with foliated capitals. Eastward of the tower the nave has on each side three very fine lofty pointed arches, still superior in their mouldings, the eastern ones having the toothed ornament; the piers are very beautiful, composed each of four large and four small shafts of black marble, disposed in lozenge form, banded round the centre, and having a general capital of foliage. There is a half-arch between that part of the aisle which ranges with the tower and the remainder of the aisle on each side.

The chancel arch is a fine one, and in its mouldings facing west presents very unusual details, viz.: a series of square ornaments resembling nail heads, raised to a point in the centre, but larger and bolder than that feature is usually found. The mouldings of this arch are altogether very fine, and spring from marble clustered shafts, with bands and foliated capitals much like those in the nave. There seems to have been an intention of groining the chancel, though the ribs were never sprung, but there are clusters of shafts in two places, those next the nave being loftier than the others, but all are of marble and banded. The western cluster has very richly executed capitals of foliage, more Decorated than Early English in its character; the others have more simply moulded capitals.

Another most striking and uncommon feature in this chancel

Stone by Dartford.   333

is the series of stone stalls * which occupy the east wall and the north and south sides of the east end. Of these, there are four at the east end, and six on each side, all similar and coeval with

MOULDING OF CHANCEL ARCH, STONE CHURCH.

the rest of the church. They are equal in height and surmounted by a string-course; each has a pointed arch with trefoil feathering enriched by a small boss of circular foliage upon each cusp, and each arch springs from black marble columns with fine moulded capitals. In the spandrels are finely wrought pieces of foliage. Within one on the south side is a small pointed

---

* Mr. Street calls this an *arcade*, not a series of "stalls." He adds: "The arcades round the chapels of the choir at Westminster are almost identical in shape and design with that round the chancel at Stone." ("Archæologia Cantiana," III., 130.)—R.

NORTH-WEST BAY OF CHANCEL, STONE CHURCH.

niche, probably a piscina. There are three steps to the altar, which is adorned with velvet cloth and candlesticks. The vestry* on the north side is Perpendicular, and contains a tomb of that style surmounted by a flat arched canopy and groining under it. In the chancel is a brass (1574) with a verse inscription to Sir Robert Chapman. The font is octagonal, but cased in wood. The roofs are very plain, the pews hideously high and inconvenient, and there is a barrel organ in a west gallery.

A small north door, near the west end, is Early English, of earlier character than other parts of the church; the outer moulding is a kind of chain, the inner has round flowers, much injured; the shafts have foliated capitals.

FRINDSBURY.

ALL SAINTS.

This church has a western tower with heavy shingled spire, a nave with south aisle and a chancel. The tower is of rough flints, without buttress, and massive, with partial repairs in brick and an octagonal turret on the south. The openings are plain and narrow; one on the north is a lancet in the belfry story, one on the west has a square head, and below it is a Perpendicular single-light window with trefoil feathering. The west door has continuous mouldings. The walls of the nave have

---

* This was not the vestry originally, but the Wilshyre chantry, erected in the 16th century. The original vestry stood further to the east, and was built in the 14th century. When Mr. Street restored Stone Church, in 1859, he found concealed within the wall of Wilshyre's chantry an original window of three uncusped lights, with tracery formed by three cusped circles. From this model Mr. Street restored the other chancel windows. He likewise opened out the east windows of the aisles, and restored the groined roof of the chancel. An important point discovered during the restoration was the fact that the side walls of the nave are finished at the top with a moulded string-course, which is returned for a foot on either side at the east, and was probably continued all round the church (vide woodcut on p. 329). R.

been in a great measure rebuilt, and covered with a modern slate roof, the original windows have been destroyed and replaced by wretched new ones. The tower opens to the nave by a plain pointed arch. The nave is divided from the aisle by three wide pointed arches springing from octagonal pillars, the aisle is not continued quite to the west end. The chancel has been comparatively untouched, and is of rough flints, partly stuccoed, with tiled roof; it opens to the nave by a plain pointed arch of Early English character without any mouldings, springing from imposts which have a course of intersecting arches. On the south side of it is a hagioscope, now closed. There is a lychnoscope on each side of Perpendicular character, square-headed and of two lights, and two similar windows nearer the east. There is a priest's door on the south; the east window is entirely hidden by a modern reredos. The font is an octagonal bowl, panelled with shields, the pedestal octagonal with small buttresses, the cover of wood with crockets. There is a barrel organ.

COBHAM.

ST. MARY MAGDALEN.

The church consists of a west tower, lofty nave with clerestory and side aisles, north porch and spacious chancel. The material is chiefly flint intermixed with Kentish rag. The north aisle is wider than the southern, and both aisles extend to the west wall of the tower. In addition to the ordinary tower-arch, handsome pointed arches with continuous mouldings open from the tower into the north and south aisles; a most unusual arrangement, with a western tower. The windows of the aisles and clerestory are all Perpendicular, but in the south aisle there is a piscina of the Decorated period. The tower, which is Perpendicular, and entirely of stone, with a battlement and octagonal turrets, is three stages in height, with a three-light west window. The north porch has a parvise over it, and a strong groined ceiling with plain ribs. The body has no battlement, but a moulded parapet, which is unusual in Kent, and the clerestory is invisible from outside, the aisles being lofty. The chancel is of flint and has lancet windows of greater width than usual. The east end has three lancets. The nave is divided from each aisle by five pointed arches with slender circular columns. The font has a plain octagonal bowl, upon four legs, with central cylindrical shaft, the whole on an octagonal plinth. There is a screen in the north aisle and another* in the chancel arch; the chancel windows have internally good mouldings and shafts, the hoods being connected by a string-course. On the south side of the chancel are three fine equal sedilia of Middle Pointed character; the canopies pedemental and crocketed, with trefoil foliation, and eastward a a fine piscina with projecting octagonal basin upon a shaft, surmounted by a canopy with three pedimental divisions, crocketed and foliated, and the back elegantly panelled.† The chancel has the wooden stalls remaining. The church contains an unusual number of fine brasses, perhaps more than any other in England, and almost all of the best period. Most of them have French inscriptions but some of the later ones are in Latin:

1. Joan de Cobham, with canopy; c. 1300.
2. Sir John de Cobham, with canopy, and headless; c. 1354.
3. Sir John de Cobham; c. 1367; holding the model of a church with transepts and spire. Figure large. (Described in Haines's "Oxford Manual of Monumental Brasses." No. 130.)
4. Sir Thomas de Cobham; mutilated; c. 1367.
5. Margaret de Cobham; c. 1375; mutilated.
6. Maud de Cobham; c. 1380. } Fine and large.
7. Margaret de Cobham; c. 1395. }

---

* Since removed to an arch in the tower. R.

† Eastward of this piscina, a short mural staircase has since been discovered. Upon its stairs were fragments of several well-carved statuettes, which probably formed part of an elaborate reredos, to the top of which this short staircase led. Opposite the piscina is an aumbry, or a credence, under an elegant arch. Immediately in front of the communion table is the magnificent altar-tomb of George Brooke, Lord Cobham, upon which lie the carved and emblazoned effigies of himself and his wife. Statuettes of their children ornament the sides of the tomb. - R.

8. Rauf de Cobham ; c. 1402 ; holding inscription.
9. Reginald Cobham ; c. 1420 ; priest in processional vestment (in the north aisle).
10. Sir Reg. Braybrook ; 1405 ; knight, with fine canopy.
11. Sir Nich. Hawberk : 1407 ; a fine armed figure, with marginal inscription. (Described in Haines's " Manual." No. 151.)
12. Joan de Cobham ; 1433.
13. John Gerne, priest ; 1447 ; much destroyed (in the north aisle).
14. Sir John Broke and Lady ; 1512 ; partly lost.
15. Sir Thomas Brooke and Lady ; 1529.
16. William Tanner ; 1418. He was first master of Cobham College.
17. William Hobson ; 1472 ; another master of the College. This brass is a palimpsest.
18. John Gladwyn ; another master of the College (in middle aisle of nave).
19. John Sprotte ; 1498 ; another master of the College.

Four " crossed " coffin slabs of stone, discovered in various parts of the church, are placed under the side arches of the tower.

On the south side of the church is the college, the buildings of which are of good character, but somewhat ragged and ruinous. The restored portions form an alms-house, built round a quadrangle ; in flint work of good Perpendicular style.

HALLING.
ST. JOHN. 1847.

This church has a nave with aisles, a large chancel, and a plain western tower surmounted by a shingled spire. The tower is of rough workmanship of mixed flint and stone, having a door on the west side but no window ; there is a large buttress on the same side, and just below the eaves of the spire are rude square openings for the belfry, which are double and foliated on the west side only. There is also a small slit on the south. The roof on the south side is tiled and slopes over the aisle ; the aisles have moulded parapets ; the walls are of flint ; the north porch is partly of brick, and has near the door in a corner a benatura. The chancel has a sloping tiled roof. The windows in the aisles are of two lights, some square-headed, and seem to be Third Pointed. The arcades of the nave are each of three acute arches with octagonal columns having caps and bases but not quite similar on the two sides. The tower arch is rude, upon a First Pointed impost. The west end of the south aisle is separated off, opening by a small pointed door to the rest of the aisle, and contains a small single window, trefoiled, with iron bars. It may have been a *domus inclusa* but is now a coal hole. The nave contains some ancient benches with square ends having buttresses. The chancel arch is a wide pointed one dying into the walls. The chancel is First Pointed; has on each side three wide-splayed single lancets. The east window is a Third Pointed insertion of three lights. On the south side is a piscina with octagonal basin upon a shaft, beneath a plain pointed arch. Within the sacrarium are several encaustic tiles. In the east wall is the trace of a pointed arch. There are portions of the original stalls remaining, and some trace of the rood door.

The nave roof has plain tie-beams. At the east end of the south aisle is a sculptured bracket by the window. The font has a plain octagonal bowl on a similar stem, close to one of the south-west piers.

CUXTON.

ST. MICHAEL. 1847.

This church has a nave, a chancel with south chapel, north porch, and western tower. The tower is a plain Third Pointed one, embattled, without buttresses, and has a square-headed belfry window. The chief features are Third Pointed; the windows of the nave are mostly square-headed, with labels; there is, however, one plain wide lancet on the north side of the chancel. The chancel arch is pointed, upon octagonal shafts, and to the south of it is a wide hagioscope. There is a Third Pointed roodscreen and the rood-door remains. The arch from the chancel to its chapel is a pointed one dying into the wall. There are benaturas near the north and south doors. There is an organ. The situation is pleasing, on a high bank, commanding a fine view over the Medway valley.

WOULDHAM.

ALL SAINTS. 1847.

This church has a nave with aisles, south transept, and chancel, with a tower on the north side of the west front. There are portions of every style, except Norman. The nave has, on the north, an arcade of four First Pointed arches, with piers alternately circular and octagonal. On the south is an arcade of three plainer arches, with one pier circular, and another large and square with First Pointed shafts. The western end of the south aisle is separated off, with access by a door, as at Halling, and is kept in a dirty state. Its west window is a plain lancet. The west window of the nave is Third Pointed of three lights. The aisles have lean-to tiled roofs and square-headed windows of Third Pointed period. The chancel arch is a plain pointed one, and there is a rood-screen and rood-door on the north. The rood steps are within the north-east pier. On the south-east respond is a Third Pointed niche, trefoiled, with spandrels panelled. The chancel has a very pretty east window of three lights, Middle Pointed in character, and rather unusual in its tracery. On the north side of the chancel are two lancets now closed. On the south only one remains, which is trefoiled. These lancets internally are contained within pointed arches with continuous mouldings forming octagonal piers. There are stone seats along part of the chancel. There is a plain pointed arch between the chancel and a dirty neglected north chapel. Over the sacrarium the roof is boarded. The south transept opens to the aisle by a good pointed arch upon octagonal shafts. In the transept is one square-headed window of Middle Pointed character, and one three-light Third-Pointed. On the outside of the transept is a very fine ivy stem. The walls are mostly of flints with stone admixed, and some parts stuccoed. The tower is strong and massive, of rag stone and Third Pointed in style. It is added on to the north aisle, is of three stages and embattled, with labelled square-headed windows; it has no buttresses, but a large octagonal turret is attached. There is an organ in the chancel.

LUDDESDOWN.
ST. PETER AND ST. PAUL. 1847.

A small church, comprising a nave and chancel with a south aisle along both, a low western tower, and a south porch. The walls are of rough flints. The tower has a pointed tiled roof, and is without buttresses; the only opening in it, seen through the luxuriant ivy, is a lancet on the west side. There is a square-headed lancet on the north side of the chancel. The east window is a single lancet, most of the other windows are Third Pointed. The nave has two pointed arches on the south side with octagonal pier. The chancel arch is pointed, dying into the wall. Between the aisle and the chancel is a pointed arch without shafts. The nave has a coved boarded roof, the chancel roof is flat. One of the northern windows presents to the interior an elegantly moulded arch with shafts and corbels to the hood. On the north side of the chancel arch is the trace of a window with sloping sill. There is a small pointed door opening to the tower. The font is First Pointed, the bowl square, charged with a range of round arches, on four shafts without capitals, two of them rather broken, upon a square plinth, attached to a south pier. The pews are very hideous.

IFIELD.
ST. MARGARET. 1847.

A small mean church, comprising a nave and chancel, with south porch and a wooden belfry over the west end. There is no chancel arch. The west gable is boarded. The east and west windows are of three lights; some others are of two and three, Pointed.

NURSTEAD.
ST. MILDRED. 1817.

A small church consisting of a nave and chancel undivided, with western tower. The tower is of stone and Third Pointed, without battlement, having a large octagonal turret on the north. It is of three stages and without buttresses. The west window is of three lights, those of the belfry are square-headed and labelled. The body of the church is of flints with tiled roof. In the nave the windows are Third Pointed with square heads. The chancel east window appears to be Third Pointed, of three lights, but rather singular. On the north of the chancel is one lancet. On the south there are two lancets.

HIGHAM.
ST. MARY. 1816.

The plan of the church is a nave and chancel with panelled north aisle, a south porch and small wooden belfry at the west end of the north aisle. The roofs are tiled and separate in each aisle. The walls of flints. The character is chiefly Middle Pointed; several windows have decidedly Flamboyant tracery, some on the north of two lights, the two at the west ends and that at the east of the north chapel are of three. Others are of a purer kind, especially those on the south, and the east window of the chancel, which is of three lights. On the north side near the west, is a Norman window, and also a Third Pointed one. The north aisle of the chancel has also Third Pointed windows. Several of them present, internally, a rear segmental arch. Between the nave and aisle is an arcade of three pointed arches, with light octagonal pillars having moulded capitals. The chancel arch is a wide pointed one springing straight from the wall; across it is an ugly modern wood-screen;* across the north aisle is one of Third Pointed work

---
* This modern screen has been removed.

which seems to have been connected with the rood-loft. The roofs are very plain, with tie-beams. The east window of the chancel is a lofty elegant one of three lights, having, internally, a segmental rear-arch well moulded, upon corbel heads. A southern window of two lights is also good, with octofoil in the head, and segmental rear-arch. On the south side is a curious piscina, the head is trefoiled and has a corbelled hood well moulded. It has a stone shelf also moulded, and below is an hexagonal basin. Westward of it is a wide sepulchral arch in the wall, with similar hood, beneath which is inserted an ugly modern tomb of black marble. The chancel opens to the north aisle by a First Pointed arch on circular shafts with moulded capitals. On the north-east side of the north chapel is a pointed arch-recess in the wall at some height. In this chapel is a late Third Pointed tomb under a flat recess in the wall with a sort of star foliation. There is a brass plate on the wall above it, commemorating Robert Hylton, 1523.[*] There are several encaustic tiles. The font is attached to the west pier of the nave, its bowl is square, chamfered at the angles, the stem cylindrical with four short legs at the angles, upon a square plinth. Some of the south windows have externally their hoods returned, some with corbels. The south doorway has continuous mouldings and returned hood. The door itself exhibits some curious tracery in wood-work, with a border of flowers, birds, and heads. There are buttresses of mixed flint and rag-stone, some intermixed with brick.

CRAY (North).
ST. JAMES. 1849.

A small church, of very little interest beyond its beautifully sequestered situation; for the modern alterations carried on in it

---

[*] Another brass upon an altar-tomb commemorates Elizabeth Boteler, who died October 15th, 1615. In the same chapel are two curious old chests. In the north aisle there is a 14th century tombstone.—R.

are very far from satisfactory. It consists only of a nave and chancel, with a modern addition on the south of the nave. Over the west end is a wooden belfry. The windows are of ordinary Third Pointed character; there is some appearance of a projection on the north for the rood turret. The roof has plain tie-beams. The chancel has no architectural division from the nave, but its roof is coved, panelled with ribs and bosses, and lately painted blue with gilt stars, which is the best thing that has been done in the church. The Decalogue, &c., are written in illuminated characters, and there are scrolls with texts beneath the chancel roof. The stained glass is not of very high order, though there is a good deal; the pulpit has some rich wood carving, and the reredos is of somewhat elaborate Flemish sculpture in wood, representing the Flight into Egypt; but it does not harmonise well, or look as if it were in its proper place. The chancel is sadly encumbered with pews quite close to the altar, the nave also abounds with pews, some of which are embellished with rich carving. There are many hatchments. The font is a plain octagon, on stem of like form.

ERITH.

ST. JOHN. 1849.

This church consists of a nave and chancel, each with wide south aisle, having separate roof, and a western tower with large shingled spire. The walls are of rough flint and rubble; the steeple mantled with ivy. There are considerable First Pointed features. The tower may perhaps be of that date, but it is very plain. The south door is decidedly First Pointed, and has shafts with foliated capitals. There is a lancet at the west end of the south aisle; another on the north side; most other windows are Third Pointed and square-headed, except the east window of the south aisle which is Middle Pointed of three lights. The nave is divided from its aisle by a First Pointed arcade, of wide arches with circular columns having moulded capitals. There is no chancel arch. The chancel is mainly First Pointed, has at the east end a triplet window, and is divided from the south chapel by a rude plain pointed arch upon imposts, with large masses of wall on each side. The roof is plain, with tie-beams and king-posts. There is a rood-screen between the nave and chancel, of five compartments, containing Third Pointed tracery somewhat mutilated. There is the semblance of a staircase on the south of the rood-screen. There is a late parclose screen between the chancel and south aisle. In the latter are several monumental remains, chiefly brasses. One with small figures of Sir Richard Walden, and Elizabeth his wife, 1506 and 1528, two others much mutilated, each of a knight and lady; another of a man between two wives, also mutilated, with inscription commemorating John Aylmer, Margaret and Benet his wives, 1511. There are several other smaller brasses, and one to "Rogerus Seneler, quondā serviens abbatis et conventus de lesney, obt. 1421."

One large figure of a lady in a triangular head-dress commemorates Emma, daughter of John Walden, Alderman, and wife of John Wode, citizen of London, merchant of the staple of Calais, obt. MCCCCLXXI.

Also an alabaster tomb in memory of Elizabeth, countess of Shrewsbury, obt. 1568. In the chancel is a sumptuous monument by Chantrey to the late Lord Eardley. There are high pews, a barrel organ, and modern font.

CHATHAM.

ST. MARY. 1852.

This church is a large structure, but has been wholly rebuilt in a bad modern style, with the exception of the west end (which, however, is much altered and patched) and a very fine Norman door on the south of the nave, which is of three orders, late in the style and almost Early English, with excellent mouldings and shafts with square abaci and toothed ornament in the jambs. The west door seems to have been Norman also; the west window late and poor Perpendicular. The church is galleried, and has a good organ.

SUNDRIDGE.
ST. ——.   1854.

This church has nave with aisles, a chancel also with aisle; and a western tower with shingled spire. The material is partly Kentish rag and partly flints mixed with stone. The nave is of considerable width; the chancel is narrower, so that its arcades are not quite in a line with those of the nave. The arcades of the nave are Early English, each of three pointed arches, with circular columns having moulded circular capitals. Over each column is a quatrefoil clerestory window within an arch, now opening into the aisles which are Perpendicular additions and loftier than the original ones. All the aisle windows are Perpendicular of three lights. The chancel arch is pointed, on octagonal shafts; in the south aisle corresponding with it appears a rood-door. The chancel has on each side two pointed arches like those of the nave. The chancel extends eastward of the aisles, and has single lancets north and south of the sacrarium. The east window is Perpendicular of five lights; those of the aisles have four lights. On the south is a double piscina. A vestry is added on the north of the north aisle, and in this aisle is a square aumbry. The chancel has been laid with handsome new tiles, and those in the sacrarium are of still richer character than the rest. The chancel abounds in monumental remains of various character, and contains several brasses. One commemorates "Rogerus   Dˢ de Sundrishe et Ffernyngham, obt. 1429." Another has a cross flory and obliterated inscription in Lombard letter. One has figures of a knight and lady and groups of children, of rather late character.

In the chancel also are marble busts of Mary Bellenden, afterwards Lady Campbell, and Caroline Campbell.

The roof has tie-beams and king-posts. The font has an octagonal bowl on a stem, with heads under the bowl. There is a gallery and barrel organ. The tower arch is pointed, from concave octagon stilted pillars. The tower is plain Perpendicular, of rough flint and stone masonry; has a west door with label and good mouldings and panelled spandrels; over it a three-light window. The belfry windows of two lights. The spire shingled, of broach form. There is a stair turret projecting on the north side.

CLIFFE AT HOO.

ST. HELEN.   1857.

A large church of considerable interest, with many excellent details. It consists of a nave, with north and south aisles, north and south transepts, and a spacious chancel; a tower at the west end of the nave; and a south porch. There is much mixture of styles, at least of the three Pointed styles, but no Norman. Part of the tower, the arcades, and the transepts are Early English. The arcades consist each of five pointed arches and include the transepts; these are of well-finished characters, and spring from circular columns having moulded capitals and bases. There is a clerestory having a single splayed lancet over each pier. In the aisles the windows are Decorated, mostly of two lights, but a good one at the west of the north aisle is of three lights; all have good hood mouldings. The transepts are curious and interesting. Between the north aisle and north transept is a large pointed arch, and beside it is a smaller one, springing from shafts which do not reach to the ground, over which is an open lancet in the wall. The west side of the north transept presents internally two good moulded Early English arches on slender shafts with bands, moulded capitals and bases. On the east wall are two larger arches of the same character, containing smaller ones on shafts with moulded capitals, and set on a bracket of foliage, beneath which is a trefoiled niche or piscina. In one of the eastern arches is a single-lancet window, with shafts. The south transept has on its east wall an arrangement of Early English arches, similar to that of the north transept, the arches containing each one lancet. On its west side is a somewhat similar arrangement: three arches are presented, one opening to the aisle of the nave, the central one shews an alteration of plan (when the nave aisles were widened), and a segmental arch is inserted within it, the apex of the original lancet occupying the space between the original arch and the segmental insertion; the piers are octagonal and filleted, but have been altered. Within the third arch is a lancet window. The end windows* of both transepts are Perpendicular. In the south wall of the south transept is a piscina, and on its east wall some ancient rude painting. There is no chancel arch, but a mutilated rood-screen remains and the rood-door is seen. The chancel is excellent Decorated and has lately undergone a very fair restoration, except the east window, which is a very ugly modern one and which we hope will soon be replaced. On the north and south sides are three good windows of two lights, of varying tracery, having excellent mouldings and hoods on corbels, and set on a string-course. There is an altar in form of a chest. On the south of the sacrarium are three beautiful sedilia, ascending eastward, having ogee canopies with crockets and finials, with double feathering and foliage at the points of the cusps; there is groining beneath the canopies, and ranging with them is a piscina of uniform character. Opposite to these on the north is a wide sepulchre, rather verging to Perpendicular character; having a foliated arch with panelled spandrels and an embattled cornice; adjoining which is a door to a sacristy now demolished, the trace of which may be seen outside. There are the ancient wood stalls

---

* These windows have since been removed, and replaced by triplets of lancets.—R.

still remaining. The interior is spacious and part of the nave is wholly clear of seats, which adds to the effect, but the existing pews are very ugly. The roof too is concealed by a modern ceiling, but the spandrels of the beams are seen; the old lead roof appears outside. There are strings in the aisles under the windows and over the doors. The pulpit is a fine carved one of wood, with the stand for the hour-glass, dated A.D. 1634. The tower arch is a plain Early English one on imposts. The tower has on the north and south in its lower part lancet windows, on the west a Perpendicular window; it also has a good stone groined roof with crossing ribs, but no boss. The lower part is decidedly Early English, and is of rough flints, with flat-faced buttresses. The upper part is later, strengthened by large buttresses * of brick. The five bells now lie on the ground within the tower, waiting to be re-cast. The exterior of the nave has rather a patched appearance, as also have the transepts. The north transept has a square end. The north aisle has a better appearance than the south, with a high tiled roof, and courses of flints on its west gable. The south aisle has a plain battlement. The south porch is Perpendicular, of flint and stone, also embattled; it has labelled two-light windows, a moulded doorway and an octagonal turret attached.

The font has an octagonal bowl, with concave sides, on a buttressed stem; it has a wood cover. There are several monumental remains. An old stone in the nave is thus inscribed—

<blockquote>
Ione la femme Johan Ram gyst ici
Deu de sa alme eit merci.
</blockquote>

A brass to Thomas Faunce, 1609, and two wives; also the print of a pillar brass on steps, and one of a priest under a canopy.

* These buttresses have since been removed, a new staircase to the tower built, and the bells rehung and increased to 8 in number.— It.

HOO.

ST. WERBURGH. 1857.

A good church, chiefly Perpendicular, consisting of a nave with north and south aisles, chancel, western tower with spire, and north and south porches. The material is mostly stone. The south aisle is embattled, as is the north porch which is of good character; its door has on each side a small labelled window. At the east end of the north aisle is a stair-turret of octagonal form. The tower is engaged with the west end of the aisles and is of large size with very thick walls of Perpendicular character, having a battlement and octagonal turret at the north-west; the belfry windows on each side are of two lights and labelled. The spire is a lofty one of shingles, and rises entirely within the tower; it is of very nice proportions, and looks very well in the views around. The tower has the wall quite solid on the north and south, without opening to the aisles. The north aisle is very wide. The arcades on both sides appear to be Early English; beyond the tower are three pointed arches on each side; the columns circular, with moulded capitals. There is a clerestory, an uncommon feature in Kent, having Perpendicular windows, each of two lights and square-headed. The roof of the nave is ceiled, but the beam brackets rest on grotesque-head corbels. There are some windows in the aisles of Decorated character, especially one at the east of the north aisle, which is of three lights and has pieces of stained glass. This window is not placed in the centre. The other windows mostly Perpendicular, of two and three lights. In the aisles the roofs are open.

The chancel arch is pointed, springing at once from the wall. The chancel is large and Perpendicular. The roof a high tiled one, and the part over the sacrarium is boarded. The east window has three lights; those on the north and south are of two lights; there are remains of stained glass. South of the altar are three good equal sedilia with double feathering upon marble shafts, with octagonal capitals, and a piscina of similar character. Part of the stalls remain, but they have been mutilated. The font has an octagonal bowl, on a stem of the same shape. There are some brasses. In the south aisle is one of a knight and lady with hands joined. In the chancel, one of a priest with hands joined in prayer, the head destroyed; with inscription: "Ricardus Bayly, quondam Vicarius." One, which is a bust, is inscribed, "Hic jacet Johēs Brown, quond. Vicarius istius ecclie, cuius aīe ppicietº Deus, Amen." Two others bear the dates 1615 and 1640.

The church is pewed, and has a barrel organ in the gallery.

www.ingramcontent.com/pod-product-compliance
Lightning Source LLC
Chambersburg PA
CBHW020223240426
43672CB00006B/400